A famous motivational speak[er] ... *do once in a while that shapes* ...

<u>*Just Thinking*</u> *achieves what many devotionals have not – offering brief, impactful messages that consistently remind us of what is true... life lessons that none of us ever outgrow. Chris, Dean & Sean have taken snippets of reality from their own lives, and mapped out a pathway to living a life that God has called us to. Don't skip a single day of* <u>*Just Thinking*</u>*!*

Brad Gibson
Business Manager, Twenty One Pilots
Sound Capital Management, LLC

"<u>*Just Thinking*</u> *is packed with engaging, easy-to-read stories, inspiring you to spend a few minutes growing your faith each day. No matter where you're at in your journey, you'll be invited to live more fully, taking next steps as you dig in. If you struggle to spend time with God daily and are ready to meet up with Him more consistently, this book is just for you!"*

Laurie Hise
Founder & President
Thepassionatepennypincher.com

"We are inundated with content that tears away at our souls. This book is counterintuitive to the information being thrown at us today, and it contains reminders of where our peace, joy, and help comes from. Sean, Dean, and Chris have managed to create content that will bring life back to your soul, gearing your mind towards the eternal, the life-giving, the abundant, and fulfilling life promised to those who follow Jesus and consume His truth."

Beth Livingston
Ohio Senate
Press Secretary

"Champions know that it's the small daily disciplines that have the greatest lasting impact. Though succinct, powerful stories, Coach Chris, Dean and Sean have provided 365 winning meditations that challenge us to daily live the victorious life – one with purpose and intentionality. Read it! Then Read it again! It will make you better."

Todd Townsend
Central Indiana Director
Fellowship of Christian Athletes

"I don't know about you, but my faith journey has me racing to catch up! I wasted a lot of years casually thinking about God, His character, and His message. Somehow, I sense God is calling to me to spend time with Him and His Word. Perhaps you sense it as well. Dean, Sean, and Chris have written <u>Just Thinking</u>, as a discipline for us to navigate the journey."

Mark R Ricketts,
President and CEO of National Church Residences,
Area Advisor for Bible Study Fellowship

"<u>Just Thinking</u> is lighthearted, engaging, and promises to encourage your soul. Dean, Sean, and Chris have filled each page with personal stories and anecdotes that will inspire your heart and point you toward truth. Take a journey with them and build your faith along the way!"

Nicole Davis
Co-Owner & Founder at Native Cold Pressed
Founder at Native Life

"Sean, Dean, and Chris are dynamic communicators with a heart to see people take steps of faith and growth in their spiritual journey. I know that this 365-day devotional will go a long way to meeting you right where you are and helping to move you closer to where God wants you to be!"

Scott Distler
Lead Pastor
E-Free Church of Northern Michigan

"I became a Christian when I was in college. Chris was my mentor. He had an ability to help me see that my faith was essential in every situation and arena of life. Just Thinking helps us interject the extraordinary power of the biblical Truth into everyday life. The devotions are thoughtful, practical and powerful."

Scott Ridout
President, Converge Churches, Missions, and Ministries

"In a world where people are drained by their jobs, disgruntled with church, and hanging by a thread in their marriage and family, Just Thinking enables the most broken and exhausted to rebound with a spiritual sense of refreshing purpose. Filled with 365 days of inspiring, funny, and purposeful devotions that will capture your heart for what really matters in life. A must read. Dean, Sean, and Chris are intentional in helping you live life with the end in sight."

Craig Peters
Executive Director
Equip Ministries International

JUST THINKING

DEAN FULKS, CHRIS JOSEPH,
SEAN PATRICK

Published by Author Academy Elite
P.O. Box 43, Powell, OH 43035
www.AuthorAcademyElite.com

Paperback ISBN-13: 978-1-64746-504-9
Hardcover ISBN-13: 978-1-64746-505-6
Library of Congress Control Number: 2020917733

Available in hardcover, softcover, e-book, and audiobook.

A NOTE TO THE READER

The simple fact you have even picked up this book shows your interest in the reality that God is interested in you.

While you might think three guys from Ohio are UN-interesting, one of us has been stabbed (with a knife at a Christian college), one of us snuck onto the set of a Bruce Willis film, and one of us barely survived crawling across a rickety bridge over crocodile-infested waters.

Actually, all of those things just happened to one of us. Add the other two of us into the mix, and you just may enjoy adjusting how you think about God.

One of the oddest characters in the Bible is Enoch. He is listed in the Hebrews chapter 11 "Faith Hall of Fame," and He's one of only two characters in the Bible who never dies. Yet, the only characteristic we know of Enoch is that he "walked with God."

Though the stories in this book may make you laugh a little or even shed an occasional tear, our real hope is that they make you THINK about your Creator.

And not just that you would think about Him, but we believe that the more you think about Him, the more you will talk to Him. And the more you talk to Him, the more you will think differently about the gifts of life—both temporal and eternal—that He has given to You.

We believe all of this can happen in a journey of 365 days, where you can find practical faith and the habits of hope.

This book is not a theological treatise. We are not saying this book is all you need to know about God. However, we are saying that walking with God begins with thinking about God. We hope that you will journey with us for the next 365 days. The world needs more Enochs. You can become one of them.

Special thanks go out to our wives and families—we all married up! We are grateful to Allison Myers for her tireless editing work, Shane Tucker (shanetucker.com) for all of the graphic/design work, and Ceci Dalton for the photo creds. We would also like to thank the team at Author Academy Elite and Kary Oberbrunner. AAE helps people like us turn books into realities. If we can do this, anyone (including you) can. Finally, we give one hundred percent of the credit for anything good that comes from this book back to our Creator, the One who has made a way for us—the One who calls us to Think.

IT'S SUPER KID WITH A TOWEL!

Psalm 28:7 – *The Lord is my strength and my shield; my heart trusts in Him, and He helps me.*

I grew up watching the original *Superman*. I didn't care that a pair of glasses distracted everyone from connecting the true identity of the world famous Superman with the mild-mannered reporter Clark Kent.

I loved when Mr. Kent transformed into a man of great strength by changing into that outfit with the large "S" on the front and the flowing cape accessory. That "S" wasn't just a cool logo; it served as a shield against bullets (I didn't even care that the bad guys only shot him in the "S." Why not aim at a shoulder or leg?). When Superman toted those tights, I felt safe.

After the show would end, little boys all across America, myself included, would wrap a towel around their necks and go into pretend mode.

Superman gave me a glimpse of how God can be my strength and shield. Spiritually, as believers, we can all put on that "outfit" of His power and protection.

PRAYER: *Father, thank You for giving the Holy Spirit to indwell me, so I can tap into Your strength to live a fruitful life. Remind me to put on that "outfit" each day by acknowledging You in prayer and asking You to live through me.*

CJ

YOU CAN SIT HERE

1 Thessalonians 5:18 – *Give thanks in all circumstances; for this is God's will for you in Christ Jesus.*

I was the last one to board, and all I wanted was to start my journey home. The first leg of my adventure required a two-hour flight from Malawi to South Africa on a now-defunct African airline company. Making my way down the aisle, my excitement turned to dismay when the steward said to me, "I'm sorry. Your seat has been oversold."

Without any seats available, my hopes of starting my journey home seemed grim. Desperate to stay on the plane, I asked the steward if there was anything he could do to help me. He thought for a moment, then pulled out a metal folding chair from the galley and said, "You can sit here—next to the lavatory."

Without hesitating, I sat down. For the next two hours, I rode without a seatbelt and next to the bathroom on a tiny, propeller-driven airplane—breaking every passenger aviation rule known to man. The ride was uncomfortable, scary, and less than ideal. Nevertheless, I was overwhelmed with gratitude.

A Word of Challenge: Don't allow circumstances to dictate your level of thankfulness. Find the silver lining. Resist the urge to complain and offer thanks to the Lord for the many good things in your life.

PRAYER: *God, help me today to be thankful in all circumstances.*

SP

THE MIKE TYSON PRAYER

Psalm 3:7 – *Arise, Lord! Deliver me, my God! Strike all my enemies on the jaw; break the teeth of the wicked.*

This verse falls into the "I can't believe that's in the Bible" category. Here is David praying, "Hit them in the face, God. Break their jaws!" Why in the jaw? Because that's where the voice of accusation comes from. In other words, it's, "Break all of the teeth of accusation out his head, God."

That is very different from how we pray. It's not, "God, please stop this, if you are able." Rather, it's much more like, "God, slug them! Mike Tyson uppercut them right in the mouth, break out all of their teeth, and shove them down their throats, God!"

I remember sports analysts saying that Trevor Berbick would give Mike Tyson a great battle, yet Berbick did not make it one half round with Iron Mike. Not surprisingly, Tyson's most famous for saying, "Everybody has a plan, until they get punched in the face."

Sometimes, it feels like God's enemy is taking ground in our lives. He's intimidating and injuring us. Remember, it's okay to pray the Mike Tyson prayer: "Punch the enemy in the mouth, God. Drown out his accusing voice in my head with Your truth. Show Your power!"

PRAYER: *God, I sense the enemy is at work today against me, against my family, against my relationships. Fight the enemy in Your power, Father, not in mine. Shut up the voice of accusation that comes against me.*

DF

ROOM TO FLOURISH

2 Timothy 4:22 – *The Lord be with your spirit. Grace be with you.*

Grace reminds me of the word "room." Grace gives us "room" to grow. Grace gives us "room" to learn from mistakes and start over.

As a basketball coach, I learned a lot from watching poor coaching. During each practice, there was usually time set aside to let the players scrimmage, and the hope was that they would attempt to apply all of the skills they had learned from the earlier drills in the practice.

I discovered that the weaker coaches continually stopped the scrimmage time to interject correction whereas the better coaches let the players work it out before stopping play. Even more, the *really* good coaches stopped play mostly to praise the players for executing a drilled skill they had been learning.

God is a great Coach. He lets us go through our lives without zapping us every time we mess up. Why? Because He's grace-oriented. Therefore, we can safely regroup during each day, pleading to Him to drill us, adjust us, praise us, and teach us. He won't force it on us, yet He longs to bless us so we can be a blessing to others.

PRAYER: *Father, thank You that You give me room. Help me to give grace to others. Enable me to put more distance between my wrongful actions, words, and thoughts.*

CJ

WEDDING DAY WINDOW WOES

1 Peter 2:12 – *Live such good lives among the pagans that, though they accuse you of doing wrong, they may see your good deeds and glorify God on the day he visits us.*

After leaving our wedding reception, Danette and I went to her parents' house to pick up a few things before departing for our honeymoon. Unfortunately, the doors were locked. Even though I was in my tuxedo and Danette was in her wedding gown, we decided to break in through the slightly elevated but unlocked kitchen window.

On my first attempt, I jumped up and grabbed hold of the window ledge, only to lose my grip and fall flat on my back. On my second attempt, I jumped, and at just the right moment, Danette used both her hands to shove my rear end forward and help me gain the leverage I needed. Not our finest hour.

Imagine what the neighbors must have thought as they watched this ridiculous scene unfold! On a less humorous note, keep in mind that people are watching our lives. Skeptics, in particular, are watching to see if Christians are living what they say they believe.

Every day we have the opportunity to show the rest of the world what it looks like to be a Christ-follower. Our attitude and actions count because they reflect on Jesus. Therefore, let's carry ourselves well and point people toward Him!

PRAYER: *God, help me today to make decisions and interact with people in a way that glorifies You.*

SP

THE GOSPEL OF SPANX

James 5:16 – *Therefore, confess your sins to each other and pray for each other so that you may be healed.*

It's an American axiom: if you want something done right, you must do it yourself. However, that's not a biblical axiom. Actually, the Bible tells us it's not good for us to be alone. We see that in James' words.

Another Stars and Stripes ideal is the American Dream, which is demonstrated in Sara Blakely's life. In 1999, Sara was going to an event and wanted a pair of control top pantyhose without the hose. She tried numerous places but couldn't find anything to suit her needs. Thus, Spanx was born. Today, Sara has over two hundred products, and the company even has a men's line now—they're called Manx (not that I'm speaking from personal experience).

Starting her company with $5,000, Sara has never gone into debt or spent a nickel on advertising. Currently, Spanx is sold in over 12,000 stores in forty countries.

Sara Blakely is a billionaire. Why? Because she can hide what no one else can.

A lot of us live *Spanx Christianity*—we hide it, stuff it, and it's terribly uncomfortable. All of this because we are trying to look like something we aren't in reality. "I'll just tuck that marital conflict in there...cram this anger problem in here." However, there's no healing in hiding.

PRAYER: *Father, remind me today that You are with me and that I need others to encourage me and sharpen me. Help me to be vulnerable to live in rhythms of confession with others.*

DF

HONEY, HOLD MY PURSE

Psalm 35:2 – *Take up shield and armor; arise and come to my aid.*

When I think of a shield, my mind wanders back to when I was a kid and watched great battle scenes of knights with lances, big swords, and whatever that ball with spikes attached to a swinging chain is called. The shield was the knights' protection.

In life, a particular scenario that I find very humorous is when an adult man has to hold a woman's purse for her. Awkward! He has to make sure that he grasps it like he doesn't really care about the purse (the loaf of bread hold is my favorite). The woman is basically saying, "You are someone I can completely trust to protect this bag of valuable belongings." She knows he will be a shield to all purse-snatchers and thieves.

We, too, all need a shield of protection from our insecurities, low self-worth, frustrations, hurts, and secret fears. God wants us to hand Him our own "purse of valuables" because He is our shield.

PRAYER: *Heavenly Father, help me to open up to You and continually hand You my valuable stuff. I know You are always there to be my help. In Jesus' name. Amen.*

CJ

MY TOOTHY FOE

Mark 14:38 – *Watch and pray so that you will not fall into temptation The spirit is willing, but the flesh is weak.*

Out of the corner of my eye, I recognized the unmistakable shape and color of a predator I had previously only seen behind glass in an aquarium. Standing knee-deep in the water at Myrtle Beach, I did a double take. Confirmation. I was standing six feet away from a shark.

For the rest of the day, I stood at the shoreline and vigilantly scanned the water for the return of my toothy foe. Thankfully, he never came back. Nonetheless, his appearance put me on guard and reminded me that I had an adversary.

When you become a Christian, you acquire an attacking enemy. Satan knows that because of your faith in Jesus, he cannot touch your soul. However, he will work tirelessly to ruin and destroy your life. And though he may have gone quietly, know that he lingers along the shore, ready to attack.

Satan is tricky and deceitful. He is a master at luring you into sin. Therefore, we have to be on guard—carefully watching the world around us and ably understanding the devil's mode of operation. Furthermore, we have to thoroughly fill our hearts and minds with the truth of God's Word. Stay alert!

PRAYER: *God, help me today to see through the devil's plans and schemes. Help me fill my head and heart with Your truth.*

SP

THE PANTS MAKE IT PERSONAL

James 4:8 – *Come near to God and he will come near to you.*

One of my favorite Bible professors used to pastor a church in California. A single lady from that church wanted to be married. She also wanted a visual reminder to pray and boldly take that request in front of God consistently.

So, she bought a pair of men's pants and hung them on the end of the bed as her reminder to pray. Her prayer was, "Lord, fill these pants with a man."

Since she was praying to a big God, she bought a particular size of pants: size 34. The pastor (who eventually became a professor) was not surprised when the woman ended up dating, getting engaged to, and marrying a man with a size 34 waist.

The pastor shared that story as a way to encourage his church that God is very personal and hears our prayers. A week later, a mother stopped the pastor after church. She said that she had walked into her fifteen-year-old son's bedroom and oddly found a very small two-piece bikini draped over the end of his bed.

Remember, if you draw near to God, He will draw near to YOU. God is very personal. Avoid the trap of comparing your spiritual life to someone else's spiritual journey.

PRAYER: *Father, I am casting off everything in my life today that's not of You. I am determined to leave those things behind to chase after You and Your activity in my life.*

DF

A LOT OF THANKS AND THANKS A LOT

Psalm 100:4 – *Enter His gates with thanksgiving and His courts with praise; give thanks to Him and praise His name.*

Having an "attitude of gratitude" is essential to a healthy relationship with our God, with others, and with "ourselves."

I remember my sister asking our dad for money. He would open his wallet, and as he was handing over the cash, she would already be headed for the door like a sprinter getting passed the baton in a track relay event. There was no "Thank you," just an expectation that the request would be granted.

As I first thought about how rude that was, I suddenly realized how I do the same thing to my Heavenly Dad. I ask for things, and He will work out answers more often than not. However, I get too busy moving on to my next prayer request to acknowledge what He has done for me.

It's the same with friends and family. Taking an extra moment to genuinely look in their eyes and thank them creates healthier relationships; it also benefits our own heart.

PRAYER: *Heavenly Father, please remind me to be a "thanker". In Jesus' name. Amen.*

CJ

HIDING UNDER THE HOOD

James 2:17 – *In the same way, faith by itself, if not accompanied by action, is dead.*

While I was on a double date in high school, my friend's car started to overheat. With steam billowing out from under the hood, we had no recourse but to pull to the side of the road. Coming to a stop, my friend looked at me and said, "Let's take a look."

Leaving our dates in the car, we got out and opened the hood. Steam was everywhere. Neither of us knew what we were doing, but for a good two minutes, we stared at the engine.

Finally, I said, "What are we looking for?" With a wry smile on his face, my buddy replied, "I have no idea—I'm totally faking it. But, with the girls in the car and the hood blocking their view, at least they can't see that we're clueless."

It's easy to fake it and live a phony version of faith. For some, it has become a lifestyle—presenting oneself as a follower of Christ but failing to back it up with the way you live. James tells us this version of faith is dead. As Christians, we are called to live what we say we believe. Put your trust in Jesus, follow His commands, and bring your faith to life!

PRAYER: *God, help me today to live what I say I believe. Help my faith to be genuine and more than just words.*

SP

SOLOMON'S SONG

Song of Songs 7:11 – *Come, my beloved, let us go to the countryside, let us spend the night in the villages.*

My wife and I led collegiate ministry together as a young couple. We consistently pointed our collegians to 65 out of the 66 books of the Bible. We joked that Solomon's Song was off limits until they were getting married. Solomon writes about God's plan for married people and sexuality in what feels like a very explicit manner.

In truth, the Israelites took sexuality seriously. Jewish people married under the *chuppah* (pronounced hoo-pah), a prayer shawl draped over four poles. The chuppah represented the fact that the marriage was done under the sacred hand of God.

When the couple made its ketubah (covenant) under the chuppah, the marriage still wasn't official. While the couple's spiritual union had been made, the covenant was yet to be consummated with physical intimacy.

In some Jewish tribes, the wedding party would walk the bride and groom to the bridal chamber, and the couple would enter the chamber to consummate the marriage while everyone waited outside. Talk about pressure!

Afterwards, when the couple walked out of the bridal chamber, the wedding party would cheer! Why? Because marriage was a spiritual covenant with a physical expression.

God also made a spiritual covenant of love with us with a physical expression on the Cross. Thus, marriage is a setup, a picture of how God loves His people.

PRAYER: *Father, help me to treat sexuality in the holy and loving way that You intended it. Help me to avoid treating it selfishly and sinfully. You intended it for good, and my prayer is to use it to bring You glory.*

DF

A DUMBBELL DUMBBELL

Luke 6:38 – *Give, and it will be given to you.*

The Bible tells us to give, and it will come back to us in some form, at some time. It doesn't always come back immediately, but once I had an experience when it did.

I went to the workout room of my apartment building, and I started my weightlifting routine in an attempt to "sculpt" my very average-sized body. In walked a very timid, thin young man who looked extremely confused. Being an athlete in high school, I had an okay idea about how to lift weights, so I decided to take the time to show this guy a few things and he was very appreciative.

I then went back to my own workout, and the next thing you know, this massive bodybuilder enters the room. He proceeded to ask me if he could show me a few things that would accelerate what he saw me trying to accomplish.

His advice was extremely helpful, and as I walked back to my apartment, I realized I had just experienced what I'd learned in Luke 6 about giving.

PRAYER: *Father, show me opportunities to give my time, encouragement, and money. Thank You for the blessings that will follow, internally, circumstantially, or materially.*

CJ

TREMONT'S FIVE AND DIME

1 John 2:1 – *My dear children, I write this to you so that you will not sin. But if anybody does sin, we have an advocate with the Father—Jesus Christ, the Righteous One.*

Michael and Maria were pretty sneaky third graders. Maria would distract the store owner, and Michael would put the candy in his backpack. Their plan only had one flaw—the owner of Tremont's Five and Dime had seen this caper dozens of times. Sure enough, just as Michael and Maria made their way to the exit, the store owner stopped them in their tracks.

At that very moment, Michael's older brother walked into the store. Realizing what had happened, he apologized and offered to pay for the stolen candy. The store owner thought for a moment and said, "Well, I suppose if you are willing to pay for it, then I can forget the whole thing even happened."

As Christians, we have an advocate who is willing to speak to the Father when we sin. His name is Jesus, and He stands ready to speak on our behalf when we fail. His work on the cross guarantees our acquittal, and His righteousness removes the stain of our sin. And while the grace and mercy of Jesus doesn't exist as a license to sin, it is good to know that when we misstep, He is there to make everything right.

PRAYER: *Jesus, thank You for covering my sin. May Your grace and mercy inspire me to greater obedience today.*

SP

LAMAZE

Psalm 9:1 – *I will give thanks to you, Lord, with all my heart; I will tell of all your wonderful deeds.*

When my wife and I were preparing to have our first child (I know, I know—my wife was actually "having" the baby), we were encouraged to go to the hospital and pay for these birthing classes called *Lamaze*.

I quickly learned that "Lamaze" is French for "Suckers!"

Here's what I learned in Lamaze: basically, I was supposed to be a coach. I thought this was awesome because in my mind, the coach is in charge. However, I quickly learned that I was not that kind of coach.

I was supposed to be a "breathing coach." Breathing coach? My wife had been breathing all of her life without coaching. She is an All-American Breather! However, I quickly learned that my wife's breathing affected what happened while she was giving birth (it's amazing how we take the small things, like breathing, for granted).

It's incredibly easy for us to fall prey to an entitlement mentality, where we take God's blessings for granted. Even more, we not only take them for granted, but we believe that we deserve them, when we should be praising God for them.

PRAYER: *God, I want to be grateful today for even the small things. I am reminded that everything I have is a gift from You. You don't owe me anything. In fact, I owe You everything. Still, You bless me, and I am grateful.*

DF

FAIL YOUR WAY TO SUCCESS

Psalm 37:23-24 – *The Lord makes firm the steps of the one who delights in Him; though he may stumble, he will not fall, for the Lord upholds him with His hand.*

The Bible is filled with messages for people to keep trying and keep starting over. We are to admit our wrongs and then ask God for the strength to get up.

A highlight of parenting was teaching each of our four kids to ride a bike. I recall my wife and me, sprinting alongside of them while barking out encouragement and instruction. Of course, there was the inevitable crash, followed by more words of encouragement (My favorite was my son plowing straight into a fluffy pine tree and completely disappearing).

Needless to say, they each got back on their bikes and tried until they could ride like the "big kids." In other words, they failed their way to success!

God doesn't want us to beat ourselves up for our mistakes and poor choices; He wants us to repent. And when we do go in the right direction, He is delighted!

PRAYER: *Lord, thank You for Your continual forgiveness. Give me the strength to keep getting back on the bike that is going in the right direction. Don't allow guilt to crush me.*

CJ

WITCH DOCTOR WALKOUT

Mark 16:15 – *He said to them, "Go into all the world and preach the gospel to all creation."*

Sharing the Gospel in the remote villages of Malawi can be wrought with distraction. I'll never forget the time a witch doctor interrupted my conversation with a family outside their hut. Dressed in a curious outfit and speaking in muttered tones, he made his presence known. After a couple of minutes, the father had heard enough and sent the witch doctor away. With the distraction gone, he asked me to continue.

Before speaking to the family, I asked our translator, "Did the father ask him to leave because he was a witch doctor?" With laughter in his voice, the translator replied, "No. He asked him to leave because his outfit was torn, and his family could see his underpants." The surprised look on my face clued the family into the fact that I'd discovered what had just happened. We had a good laugh together.

Over the years, I have discovered that if you are going to be active in sharing your faith, the devil will try to distract you, delay you, and stop you. My response, in these circumstances, is to persevere.

The world needs to hear about Jesus Christ. Don't let anyone or anything stop you from talking about Him.

PRAYER: *Jesus, today I ask You to energize my passion for talking to people about You. Help me persevere when distractions come.*

SP

JEREMIAH & JAGGER

Jeremiah 2:13 – *My people have committed two sins: They have forsaken me, the spring of living water, and have dug their own cisterns, broken cisterns that cannot hold water.*

I can't get no satisfaction
I can't get me no girly action
And I try, and I try and I try, t-t-t-t-try

I'm sure it's a sin to quote Mick Jagger in a devotional book (I bet it's listed somewhere in Leviticus). But what Mick sang about *FOR* the Stones, the Hebrew prophet, Jeremiah, taught about *IN* the stones.

Jagger crooned the Stones' problem: no matter how hard they tried, seeking soul satisfaction left them "on a losing streak." Thousands of years earlier, Jeremiah had previously answered their problem with a stone of his own.

Jeremiah says that we left God's spring for broken cisterns. Modern translation: don't trade an Artesian well for a cracked cup. You will always end up thirsty.

And yet, we try, and we try, and we *t-t-t-t-try.* One way that we whiff regularly looking for satisfaction is in romantic relationships. Men, it doesn't matter how hot she is (or how much she cooks, cleans, and works); she will never heal your soul. Ladies, there are not enough dimples, security, humor, and Hallmark Channel-watching to fill you.

And the beat goes on. It's not just Jeremiah. Elijah, Stephen, Peter, and Mary all came to the same conclusion about where true satisfaction is found. Paul said it this way: "This one thing I do…forgetting what lies behind, I press on toward the prize of the upward call of God in Christ Jesus."

PRAYER: *Father, please forgive me for my failures. Help me to forget what is behind me and live for what's ahead of me—to know You eternally. Only You can satisfy.*

DF

PAPERS IN THE WIND

Ephesians 5:15-16 – *Be careful, how you live, not as unwise but as wise, making the most of every opportunity...*

Dropping papers in the wind is always an adventure. My last episode found me briskly walking after a note that was skipping along the parking lot. The paper seemed to be trying to escape, and when I bent over to pick it up, it sprung forward as if it knew it was about to be captured.

I have learned to use the "stomp method" on my paper chases. Don't bend over; just stomp on that pesky, little fluttering runaway.

Sometimes life can feel as though we are chasing papers in a breezy parking lot. While our goal is to get from the car to the building, we find ourselves chasing distracting pleasures or time wasters. We know where we want to end up, but we just keep getting pulled in other directions.

In order to combat such distractions, I started to pray consistently about my time management, and slowly, I have gained control of my discipline in the area. As believers, being disciplined with our time is crucial in order to live wisely and make the most of every opportunity. As motivational speaker Jim Rohn says, "Discipline is the bridge between goals and accomplishments."

PRAYER: *Father, I hand You my ability to use my time well. Give me goals that will glorify You and assist others.*

CJ

40-YARD FAIL

1 Timothy 4:8 – *For physical training is of some value, but godliness has value for all things…*

I thought I could help. My son, Emerson, was working to improve his 40-yard dash time for an upcoming football camp. Usually, my job was to hold the stopwatch. But on this day, I decided to show my 17-year-old son a thing or two.

Bolting from the starting line, I felt like I was flying (the words "bolting" and "flying" may be slight exaggerations). My first four strides were powerful and swift. As I hit my fifth, I felt the unmistakable pull of my hamstring. As I collapsed to the ground, my days as a sprint coach came to a screeching halt.

It's good to place value on physical fitness and training (Obviously, I had not done enough to prepare myself). I know people who spend hours each week training their bodies. They put in the work, and they get the results. I admire their dedication.

As Christians, we're called to a life of spiritual fitness—endeavoring to be more like Jesus Christ. Creating a routine of Bible reading, prayer, and worship will help us get the results we want. Scripture is clear; physical strength is important, but spiritual health is more important. My advice: Work on them both.

PRAYER: *God, help me today to pursue spiritual health and fitness.*

SP

JESUS CHRIST AND WOODY HAYES

Colossians 1:15 – *The Son is the image of the invisible God, the firstborn over all creation.*

Today's verse teaches us that as you study Jesus, you are looking at God. The word "image" means "icon." When you look at your computer screen and see a bunch of icons, those small boxes represent larger files. Jesus is the exact icon of God, *and* He is the firstborn over all creation. This is precisely why Christmas is such a big deal—God wasn't content to stay in Heaven. He became one of us!

If you've read much about Woody Hayes, then you know that there were times when he would lead practices, while watching from the bleachers. From there, he would yell instruction down to the players to make sure they got it right.

But when they consistently couldn't figure something out, Woody would go down onto the field and show them what he wanted instead of just coaching from on high. Coach Hayes knew at times that his players needed his presence, in addition to his words.

When humans couldn't fix themselves, God wasn't content to merely send us commands from the heavenly bleachers. Because we could not fix ourselves, He joined us on the field by becoming one of us. We were blessed to see the Invisible God in the icon, Jesus the Messiah.

PRAYER: *Jesus, if You were willing to leave Heaven for me, that means You will never leave me alone. I believe that You are with me right now, and that You will come again for me.*

DF

ON STAGE

Acts 4:13 – *When they saw the courage of Peter and John and realized that they were unschooled, ordinary men, they were astonished and they took note that these men had been with Jesus.*

My first child was born with a certain kind of staph infection that gave him a 1 in 6,000 chance of surviving. I recall the heart-wrenching hours I spent beside his intensive care bed, praying to Jesus. After a desperate blood transfusion, the doctors and nurses got to witness a "1 in 6,000 miracle."

Fast forward twenty-eight years, and I find myself, on Father's Day, in front of 60,000 people. This child of mine brought me up on stage to lead the hand motions to a song he was performing. The event brought to mind that while I'm just an ordinary man and my son is unschooled in music, we had both been with the extraordinary Jesus in that intensive care room all of those years ago.

People continue to be astonished that my son, Tyler of Twenty One Pilots, fills arenas around the world for people to experience his shows. However, it's not surprising when you consider that we have a big God who can easily fill Madison Square Garden if He wants. All of us can have courage in what we do when we've been with Jesus.

PRAYER: *Lord, remind me of Your might. Remind me to walk with You and spend alone time praying with You.*

CJ

HE LOST HIS HELMET

Hebrews 12:1 – *Therefore, since we are surrounded by such a great cloud of witnesses, let us throw off everything that hinders and the sin that so easily entangles. And let us run with perseverance the race marked out for us...*

At the age of six, I played my first year of organized baseball. Since I grew up in Ohio, my hero back in 1977 was Pete Rose of the Cincinnati Reds. I used to love watching Pete's helmet fly off his head as he ran around the bases—I thought it made him look fast.

In my attempt to emulate Pete, I discovered that I could make my helmet come off by leaning back and violently shaking my head as I ran around the bases. I must have looked ridiculous. After two games of this nonsense, my coach pulled me aside and explained that my effort to lose my helmet and look fast was actually causing me to run slower.

As Christians, we have been instructed to let go of the things in our lives that slow our pursuit of Jesus Christ. If we are to chase after Him with maximum speed and efficiency, we must be willing to stop connecting ourselves with people and activities that cause us to slow down, stumble, or sin. Sometimes, this requires us to make difficult decisions related to friendships and habits of life.

Let go of your hindrances and experience the freedom of fully chasing after Jesus.

PRAYER: *Father, help me today to let go of people and activities that hinder my relationship with You.*

SP

SPIRITUAL PUBERTY

1 Corinthians 13:11-12 – *When I was a child, I talked like a child, I thought like a child, I reasoned like a child. When I became a man, I put the ways of childhood behind me. For now we see only a reflection as in a mirror; then we shall see face to face. Now, I know in part; then I shall know fully, even as I am fully known.*

Honest moment here—I have often wondered what God was thinking about when He invented puberty. Was He having the worst of all of His perfect days? Was He frustrated with some angels?

How did God explain what He was going to do to everyone else in Heaven?

Watch this! These children have lived relatively normal lives. Then, all of a sudden, their bodies will totally freak out. They'll get pimples; their voices will crack; their hormones will rage! But don't worry. They will grow through it and become wonderful adults—just in time to leave their parents!"

This life that we are living is only a dress rehearsal for real, eternal life. I think what we currently have on this earth is like spiritual puberty—sometimes fascinating, sometimes exhilarating, but mostly confusing and exhausting. But all of it is preparing us to move out of this world and making us ready to meet our God.

PRAYER: *Father, thank You for the reminder today that this world is not all there is. I have so much more in You. I cannot wait to see You in person—face to face!*

DF

FORE!

Psalm 5:11 – *But let all who take refuge in You be glad.*

As a kid, I played my local golf course hundreds of times. On it, there was a long, par-5 hole that took you far away from the clubhouse, and behind the green sat a little, old shelter that was overgrown with vines and weeds. The unkempt little shelter used to bother me, but over time, it just became part of the background.

One summer afternoon a rainstorm hit the golf course hard and fast. I felt helpless until I remembered the shelter. I sprinted to my place of *refuge and remained there* during the thirty minutes of driving rain. I was safe, I was glad, and I never looked at that dingy, little building the same.

In life, we all need refuge, a shelter, a place where we are safe. Even more, we all need to take *refuge* in the One who can truly shelter us from life's pressures and attacks. If we do, our affection for God will always grow.

PRAYER: *Heavenly Father, shelter, comfort, and protect me. I need You in the midst of life's stresses. In Jesus' name. Amen.*

CJ

TODAY IS YOUR DAY

2 Corinthians 6:2b – *I tell you, now is the time of God's favor, now is the day of salvation.*

As a marine serving in Vietnam, Jim kept a pocket New Testament with him for good luck. He wasn't a religious person, but the chaos of war made him consider spiritual things.

Jim's chaplain often spoke with him about Jesus, forgiveness, and eternal life. Though each encounter made him think, Jim was still reluctant to take the final step and invite Jesus to become his Lord and Savior. After one such conversation, the chaplain took Jim's New Testament, wrote "Today is the day of salvation" on the inside cover, and gave it back.

That same evening while on patrol, Jim's unit was ambushed, and he was hit with enemy fire. His buddies pulled him to safety, and a medic stabilized his condition. The next morning, Jim woke up in a military hospital. Tucked into the fold of his recovery blanket was his New Testament. As the anesthesia faded, Jim opened the book and saw his chaplain's inscription for the first time. Tears came to his eyes as he prayed to receive Jesus Christ.

We all need Jesus. We need His love, forgiveness, and salvation. Turn from your sin, ask Jesus to forgive you, and invite Him into your life. Don't delay. Today can become your day of salvation (see Appendix).

PRAYER: *Jesus, today I ask You to enter into my life. I ask You to forgive me of my sin and be my Lord. Today, I ask You to save me.*

SP

WHY IS SHE WITH HIM?

Romans 5:12 – *Therefore, just as sin entered the world through one man, and death through sin, and in this way death came to all people…*

Most of us would never say the words out loud, but we have all met couples and thought, "Why is she with him?" We just don't see it. She has her life together; she's headed in a solid direction; he's thirty, and still living in his parents' basement and playing Call of Duty all day.

Why is she with him? (I wonder how many people thought this about my wife and me!) Maybe she loves him, or she sees what no one else can see.

I also wonder how the angels feel about us. Angels see blessed, eternal things that humans cannot see, and they serve in ways that humans cannot yet.

However, humans have advantages over angels. Humans uniquely bear God's image. Only humans can experience grace and forgiveness. Only humans ultimately reign with Christ.

Assuming angels CAN see human events, I do wonder if one angel ever says to another, "Why is God with them? What does He see in humans? They are so—wrong." And the angels would be right.

They would rightly be jealous of the love God has placed on us through Christ. Charles Spurgeon once said, *"A soul in converse with God is the admiration of angels."*

Why is God with you? He loves you…He sees beyond who you are to who you can become.

PRAYER: *God, I want to live out of Your love today. I want to let Your love change my desires to reflect what You want. I pray for consistency between who I am and what I do.*

DF

REF, ARE YOU BLIND?

James 1:2-3 – *Consider it all joy when you encounter various trials, knowing that the testing of your faith produces endurance.*

Back when I coached high school AAU basketball, my team traveled during the off-season to another city that used their own referees to officiate the games.

Needless to say, we got the short end of many calls. One team we played really took advantage of the situation and played very rough and dirty. Our players were encouraged to play through it, and they did. We ended up losing the game even though we had outplayed the opponent.

My postgame talk was similar to today's verse, as I let the players know, "Even though you are upset with the loss, each of you got more out of this experience than the home team we played. You got tougher, played together, and worked harder than ever. Getting better and growing as a person and a player is why we play in the off-season."

We often will come across difficult experiences that shouldn't be viewed as a hassle or a waste of time. God can use those trials to develop us and make us "strong players" in the game of life.

PRAYER: *Lord, help me to see unfortunate experiences as times of personal growth. Teach me to lean on You.*

CJ

FIGHT BACK

1 Peter 5:8 – *Be alert and of sober mind. Your enemy the devil prowls around like a roaring lion looking for someone to devour.*

After parking my car near a ravine, I turned off the engine and got out of the car. Taking my backpack from the trunk, I turned around as an unknown person stepped out of the shadows and punched me in the face. Immediately, another man grabbed me, held me up, and pinned my arms behind my back. I was in serious trouble.

As the low-life thugs looked through my wallet, they became frustrated by my lack of cash. Out of anger, the man in front of me took out a knife and stabbed me in the chest. I collapsed to the ground, and they disappeared into the ravine.

My assailants came out of nowhere. They snuck up on me and used overwhelming force. Before I even realized what was happening, they had assaulted me. I was in the dark, unaware of my surroundings, and alone. I didn't stand a chance.

Check out this parallel: Temptation operates the same way, and we have to take steps to protect ourselves. We must fill our hearts with the light of God's Word, remain aware of our vulnerabilities, and walk with someone who will ask hard questions and hold us accountable. It's time to fight back.

PRAYER: *God, help me take steps today to fight back against the plans and schemes of the devil.*

SP

YOU ARE KEN WALTER

Matthew 23:11 – *The greatest among you will be your servant.*

The Westminster Catechism says, "A man's chief end is to enjoy God and glorify Him forever." You were created with a purpose and gifted to play a role in God's Kingdom. Today is the day to employ your gift.

When someone mentions the New England Patriots and their five Super Bowl wins, we think about Brady, Belichick, Vinatieri, and Gronkowski. The last name that comes to your mind is Ken Walter.

Walter was born in Cleveland, Ohio and blessed to be the punter at Kent State University. Walter played three seasons with the Patriots from 2001-2003. As the punter, his secondary role on the team was to be the holder for Adam Vinatieri.

Remember Vinatieri's famous 45-yard Snow Bowl kick to win the division in 2001? Or the Patriots' first Super Bowl win that came from a 48-yard kick from Adam Vinatieri the same year? Or the Super Bowl win in 2003? All of those kicks were held by Walter— behind the scenes, faithfully playing his role.

You can glorify God today with your gifts—your service, your teaching, your encouragement, your caring AND enjoy your relationship with Him along the way. You may not be Brady, Gronk, Vinatieri, or Belichick. Most of us aren't, but all of us can be Ken Walter.

PRAYER: *God, help me to see ways to serve others today. Thank You for the ways that You have gifted and equipped me to make a difference in the world.*

DF

BLUEBERRY PRAYERS

Jeremiah 33:3 – *Call to Me and I will answer you and tell you great and unsearchable things you do not know.*

Thinking about my life as a young boy, I remember our rotary telephone that sat on a hallway desk. Its loud ring would sound, and we had to race to pick it up from all areas of our big, old house.

Then one day, car phones became popular, all thanks to a huge car antenna that made mobile communication possible.

There is another phone I have to mention—the BATPHONE. When trouble occurred in the fictional Gotham City, its citizens would pick up this emergency red phone to reach Batman. When all else fails, use the batphone!

And now today, it seems as though everyone has a cell phone. Communication is right at our fingertips, and if that weren't enough, I see people wearing an earpiece for even quicker use.

When it comes to prayer, is our "prayer phone" an old rotary? A car phone? Is the emergency batphone the only time we talk to God? Or do we use an earpiece that's always dialed into the One who can "tell us great and unsearchable things we do not know"?

PRAYER: *Father, help me be aware of Your continual ability to guide and teach me about life. Remind me and help me to stay dialed in.*

CJ

A LIST OF MY OWN

2 Timothy 4:7 – *I have fought the good fight, I have finished the race, I have kept the faith.*

I had my share of eccentric professors in college. One such educator routinely said, "Write this down. You don't need it now, but you might need it later."

In honor of his memory, I have created a "You don't need it now, but you might need it later" list of my own. Consider the words below as we face a world with an ever-increasing disdain for Jesus Christ.

How To Respond In The Face Of Persecution:

Pray for those who persecute you. - Matthew 5:44
Rejoice when persecuted. - Matthew 5:11-12
Fulfill your calling despite persecution. - Acts 20:22-24
Bless those who persecute you. - Romans 12:14
Endure persecution with courage. - I Corinthians 4:12
Acknowledge God's presence when persecuted. - II Corinthians 4:7-9
Be faithful when persecuted. - II Thessalonians 1:4

Fight the good fight, finish the race, and keep the faith.

PRAYER: *God, help me today to remain strong and committed to You in the face of persecution.*

SP

SOFTBALL GUY

1 Peter 1:13 – *with minds that are alert and fully sober, set your hope on the grace to be brought to you when Jesus Christ is revealed at his coming.*

We all know Softball Guy. He shows up at the ballpark on opening day in midseason form. That's because he spends his winters at the indoor batting cages, honing that perfect swing.

Not only does he roll with the perfect uniform and the perfect swing, he always has the perfect gear—the latest carrying bags, glove, and triple-walled aluminum bat.

He yells at the umpire a little too much and encourages others too little, but he has perfected his home run trot.

Most people think that he is hiding insecurity, struggles with anger, or has never left high school ball behind. However, I would suggest there's something else going on in some Softball Guys—and in some of us.

What the wannabe Babe Ruth of the local league doesn't even realize is that the reason he loves softball so much is that on the diamond, he can feel something. He can express the anger of failure, the exhilaration of success, the joy of friendship, and the intensity of a comeback.

Most of us comfort ourselves in ways outside of the softball diamond, but they are just as destructive. Be sober-minded and fully alert. Play for an eternal win.

PRAYER: *Lord, I don't want to become phony or complacent. However, I am not perfect. I want to feel what You felt as You walked in this world and learned to lean into Your Father. I trust You today.*

DF

CAN'T OUTRUN GUILT

Psalm 32:5 – *I will confess my wrongdoings. And You forgive the guilt of my sin.*

When I was a little, ten-year-old boy, my friends and I would play basketball in a neighbor's driveway. One day the ball took a bad bounce and broke the antenna off the neighbor's car.

Our first instinct was to run to avoid punishment. So, nine little gutless wannabe NBA stars fled, and one stayed behind. Me.

I fearfully approached the neighbor's front door with the antenna in hand. When the neighbor came to the door, instead of being upset, she surprisingly said how proud she was of me. You see, she'd seen the whole thing transpire through the window.

There are times when we "run" after a wrongdoing, habitual sin, or offensive act. We can think, as those little boys did, that we can run to avoid getting blamed, but guilt will track us down. We then run from the guilt and turn to activities that help us not think about it. In the end, guilt finds us eventually.

PRAYER: *Father, give me the guts to pick up the "antenna" and admit my mistakes and wrongdoings to You and to others. I want the freedom from guilt.*

CJ

BAXTER HAS LEFT THE BUILDING

Psalm 37:23 – *The Lord makes firm the steps of the one who delights in Him.*

Our family is the proud owner of a Jack Russell Terrier named Baxter. Baxter eats excellent food, sleeps whenever he wants, goofs around all day, and has absolutely zero responsibility. In addition, my wife and daughter treat him like royalty. I'm telling you, this crazy dog has a better life than I do.

I say "crazy" because he is rambunctious, spunky, and quite an escape artist. One afternoon, Baxter escaped and was gone for twenty minutes before anyone realized it. For over an hour, we scoured the neighborhood in cars, on bicycles, and on foot. Unfortunately, we couldn't find the pup.

Fearing the worst, we regrouped on the front porch to figure out our next move. Within seconds, my wife spotted Baxter. He casually strolled up the sidewalk and into our driveway, as if to say, "OK, I'm ready to be home."

Baxter has it made as a member of our family. Still, his instincts tell him to check out the rest of the world. He's like the Prodigal Son who ran away and figured out life was better back home. Don't stray from God's provision and protection. He has an amazing purpose and plan for your life.

PRAYER: *God, help me today to find contentment in Your provision and protection.*

SP

SLIP SLIDIN' AWAY

2 Corinthians 4:8-9 – *We are afflicted in every way, but not crushed; perplexed, but not driven to despair; persecuted, but not forsaken; struck down, but not destroyed; always carrying in the body the death of Jesus, so that the life of Jesus may also be manifested in our bodies.*

We are "*always* carrying in the body the death of Jesus." On the day you are born, your heart has a certain, specified number of tics in it. Encouraged yet?

What about your physical appearance? Behold, the wrinkle monster cometh! You can tuck it or botox it, but eventually, you'll either look old or weird or both. And someday soon, someone will look at you and say, "She's your wife? I thought she was your daughter!"

Your relationships also are wearing away. You grow up playing with cousins at family reunions, but you grow older, divide up, and go your own ways. Time and circumstances pull you apart, then you're separated, and you die off—one at a time. Aren't you glad you bought this book?

Your skills are falling apart, too. Right now, someone younger than you in your organization thinks you are over the proverbial hill, and he/she cannot wait to replace you.

The great Apostle Paul (Simon) said it this way:

> *God only knows, God makes his plan. The information's unavailable to the mortal man. We work our jobs, collect our pay, believe we're gliding down the highway. when in fact we're slip slidin' away.*

Your *today* needs to be rooted in your "Someday." This life is a mere dress rehearsal for the real life to come!

PRAYER: *God, I believe that the more things seem to fall apart, the more they come together. Every day brings me closer to You. Help me to not waste one day.*

DF

GIDDY UP!

Hebrews 10:24 – *Let us consider how we may spur one another on toward love and good deeds.*

When I was a little kid, I was always fascinated with cowboys on TV. I had no idea that all of the equipment they wore had a purpose; I just knew they wore it, and it was so cool!

The hat, chaps, scarf, boots, gloves, and, most importantly, the spurs all caught my eye! They would jingle, jingle as the cowboy strutted through those swinging saloon doors. It wasn't until later in life when I realized the spurs weren't just a form of the early western bling. They were used to jab into the sides of a horse to jolt him to go faster. I guess we could say they were the horse's form of an energy drink.

Today's verse is telling us to "spur" others. Words of praise or encouragement, acts of kindness, and gifts can all give that jolt of energy needed to keep others going. When people see us, I hope they are hearing that jingle, jingle coming their way.

PRAYER: *Father, help me be convinced of how much You love me, so that I will be used to spur others.*

CJ

February 7th

I CAN'T MAKE IT

Psalm 107:19 – *Then they cried to the Lord in their trouble, and he saved them from their distress.*

While snorkeling and cliff jumping in Maui, my thirteen-year-old daughter Maddie and I found ourselves nearly a hundred feet from shore. The water was calm but twenty feet deep. As I was about to suggest moving into shallower waters, Maddie said, "Dad, I need your help."

Treading water, climbing up cliffs, and jumping off rocks had worn Maddie out. Without warning or explanation, overwhelming fatigue came over her. With arms thrashing and fear in her voice, Maddie exclaimed, "I can't make it."

Without hesitation, I swam to Maddie's side, grasped her shoulders, and held her up. I was able to keep her head above water, but Maddie was unable to swim. Unfortunately, we were still a long way from shore. With one arm around her upper body, I positioned Maddie so the rest of her weight would be on my back and side. For nearly eighty feet, I swam to shallow waters with Maddie on my hip.

If you find yourself in trouble and the water is over your head, cry out to God for help. He will hear your voice and, without hesitation, move to you. He is in the business of rescuing His children from their distress—it's what fathers do.

PRAYER: *God, hear my voice today and rescue me from my trouble.*

SP

HAPPY TREES

Proverbs 29:18 – *Where there is no vision, the people perish:* **(KJV)**

As a kid, sometimes the weather interrupted our TV antenna. In such cases, the only channel we had was PBS. And PBS didn't have the Superfriends on Saturday morning cartoons.

However, they did have a show called *The Joy of Painting* with Bob Ross. He had an afro that made 1970s disco kings jealous. Bob would start with a blank canvas and say, "You want a tree? Make it a happy tree." And in thirty minutes, he could create a picture that would leave you saying, "I don't know where that is, but I want to go there." He had vision.

Spiritual vision is God's picture of your preferred future. According to the Bible, you'll die without it. God's provides the canvas, brings the brushes, and has wired you to excel in certain areas. Vision allows you the opportunity to assure that some things will end up on your canvas *someday* by taking solid steps *today*.

You want a career? Make it a joyful career…not perfect or always happy. But you can choose joy. You want a great marriage? Make it a faithful one. You cannot control or change your spouse, but you can become the kind of spouse who sees the best in their mate.

Today, the brush is in your hands.

PRAYER: *Father, help me to see right now the vision that You have for my day, and not for all of my days—just enough vision to paint within Your lines for my life today.*

DF

SWISS ARMY KNIFE

1 Peter 2:11-12 – *I urge you to abstain from sinful desires, which war against your soul. Live such good lives among unbelievers that they may see your good deeds and glorify God.*

Sinful desires (wrongful actions, thoughts, and words) shouldn't be taken lightly. Sometimes they are reactions or impulses: the urge to lash out, gossip, watch bad shows, buy that ultra-sized Snickers bar, spend too much, hate, lie, and so on.

While our sinful desires can give us short-term satisfaction, they result in our inner-erosion in the long-term.

Comedian Jerry Seinfeld once talked about the Swiss having an interesting army:

> *Five hundred years without a war. Pretty impressive. Also pretty lucky for them. Ever see that little "Swiss Army Knife" they have to fight with? Not much of a weapon there. Corkscrews. Bottle openers. Come on, buddy, let's go! You get past me, the guy in back of me, he's got a spoon. So back off! I've got the toe clippers right here.*

Unlike the Swiss Army Knife, we, as believers, have powerful and effective weapons at our disposal in order to fight our sin. God wants us to keep asking for His strength to fight our battles and to continue to confess and start over when we fail.

PRAYER: *Lord, keep convincing me that entering the war against our wrongful desires is worth it. Give me the power to win and the humility to confess and start over when I lose.*

CJ

SHOCKING

Psalm 107:1 – *Give thanks to the Lord, for he is good; his love endures forever.*

In the spring of 2003, I was using a pair of long-handle hedge shears and an electric hedge trimmer to shape the bushes in our yard. My five-year-old son, Emerson, joined me outside as I wrapped up the project. Turning my back for a moment, I walked into the garage to get a rake. Immediately, the lights flickered, and I heard the unmistakable sound of an electrical surge. Emerson had cut the extension cord to the trimmers with the metal shears.

Terror gripped my heart as my son's life flashed before my eyes. Not knowing much at the time about grounded outlet plugs and circuit breakers, I thought for sure Emerson had electrocuted himself. Sprinting to him, I expected the worst.

Thankfully, the shock only knocked him on his backside. As my heart raced and tears filled my eyes, I picked him up and tried to catch my breath. Having feared the worst, I looked to Heaven and thanked God for his protection.

God protects and provides. He gives us more than we deserve, and I am amazed by His goodness. Take time today and reflect on what He has done in your life. Then, pause and say, "Thank You."

PRAYER: *God, I want to thank You today for Your protection, provision, goodness, grace, and mercy.*

SP

THE LAST DANCE

Hebrews 9:27 – *Just as people are destined to die once...*

The documentary series about the 1990s Chicago Bulls dynasty centered around their final championship. The team was expensive and aging. They were given a gift, but they knew their future. The general manager, Jerry Krause, vowed to break up the team following their '97-98 season. Their coach, Phil Jackson, told the team, "This year, this season, is the last dance."

America's greatest theologian, Jonathan Edwards, had 70 life-resolutions (I'd like to have 7).

Resolution #9 was, "Resolved, to think much on all occasions of my own dying, and of the common circumstances which attend death." Morbid? Possibly. Maybe *sobering* is a better word.

Jonathan Edwards and Phil Jackson had something in common. They knew the future. And knowing your future shapes your present. Knowing your tomorrow shapes your today. Life is a one-lap race...our only dance. Make today count.

PRAYER: *God, help me to be reminded that today matters. Someday... maybe today...I'm going to see You face-to-face. As I live today, help me to slow down and make a difference in people's lives...to see people the way You see them and love them the way You love them.*

DF

"UP!"

Micah 6:8 – *What does the Lord require of you? To act justly and to love mercy and to walk humbly with your God.*

What does God want us to do?

- Act justly — be fair; don't cheat.
- Love mercy — we don't have to get back at those who wrong us.
- Walk humbly with our God — hang out with Him as we go through our day.

I remember taking walks with my toddlers. My favorite part was when they would tug on my pants, extend both arms, and proclaim the magic word, "Up!" That one, little word was like a humble acknowledgment that they needed a break. It's almost as if they'd said, "I've done my own thing. Now I need a hug and a ride to where we are going."

God longs to walk alongside us. He will redirect us when we take a poor turn, pick us up when we trip, gently take away sharp objects, and steer us around the deep puddles if we would merely humble ourselves to acknowledge His presence, assistance, and wisdom.

When we need a break, we must be humble enough to extend our arms to Him and say, "Up."

PRAYER: *Lord, give me the strength to treat others well. Remind me to walk and talk humbly with You. Thank You that You want to direct me in life and carry me when I need a break.*

CJ

LOST

James 1:5 – *If any of you lacks wisdom, you should ask God, who gives generously to all without finding fault, and it will be given to you.*

Several years ago, I found myself lost in a remote village in Malawi. A flash storm and subsequent torrential rain had sent my team running for shelter. Unfortunately, while everyone ran one direction, I ran another.

After I'd sheltered for more than an hour by huddling under a leaky, thatched lean-to, the storm finally subsided. In search of my team, I set out on foot. As I trudged through the muck and the mud, it didn't take long to realize that I was lost.

Over the course of the next forty-five minutes, I asked three villagers if they had seen my team. The first villager couldn't speak English. The second villager spoke English but hadn't seen my team. Fortunately, the third villager was the local chief's son, and he pointed me in the right direction. Once I had found the right source, finding my team was easy.

As a believer, there will be times when you need to seek direction related to your education, career, relationships, family, and faith. When these moments come, be sure to go to the right source. Seek wisdom and direction from the Lord. He promises to give generously.

PRAYER: *God, today I ask for Your wisdom. When I don't know the answer or the next step to take, remind me to seek Your insight and direction.*

SP

THE TALK

Genesis 2:24 – *That is why a man leaves his father and mother and is united to his wife, and they become one flesh.*

Happy Valentine's Day! Between the third and tenth centuries, the institutional church issued decrees to ban husbands and wives from having sex on Fridays, because that was the day of the week when Jesus was crucified. And then on Thursdays, because that was the day Jesus was arrested…and on Sundays in memorial of the past saints.

Eventually the church added the feasts, and there were no sexual relations between husbands and wives during the forty days of Lent—and then during the forty days of Advent—or during the forty days of Pentecost. Writer Philip Yancey added those dates up on the annual calendar and concluded that the institutional church only allowed forty-four days a year for marital sexual relations.

Needless to say, the church has not always done a great job of handling this topic. Because of fear, the church has often been more conservative than God about sexuality. At the same time, the culture is always more liberal in its views.

The Bible teaches that sex is merely an echo of the eternal delight that we will share living in relationship with God. It's a gift that God has given to married men and women who have made a commitment to each other. Inside of God's boundaries, it's a beautiful reward.

PRAYER: *God, help me to see sexuality the way You see it. I don't want to make an idol out of sex. It is not the most important thing in the universe. You are. Help me to be reminded that You alone are my eternal reward.*

DF

HANG ON TO THE TOWEL

Galatians 6:9 – *Let us not become weary in doing good...we will reap a harvest if we do not give up.*

"I never talk poorly about them, yet they get away with making me look bad."

"I don't cheat on my tests, so the cheaters get better grades than me."

Many times we can become tired of doing good. Plus, it can seem as though others are enjoying themselves more as they live their lives of unclean pleasures and unethical practices. However, God tells us not to throw in the towel.

A young lady I once coached in high school basketball was truly dedicated to doing what was right in God's eyes. While this intimidated the boys, they respected her. Still, one day her father told me that Julie never gets asked to Homecoming or Prom, and it breaks his heart. Clearly, Julie experienced a lot of hurt in her pursuit of God, but she never threw in the towel.

Years later I recall sitting at Julie's wedding, and her dad told me that the man Julie was marrying was perfect for her. I could see the joy on her face, and it continues to this day.

God promises a harvest of blessings if we hang in there and don't give up.

PRAYER: *Father, I need Your strength to not give up or give in. I want Your harvest of blessings.*

CJ

EXTRACTION

1 Corinthians 15:57 – *But thanks be to God! He gives us victory through our Lord Jesus Christ.*

The novocaine had taken effect, and at the age of thirty, I was just moments away from my first tooth extraction. Immediately, my dentist had a grip on my tooth, and I felt him pull. Nothing happened. He tried again, and still nothing happened. My tooth refused to budge.

When the dentist stood to his feet, my anxiety peaked. Again, he pulled, and no dice. I lost my mind when he placed his knee on the edge of the dental chair to gain better leverage. With one final tug, he said, "Wow. Those are some deep roots!"

Once sin takes root in our lives, it never wants to leave. It digs into our soul and sets up residency. In our attempt to remove it, we become frustrated because no amount of pushing, pulling, or straining seems to work.

Despite your frustration, you cannot quit. As a follower of Jesus Christ, you have been promised victory over sin. Know that it won't be easy, but you have to remain engaged in the battle. Commit God's Word to memory, find an accountability partner, speak to your pastor, or see a counselor. Do whatever it takes to extract any deep-rooted sin from your life!

PRAYER: *God, give me victory over sin today and help me be determined to fight the battle each day.*

SP

February 17th

MARTHA MAYHEM

Luke 10:40-41 – *But Martha was distracted by all the preparations that had to be made. She came to him and asked, "Lord, don't you care that my sister has left me to do the work by myself? Tell her to help me!" "Martha, Martha," the Lord answered, "You are worried and upset about many things."*

March Madness causes a ripple effect everywhere in the U.S. from workplace attendance to Vegas gambling. It's the wonderful chaos of Cinderella teams, unknown young men suddenly becoming household names, and bracketology. It's NC State and Jimmy V. It's Christian Laettner simultaneously becoming the most loved player in Duke history and the most hated in Kentucky history. And it's 98-year-old nun, Sister Jean, with Loyola-Chicago. It's organized chaos, and we love it!

Another kind of organized chaos occurred when Martha invited Jesus and the Disciples to dinner at her house. Maybe she had a bracket in her mind about which Disciple would complement her cooking first or thank her last. St. John was a one-seed—so caring. Judas was sixteen-seed, always looking out for himself.

I imagine that she envisioned the banner that would be hung in Bethel. Everything was perfect—she just needed a little help. She heard the laughs in the next room. You can imagine her thoughts, "Here I am doing all of the work, and where's my sister?!?" You realize there's more cooking in the kitchen than dinner.

When Jesus says that Martha is "worried," the word means to "choke." She is being smothered by life. Who is Martha serving? Jesus or herself? Are we the ending of our own serving? Like Martha, we are worried and choked about many things, when we only need One thing.

PRAYER: *Jesus, help me to live in freedom today. Right now, I am embracing the fact that You are in charge of the universe and I am not. I am letting go of the responsibility of the results and entrusting those to You. I will follow where You lead.*

DF

JUST THINKING

ROLL THE LOG

Ephesians 5:11-13 – *Have nothing to do with the fruitless deeds of darkness, but rather expose them. For it is shameful even to mention what the disobedient do in secret. But everything exposed by the light becomes visible.*

We all have those secret thoughts, actions, or words that we keep in the dark closets of our lives. I remember a famous preacher stating to his audience, "If you knew everything that I thought, you wouldn't be here to listen to me. And if I knew all your thoughts, I wouldn't want to be here to speak to you."

One day, I rolled over an old log in my backyard, and underneath was an infestation of pinching-like bugs, worms, and other creepy critters that had lived in the darkness beneath the log. When the sunshine hit the area, all of the critters hurried away to seek shelter from the exposing light.

Similarly, we can allow God to shine His light and expose those secret areas of our lives by confessing and handing them over to Him. Instead of ignoring our dark areas, we can invite Him to empower us to overcome and ask Him to change us. It all starts with turning over the log and letting the light do its job.

PRAYER: *Father, I hand You most private thoughts and actions. Shine on them. I know it can take time, but keep changing me. Thank You that You still love me.*

CJ

NOT AN EASY CLIMB

Hebrews 10:36 – *You need to persevere so that when you have done the will of God, you will receive what he has promised.*

While on our honeymoon, my wife and I decided to hike Diamond Head Crater in Honolulu, Hawaii. While I wasn't initially interested in making the trek, the hotel concierge promised a magnificent view at the top.

The adventure required more effort than I'd anticipated. The ascent was arduous and steep, and about halfway up, I could tell my perseverance meter was getting low. I started to wonder if the view was going to be worth the climb.

My wife never waned in her enthusiasm to get to the top, and together we finished the hike. Reaching the top, I immediately realized that our effort was not in vain. It wasn't an easy climb, but the view was out of this world.

Spiritually speaking, the reward for persevering in our faith is much greater than the view from atop Diamond Head Crater. In fact, God promises to richly reward those who persevere. Through trials and persecution, we are encouraged to cling to our confidence in Christ—believing that He has prepared an eternal home for us. Knowing what awaits us in Heaven should inspire us to finish the climb.

PRAYER: *God, help me today to draw strength and resolve from the promises found in Your Word. Help me to faithfully endure the challenges of each day.*

SP

NO OFFENSE

Proverbs 15:1-2 – *A gentle answer turns away wrath, but a harsh word stirs up anger. The tongue of the wise commends knowledge, but the mouth of the fool gushes folly.*

You can be honest without being hurtful, truthful without being rude, and straightforward without being mean.

One time, I was discussing a minor health issue with my wife, and I had not followed up on it with a doctor. Somehow our five-year-old, who usually couldn't hear me from two feet away when asked to pick up her toys, suddenly called on her Superman-like, supersonic hearing from two rooms away to say, "Daddy, why won't you go to the doctor?"

"Well, honey, daddy's not always a good listener." Her response? "Well, you better start listening, or God is gonna get mad at you." I believe I replied with, "Thank you. No fears about you having the gift of mercy, Ms. Prophecy."

Our family has a running joke about her. As a child, her favorite way to start a sentence was, "No offense, but…"

One of the most amazing traits of Jesus is that He was simultaneously the most powerful human who ever lived AND He never intentionally hurt anyone with it. The Scriptures are clear that He was FULL of both grace and truth. He never tried to win an argument simply to boost His ego.

Don't let your demeanor trump your message.

PRAYER: *Spirit, help me to have the same kind of grace for others that You give to me. Bring the conviction into my life today that others need Your message more than my arguments.*

DF

REV UP THE JET SKI

Ephesians 6:10 – *Be strong in the Lord and in His mighty power.*

Let's say there's an alligator swimming after you in a river (I hate it when that happens). The shore is one hundred meters away, and you are given the following choices:

a) swim as fast as you can
b) hang on to a Jet Ski that just so happens to be offering you a ride
c) do nothing and hope that the gator just wants to have tea and chat (It's like the Bob Hope joke about the man falling down a hill and ending up right under a bear. The man thought, "I sure hope this is a Christian bear." He looked up to see the bear kneeling and praying, "Lord, thank You for the food I'm about to receive.")

The point of this illustration is to say that God isn't here to just stand beside us and cheer us on in life. He wants to be our Jet Ski; He is our help. He also gives us His *mighty power* to tap into through prayer, faith, and dependence. With every task, relationship, athletic contest, job, problem, crisis, daily routine, and so on, ask Him to empower you and work with and through you.

PRAYER: *Father, I need You and Your power to do this life. Help me to be strong in You.*

CJ

THERE'S NOTHING WE CAN'T DO

Romans 12:11 – *Never be lacking in zeal, but keep your spiritual fervor, serving the Lord.*

Several years ago, I was sitting in the passenger seat of a 4x4 truck at the bottom of a steep 500-foot mountain path in Malawi. My Malawian brother, Love Kaphesi, was in the driver's seat waiting for the rain to stop so that we could make our climb to the top. At the top of the mountain was a church with more than three hundred people awaiting our arrival.

After fifteen minutes, the rain subsided, but the deluge left the mountain path nearly impassable—or so I thought. Without warning, Love gripped the wheel and revved the engine. Before I knew what was happening, we were slipping and sliding up the hill.

Lips pursed with determination; Love drove the truck like he was in the Baja World Championships. After nearly two minutes of adrenaline-charged acceleration, the vehicle crested the ridge and came to a sudden stop. I looked at Love and said, "I can't believe we just did that." He looked back at me and said, "Brother, we're alive. God has given us this day. There's nothing we can't do!"

Take a risk for Jesus. Serve Him with all you have. Make an eternal difference in someone's life.

PRAYER: *God, help me today to passionately serve You and make an impact on someone's life.*

SP

LINE JUDGING

James 4:12 – *There is only one Lawgiver and Judge, the one who is able to save and destroy. But you—who are you to judge your neighbor?*

When my daughter played middle school volleyball, my wife was asked to be a line judge one evening. Now, one of my wife's primary spiritual gifts is mercy. Volleyball line judging is not included underneath the suggested areas of service for the mercy gift. Line judging is very black and white. The ball is in or out—not a good match with mercy.

The chair judge who gave my wife instructions before the game just said, "Use this flag. Be definitive: 'in' is flag down and 'out' is flag up." The game was close. The parent-fans were cheering, and the score was 23-24 in a game to 25 where you had to win by two.

Our team hits a great shot that bounces near the line. Everybody in the gym is waiting on my wife's call. As the crowd waits on flag up or flag down, my wife shrugs her shoulders and puts her flag right in the middle!

The teams replay the point, the other team scores, and we lose. But the genius of my wife is that she has never been asked to be a line judge again.

Remind yourself today that God is the only qualified Judge. We can step off of the judge's bench and trust Him.

PRAYER: *Father, I believe that You are a righteous, just Judge. You will do what is right at the exact right time in the best way for Your glory and my eternity.*

DF

TOOSDAY, TEUSDAY, TUESDAY!

John 10:10 – *The thief comes only to steal and kill and destroy; I have come that they may have life, and have it to the full.*

In today's verse Jesus reveals that He came not only to give us eternal life in Heaven when we die but also to give us a *full* life right now.

I have concluded that a major part of a "full life" is having good, solid relationships. These relationships need to be handed over to Him continually by praying for the needs of others, looking to encourage others, and especially forgiving those who offend, bother, or hurt us.

Unforgiveness and fault-finding will truly *steal, kill and destroy* a most precious commodity—our relationships. I admire the character of Winnie the Pooh who looked for the good in others when he said, "You can't help respecting anybody who can spell TUESDAY, even if he doesn't spell it right; but spelling isn't everything. There are days when spelling Tuesday simply doesn't count." Those words are a good reminder to us of the importance of valuing people and understanding what truly matters in life.

PRAYER: *Father, help me to forgive and not criticize or complain when others bother me. Thank You that You accept me when I "misspell Tuesday." Help me to do the same with others.*

CJ

CURBSIDE CRASH

Deuteronomy 31:8 – *The Lord himself goes before you and will be with you; he will never leave you nor forsake you. Do not be afraid; do not be discouraged.*

It was a picture-perfect Saturday afternoon in our neighborhood when my daughter, Maddie, asked if she could ride her bike around the cul-de-sac with her friends. Though she had only been riding her two-wheeler for a little while, I felt comfortable with her abilities.

Standing on the sidewalk, I watched Maddie hop on her bike and join her friends. She smiled and laughed as she pedaled her way around the circle with the rest of her pint-sized bike brigade. Everything was going great until Maddie caught the edge of her wheel against the curb, lost her balance, and crashed violently to the ground.

Though I was standing only a few feet from her, there was nothing I could do to keep my daughter from falling off her bike and breaking her arm. I felt helpless.

One of the many realities of life is that some things are just out of our control. As much as we would like to make our lives void of accidents and illnesses, we realize it's impossible. In these moments, we have to trust God, believe He has our eternal best interest in mind, and know that He is with us in the storm.

PRAYER: *God, help me today to remember that You are in control. Help me to sense Your presence and trust Your plan.*

SP

THE TROPHY SPOUSE

Ephesians 2:7 – *In order that in the coming ages he might show the incomparable riches of his grace, expressed in his kindness to us in Christ Jesus.*

Even though we would not *say* it, we have all *seen* it: billionaires in their 80s with uber-attractive spouses in their 20s. But it's rarely happily-ever-after. Best-selling author, John Grisham, famously said, "The mother of a trophy wife is not automatically a trophy mother-in-law." Historically, we have applied terms such as "gold digger" to the much younger spouse. We quietly think, "He's going to die, but she will get everything!"

Paul tells the Ephesians that God will save you in order to show off His love eternally. More than one well-known Bible commentator has used the idea of a trophy to explain this reality. I don't want to go so far as calling you God's trophy wife—only because there's nothing spiritually attractive about us.

But Jesus left Heaven, came to earth and died. And because He died, you get everything. No matter who you are or what you've done, you can have it all. You only have to be willing to give up everything.

God's grace is wonderfully uncomfortable. It is just as available for the most crooked snakes, as it is for the straightest arrows.

PRAYER: *God, I am so grateful for Your grace. Thank You for the reminder that I cannot earn it…I do not deserve it…but I will enjoy it forever. As You have given it to me, help me to extend it to others!*

DF

TAKE A HIKE

Genesis 6:9 – *Noah was a righteous man, blameless among the people of his time, and he walked with God.*

When I was first married, I tried to think of creative dates for my new bride and me. My wife mentioned to me that a great date would be to simply go on a walk together.

Not only was my wife's suggestion inexpensive, but it also made sense. She wanted to walk and talk, so we could get to know each other better. It turns out that walking together proved to be a very good time for our relationship.

Today's Scripture speaks of how Noah "walked with God." Walking with God is a figurative way to say that we are acknowledging His presence as we stroll through our daily routine, while intermittently chatting with Him.

Additionally, there are times in life when we can actually get away and take a literal walk. Those can be great opportunities to pour out our hearts to God, share our concerns, ask for His guidance, and talk to Him about others. Even more, those walks are especially helpful to get a sense of what He has to say to us and to help us know Him even more.

PRAYER: *Father, teach me how to truly "walk" with You.*

CJ

DARBY IS ON THE LOOSE

Genesis 39:12 – *But he left his cloak in her hand and ran out of the house.*

Darby was fast and ferocious. As a third-grader, I wanted nothing to do with our neighbor's Doberman Pinscher. On most days, a six-foot-tall fence kept Darby confined to his backyard. His bark was fierce, my fear was real, and I knew I never wanted to meet Darby face to face.

One afternoon, the beast broke free, and I heard the panicked shout of my best friend, "Darby is on the loose!" I took off like a shot. After just a few steps, I was in a full sprint toward the safety of my home. I wasn't taking any chances.

When danger rushes toward us, our instinct is to flee. Intuitively, we know that if we stick around, we might end up paying a price. Temptation, on the other hand, has the unique ability to paralyze. Often, our curiosity causes us to stop, stare, and consider the consequences. But this slight hesitation could end up costing us a great deal. In Genesis 39, Joseph finds himself in a remarkably tempting situation with Potiphar's wife. However, he didn't pause, ponder, or contemplate. Instead, he vigorously broke free from her grasp and sprinted from her presence—a smart move.

Don't underestimate the power of promptly removing yourself from tempting situations. Don't hesitate. Move your feet. Flee.

PRAYER: *God, help me today to recognize temptation and its attempt to paralyze and destroy. Help me run from situations and people who cause me to sin.*

SP

THE GRASS IS ALWAYS GREENER OVER THE SEPTIC TANK

Psalm 37:1-2 – *Do not fret because of evil men or be envious of those who do wrong, for like the grass they will soon wither, like green plants they will soon die away.*

Why do the worst people sometimes end up in the best circumstances? We aren't the only ones to ever feel that way. David and Jeremiah asked the same question.

Growing up, my family had a septic tank. When I began mowing the yard, I noticed that the grass grew the greenest and fastest over the septic system. However, looks were deceiving because there was death underneath that beautiful grass. You just had to get close enough to smell it.

When we ask questions about bad people getting good stuff, we make some false assumptions:

1. "Because things are the way that they are today, they will always be this way." This is not true; your condition is not your conclusion.
2. "Just because something looks pretty on the outside, it's thoroughly beautiful." This is also false. For examples, see Hollywood lives.
3. "I am one of the good people." Unfortunately, this is a third false narrative. The Scriptures are clear that none of us is righteous (good) of our own merit. G.K. Chesterton once responded to an op-ed article entitled "*What is wrong with the world?*" with the simple answer, "I am."

We are all flawed people who are prisoners of broken moments, but a better eternity is on the way.

PRAYER: *Jesus, help me to see that You are far better than anything that I could achieve or receive in this world. Help me to believe the truth that better days are coming!*

DF

THE APPROACH

Hebrews 4:16 – *Let us approach God's throne of grace with confidence, so that we may receive mercy and find grace to help us in our time of need.*

When I think about thrones, it takes me back to those famous Knights of the Round Table and movies with dragons. I picture a handsome, square-jawed, gray-haired King sitting on an oversized golden throne that's placed at the end of a long aisle. In this scenario, I gingerly walk toward Him, but along the way, feelings of intimidation come over me.

Suddenly the majestic King notices that I am approaching, and the smile on His face finally puts me at ease. It's almost as if He was looking forward to seeing me. As I amble even closer, a gush of comfort pours out of His countenance and coats my heart with a unique certainty that this King completely forgives and cares about me.

This is how we approach God the Father. No matter what I've done, thought, or said, He is always so glad to have me approach His throne of grace. And the more I approach this gracious King, the more I look forward to our conversations, my confessions, and especially those times when He reassures me because I'm hurt, frustrated, helpless, or feel like giving up.

PRAYER: *Father, thank You for allowing me to approach You with confidence. I need the forgiveness, strength, and understanding that You provide.*

CJ

GRIT AND GUTS

Philippians 4:13 – *I can do all this through him who gives me strength.*

Starting a football program from scratch is challenging under optimum conditions. For an underfunded private school, it's almost impossible. My son, Emerson, and his brand-new, eighth-grade teammates were about to discover this fact for themselves.

Injuries, inadequate facilities, and a lack of players plagued the first three seasons. During their eighth, ninth, and tenth-grade campaigns, the team lost many more games than they won. At times, Emerson and his teammates were so physically beaten up and mentally defeated that they considered throwing in the towel. With grit and guts, they pressed forward.

During their junior campaign, the squad made vast improvements. In their senior season, Emerson and his teammates won the final game in dramatic fashion to secure their first winning record. Today, the program excels beyond anything this group of young men could have ever imagined when they helped launch it back in eighth grade.

It's not easy starting something new. Sacrifice, dedication, and courage are required. Make a plan, put in the work, and don't be afraid of the results. If God has given you a vision, chase after it with determination, grit, and guts. You can do all things.

PRAYER: *God, help me today to boldly chase after the vision You have for my life.*

SP

A PRAYER FOR MY REPAIR

Genesis 22:13-14 – *Abraham looked up and there in a thicket he saw a ram caught by its horns. He went over and took the ram and sacrificed it as a burnt offering instead of his son. So Abraham called that place The Lord Will Provide. And to this day it is said, "On the mountain of the Lord it will be provided."*

Just after painting our garage, one of our family members (who shall remain nameless) drove into one of the garage walls. So, I found myself trying to make a large drywall repair, and I think I was responding emotionally. Even though it was cold outside, I was in our unheated garage, cutting out the broken drywall with an x-acto knife, while wearing sandals—home repairs are not my strength.

As my repair was deteriorating, my friend, who is a contractor, calls me. He says, "Hey! I've got a few minutes; thought I'd stop by your house." I looked up at Heaven and said, "Thank You, Lord for *providing* for my needs out of nowhere!" I later found out that my wife had called his wife and asked for "prayer" for my repair.

In today's verse, the word "Provide" is two Latin words smooshed together. "Pro" is the prefix that means "before," and "vide" comes from the Latin word "videre," which means "to see" (where we get our word *video*).

That means our God is the God Who Sees Before—He sees our needs before they ever exist. Today, you may be pressured in numerous ways or have many needs. In the middle of confusion, don't forget to look around. Jehovah-Jireh will be there providing in ways you may have never expected.

PRAYER: *God, thank You for how You have provided for so many of my needs that I have taken for granted. Thank You that You have already provided for my need for today. Help me to see Your provision!*

DF

THE CUT LIST

Psalm 139:13-14 – *For You created my inmost being; You knit me together in my mother's womb. I praise you because I am fearfully and wonderfully made.*

I once coached a seventh grade basketball team where I could only keep twelve players, which meant I had to cut fourteen players. Those fourteen kids felt like losers, and their self-esteem was shaken to be cut from the team. While it seemed unfair, there was only room for twelve.

However, there was a blessing for those kids, if one is able to see it. The blessing is that those "cut" guys now have more time to find a niche in life that better fits them. Actually, making the team could have stunted their growth and kept them from discovering a true passion or talent.

We tend to do the same thing and become discouraged easily. We must remember that every person is uniquely valuable, and failure can be God's way of redirecting us. One person defined success in a very helpful way by saying that it's, "Going from failure to failure and not losing your enthusiasm."

PRAYER: *Father, don't let my culture define my value and worth. You see me as valuable. Help me to see through Your eyes what and who You want me to be.*

CJ

ADAM'S ASSOCIATES

Proverbs 13:20 – *Walk with the wise and become wise, for a companion of fools suffers harm.*

When Adam was twenty-two, he walked with God, and his faith was vibrant and real. Having just graduated from college, he had plans to get married and start a career. Everything was perfect.

By the time Adam was thirty, his life was a mess—he had destroyed his marriage, lost his career, and started using drugs. At age thirty-one, with heroin coursing through his blood, Adam lost control of his car and hit a telephone pole at a high speed. He died alone on a country road in the middle of the night.

I knew Adam well and watched his life spiral out of control. Sadly, he refused help. Reflecting on his life, I'm confident in this statement: Adam's life began falling apart when he started surrounding himself with friends and colleagues who lived in the fast lane.

The people we spend time with have an enormous impact on our lives. They can shape our thinking and influence our choices. You can't always control who you work with, but you can take charge of the rest of your life. Surround yourself with people who build your faith. Make your best friends those who aspire to live for Jesus Christ.

PRAYER: *God, help me today to choose friendships that strengthen my relationship with You.*

SP

WEDDING DAY

Revelation 19:7 – *Let us rejoice and be glad and give him glory! For the wedding of the Lamb has come, and his bride has made herself ready.*

I have officiated my fair share of weddings and witnessed many couples make covenant vows such as, "I will love, honor, and cherish" and "for better or worse, for richer for poorer." Those are very lofty goals.

Sometimes, I think we should give couples something more practical at first, perhaps lower the bar a little. "Austin, do you solemnly swear to give up control of the remote, actively listen, make eye contact when the game is in fourth quarter, and pick up your underwear?"

When God introduces the idea of covenant with Abraham and Sarai, God says, "I will make a covenant with you." He does NOT say, "We will make a covenant together." God knew they wouldn't keep up their end of the deal. Instead, God says, "I will keep my end of this agreement, even when you do not."

Every time a couple stands in God's sight and makes covenant vows, two people become one, spiritually speaking. When they kiss and walk down the aisle, the newlywed euphoria (no matter how short-lived it may be) is a reminder to us of a better covenant—God is preparing His church to experience His love for all of eternity. If we believe that our future is that secure, we can face anything today.

PRAYER: *Father, I'm forever loved by You today. No matter what happens to me on this earth, I will never stop being loved by You. I can face anything with You on my side.*

DF

THE GIVE UP POINT

Psalm 31:24 – *Be strong and take heart, all you who hope in the Lord.*

My paraphrase of today's verse would go something like this: "Hang in there when things get tough; God will rescue you."

The biblical term "hope" is different from how the word is used today. Hope isn't just a desire for something to happen, which is how it's commonly used today. In the Bible, the word for "hope" is actually interpreted as something that will, in fact, happen.

Once there was an experiment done with rats in deep, sewer water (sounds disgusting, right?). The experiment was centered around the question, how long can a rat swim before it gives up and drowns? During the experiment, some of the rats were rescued right before they reached their giving up point. Interestingly, the next day, those rats swam farther than their initial giving up point. Why? Those rats had hope! They knew, unlike the first timers, that if they hung in there, they would be eventually rescued.

Hope is a powerful thing, indeed!

PRAYER: *Heavenly Father, I need Your strength to not give up. I place my dependence and hope in You. I know You won't let me drown. In Jesus' name. Amen.*

CJ

IF THESE WALLS COULD SPEAK

Psalm 78:4 – *We will tell the next generation the praiseworthy deeds of the Lord, his power, and the wonders he has done.*

Don and Lisa were ready to leave their home of forty years for the last time. Headed south for retirement, the couple had made peace with their memories. Still, tears filled Lisa's eyes when Don said, "If these walls could speak."

Together, they had raised a family in the now-empty rooms of their modest home. As people of faith, the couple did their best to establish Jesus Christ as the head of their household. Collectively, they laughed and cried through peaks and valleys. As a family, they sought after dreams, gave God the glory, and created a lifetime of memories.

And though they were far from perfect, they endeavored to leave a legacy of faith for their children and grandchildren. More than anything, they wanted the people whom they loved the most to remember the work Jesus Christ had accomplished in their lives. What a noble intention!

As parents and grandparents, we create a legacy of faith in the hearts and minds of our children and grandchildren when our words and actions reflect the love of Jesus. We help cement a godly heritage when we teach His principles, worship together, and put our faith above everything else. A noble intention indeed!

PRAYER: *God, help me today to be a legacy builder. Help me make decisions that will forever point my children and grandchildren toward You.*

SP

SCARED TO LIFE

Luke 5:8 – *When Simon Peter saw this, he fell at Jesus' knees and said, "Go away from me, Lord; I am a sinful man!"*

Numerous times a month, something odd happens, when I walk into another room of my house. As I stride into the room, my wife will jump into the air and yell, "Oh! You scared me!"

I'll never figure it out. My wife knows that I'm home—that I'm the only one home—so I respond, "You know I'm here." She replies, "I know you're here. I just didn't know you are right here!"

I think Christians generally know God is here. He's omnipresent, so He's everywhere all of the time. However, I think we forget that God is right here...next to you right now.

In today's verse, Simon Peter told Jesus to leave Him, but couldn't Peter have left Jesus? However, what Simon Peter was really saying is, "Jesus, my sin means I don't belong with You." Aren't you grateful that Jesus does not leave?

Rudolf Otto referred to God as, "Mysterium Tremendum," that which is mysterious and tremendous.

You cannot escape from God today. There's no hiding place or back alley, not to mention that you may be surprised when you realize, "He's right here."

PRAYER: *God, thank You that You never leave. No matter what my sin is, Your love always pursues me. I cannot escape Your Presence today. And I don't want to. I want to be right here with You!*

DF

THE CAR WASH OF LIFE

Proverbs 4:26 – *Give careful thought to the paths for your feet and be steadfast in all your ways.*

I recall my first automated car wash. All I had to do was drive my '72 Oldsmobile front tires up to the rails, put her in neutral, and let the spinning brushes do their thing as my car was pulled through.

Sometimes, I find myself having whole weeks where I seem to live as though I've pulled up to the "car wash of life": I put my brain in neutral, I autopilot my daily routine, and I allow the world around me just to happen.

One challenge in life is to set aside time to just think. As today's Scripture tells us, we are to "Give careful thought to" what is going on around us, the feelings of those we encounter, the dreams we have, the help we could give, the problems we need to be fixed....

Taking these thoughts and turning them into conversations with God makes for a secure and significant life. We need to be careful not to let texting, Instagram, YouTube, TV, movies, and surfing the web steal all of our "think time." We have much to consider.

PRAYER: *Lord, remind me to take time to stop and think often. Thank You for the blessings that will follow as You join me in my think times.*

CJ

TWENTY-ONE PEOPLE

Matthew 28:19 – *Therefore go and make disciples of all nations, baptizing them in the name of the Father and of the Son and of the Holy Spirit.*

As a teenager and college student, I was fortunate to have wonderful people invest in my life. Humanly speaking, they used their own time and spent their own money. Spiritually speaking, they offered wise counsel, much-needed encouragement, and biblical instruction.

Who were these incredible human beings? Recently, I made a list, and twenty-one people came to mind. Apart from my parents, these folks made the most significant impact on my life as a young person. Interestingly enough, only three were pastors, while the vast majority were regular people with ordinary jobs. Some were construction workers and farmers, while others were computer programmers and business owners. And as you might imagine, there was everything in between.

Though these amazing people came from various backgrounds, they all had the same thing in common. They had a great desire to make a lasting difference in people's lives. They were selfless investors who chose to be disciple-makers.

As believers, we are called to make an impact in this world, and we are called to make disciples. You don't have to be a pastor or ministry leader to make a difference in someone's life; you just have to be willing to do so.

PRAYER: *God, help me today to be a disciple-maker.*

SP

MOMS WIN

John 13:34 – *A new command I give you: Love one another. As I have loved you, so you must love one another.*

On one occasion, my wife went to spend time with her family for a week. As she was leaving, one of our kids said, "Mom, how are we going to make it without you?" That is code (or not so code) for, "Please don't leave us with Dad!"

It reminded me of another time when our kids were young, and my wife was gone for a few days. The kids woke up, and I had cereal sitting out for breakfast. They said, "We want waffles and eggs and bacon and French toast. We don't want cereal." I responded, "So, what you're saying is that you don't want breakfast?"

On the day my wife was returning home from that particular trip, my children and I sat down to eat. I asked my oldest child to pray, and she prayed, "Lord, thank You for the food, and please bring Mom home safely." My youngest child, who was five years old, quietly commented, "Yes, Jesus! Oh, praise Your name!"

Moms win, because they sacrifice for their families. Dads sacrifice too, but moms just do it better generally speaking. You will influence people's lives in relation to how much you are willing to sacrifice for them. While they won't always appreciate it in the moment, it will make a difference eternally.

PRAYER: *Father, help me to love others today the way that You love them: to the point of sacrifice. Grant me the grace to see my sacrifice as joyfully giving to eternity.*

DF

A STOMACH THAT DOESN'T JIGGLE

Psalm 71:20 – *Though You have made me see troubles, many and bitter, You will restore my life again; from the depths of the earth You will again bring me up.*

God knows we are inherently knuckleheads by nature. He doesn't expect perfection from His people. Rather, He expects believers to attempt, while leaning on His strength, to strive in the right direction. However, because of our many flaws, this entails continual "start overs."

Overweight Comedian Kevin James once said, "My fitness goals are different than most peoples. Most people want to lose enough weight so they look good in a bathing suit or they want to lower their cholesterol. I just want to lose enough so my stomach doesn't jiggle when I brush my teeth."

Pulling off perfection and a faultless, error-free existence isn't possible. It's more so that we join God in the process of going in the right direction, a little at a time, and live with a heart of forgiveness towards others as we remember how much we have been forgiven.

PRAYER: *Father, give me the heart to be a forgiver. Give me the eyes to see when I need to ask forgiveness. Thank You again and again for "bringing me up."*

CJ

AIR TRAFFIC CONTROL

Psalm 121:7-8 – *The Lord will keep you from all harm—he will watch over your life; the Lord will watch over your coming and going both now and forevermore.*

"Folks, we've been instructed to move into a holding pattern as Air Traffic Control has indicated a complication on the ground. We're not exactly sure what the problem is, but we're going to trust the good people in the tower to bring us home when the time is right."

After spending the last four hours in the air, these were the last words I wanted to hear from our captain. More than anything, I just wanted the plane to land so I'd be one step closer to getting home. To my dismay, we spent the next hour circling the skies.

Upon our landing, the airport was buzzing with police and security officials. As it turns out, about thirty minutes before our scheduled arrival, two men were arrested for shining high-powered lasers into the cockpit windows of planes trying to land—an activity known to be extremely dangerous to pilots. After hearing this, I was thankful for the time spent in the holding pattern.

It's important to remember that God often places us in a holding pattern to protect us. Like the air traffic controller, He sees the big picture and works to keep us from danger.

PRAYER: *God, thank You for protecting me today. Help me to be patient and trust You in moments when You ask me to wait.*

SP

THE HOBBY LOBBY

Psalm 86:11 – *Give me an undivided heart* **(NASB)**

Frustrated and angry during my first round of golf, I remember my partner saying, "If golf is relaxing, it's because you are cheating."

So, let's say you have two guys. One owns a landscaping business, loves running it, AND enjoys golf for fun. The other guy lives for golf and works just to make ends meet. Being on the PGA Tour is his dream.

Now, let's say both play a US Open qualifier but miss the cut by one stroke. The two of them will experience completely different levels of discouragement. Why? Because one has a hobby and one has an obsession.

What is your obsession? Your primary pursuit? Are you primarily in love with Jesus and grateful when happiness is thrown in as a bonus? Or are you primarily pursuing happiness, and God is just your hobby?

A good friend of mine once fell off of a ladder and got not one, but two compound fractures in his ankle. I texted him the next morning to see how he was doing, and he sent me a picture of his ankle post-surgery.

In the picture, I noticed his Bible was opened and his journal was out. He was reading (and journaling) Deuteronomy! When was the last time you said, "I need more Deuteronomy in my life." It was a good reminder that we must lobby our hearts to be undivided towards Him or God will just become nothing more than another hobby.

PRAYER: *God, I want to have a singular heart and vision for my day. I'll encounter tough circumstances and tough people. I want to face both of them with You on the throne of my heart.*

DF

March 17th

NOT DISCOURAGED BUT HIS-COURAGE

Joshua 1:9 – *Be strong and courageous. Do not be terrified; do not be discouraged, for the Lord your God will be with you wherever you go.*

The reason we can be courageous is because God goes with us wherever we go. Thus, we don't have to remain discouraged because we can tap into "His-courage."

I once talked with a young man who had biked across the United States. Along his journey, he made his way to a road sign in Florida that read, "Bear crossing, next 16 miles." After a few moments of debate and some serious reflection, he chose to continue on the path.

Just as this nerve-racking, 16-mile stretch had come to an end and relief was beginning to set in, *another* sign appeared: "Bear crossing, next 14 miles." His first reaction was, "Are you kidding me?!" The young man then realized that had the first sign said, "Bear crossing, next *30 miles*," he probably would have given up and missed out on the rest of his life-changing ride.

God puts just enough fearful situations and difficulties in our paths that require us to tap into "His-courage" to go on. He wants us to push through the difficulty in order to make us stronger.

PRAYER: *Lord, I need the courage that You can supply. Thank You that You will be with me wherever I go.*

CJ

YOU'RE ON THE TEAM

1 Corinthian 12:27 – *Now you are the body of Christ, and each one of you is a part of it.*

With one lap to go in the 4x800 meter relay, my daughter, Maddie, needed to pass one more girl in order for her team to advance to the regional track meet. Standing along the track, I wondered if she had the strength and stamina to make it happen.

Along the backstretch, Maddie overtook the runner in front of her. Coaches and teammates cheered as she passed. Now, I wondered if my daughter could hold her position. With 100 meters to go, Maddie found another gear, separated from her opponent, and removed any doubt in my mind. Her team qualified!

In a relay race, each runner has a specific role in helping the team achieve victory. Maddie did her part, but so did each of the girls who ran before her. Their combined effort made the difference.

As a Christian, you have a spot on the team—a role we need you to play. Your unique gifts and abilities can contribute to a larger purpose. You can be a part of helping someone come to faith in Jesus Christ. If you're sitting on the sidelines, jump in, and start making a difference. The Gospel depends on it!

PRAYER: *God, help me discover today how I can serve You and make an eternal impact in the lives of the people around me.*

SP

March 19th

SINGLE SHEET

Matthew 6:9-10 – *"Our Father in heaven, hallowed be your name, your kingdom come, your will be done, on earth as it is in heaven."*

When I lived with five other guys in college, I had this problem. As my own kids grew older, the same issue suddenly began surfacing at my house, as well.

As parents, we try to teach our kids to be responsible. You get something out; you put it away. You use something; you replace that "something." Here's where the problem comes into play.

You finish off a roll of toilet paper? You put a new one in its place. However, I began seeing a lot of toilet paper rolls with one sheet left. That way, there was justifiable deniability to replace the roll. What are you going to do with one sheet of TP? That says, "I'm going to take care of my business, give you the minimum I have to, and still be right."

That's exactly what religion says: "God, there's all this stuff I want you to give to me. However, I'm only giving You the minimum I have to, so that I can get what I want." It's toilet paper religion.

That doesn't remotely resemble, "Hallowed be Your name." God is the great Creator of the universe. Instead of acting as though we are entitled to His blessings, we can bring Heaven's values to earth today.

PRAYER: *Father, I don't want religion today. I want to adore You by living in relationship with You right now. I want to do everything I can to bring Heaven's Kingdom values to earth today.*

DF

OLD SALAD DRESSING

Psalm 26:2 – *Test me, Lord, and try me, examine my heart and my mind.*

I have friends who recently had a refrigerator die, so they had to clean out all of the ruined contents. After hearing about their situation, I thought it wouldn't be a bad idea to go through and restock my own fridge.

Well, I didn't realize how much stuff had accumulated in my fridge, especially the door items. There were hot sauces, ketchup, salad dressings, jars of random items like diced garlic, a plastic lemon filled with juice, and so on. Then, I looked deeper inside at all the items that just have become routine foods that we consume. However, if I took the time to read the ingredients on these items, I'd most likely change to healthier options.

Just like the refrigerator, our routine needs to be examined—what we say, what we watch, how we use our time, how we talk to others, how we exercise, what we eat, and even our occupational pursuits. The good thing is that we aren't left alone to make adjustments in our lives. We have a God who gives us the strength to make change happen.

PRAYER: *Father, test me, try me, and examine my heart and mind. Lead me into an even more fulfilling life.*

CJ

GRANDMA'S GOODNESS

Philippians 2:5 – *In your relationships with one another, have the same mindset as Christ Jesus.*

In 2012, I met with the pastor of a large church in Pennsylvania. Taking a seat in his office, I was intrigued by a large placard on his wall. When I asked him about it, he told me that it was a gift from his grandma who always wanted him to remember how to treat people. The words inscribed are worth passing along today:

> God is gracious with you; extend grace to others.
> God is merciful with you; extend mercy to others.
> God is kind to you; extend kindness to others.
> God forgives you; extend forgiveness to others.

The way we treat people speaks volumes about how much we understand and appreciate God's all-encompassing love for us. Despite our weaknesses, weirdness, and failures, He chooses to love us. Likewise, we should determine to love those around us despite their shortcomings, peculiarities, and missteps.

Let's not live in a world of revenge, put-downs, and grudges. Instead, may we choose to pattern our relationships with one another after the humility, love, and selflessness of Jesus Christ.

PRAYER: *God, help me treat people today in a way that reflects the kindness, grace, mercy, and forgiveness You have given to me.*

SP

DIY CHRISTIANITY

Romans 12:1a – *Do not be conformed to this world, but be transformed...*

The DIY revolution has made everyone a contractor. Every home older than twenty years is a potential flip! But even Chip and Joanna Gaines will tell you that not every flip is the same.

Flips can easily become flops, when the "flippers" decide to only make cosmetic changes. Instead of taking old walls down to the studs, you can just cover up old problems with fresh paint. But the problem is still there, lurking just below the "Behr minimums." (See what I did there?)

There's a similar parallel in Christianity. We have the tendency to settle for cosmetic changes...quick spiritual flips. This verse says that we should not "conform." It's the word "skema," our root word for *scheme*.

Jesus didn't ask for people to simply be converted, walk an aisle, or pray a prayer. He said, "Follow me." In other words, Christianity is not a human scheme to work our way into Heaven with the least amount of change possible.

God gave all of Himself for us on the Cross. We don't have the option of giving Him bare minimum changes. Our hearts need to be taken down to the studs. We need to be transformed—made into something brand-new by God's Spirit.

PRAYER: *Father, I want to be a follower, not a simple flip. Right now, I'm putting my life in Your hands today. Change me. Transform me into Your image.*

DF

MUSICAL BOWL

Romans 12:16 – *Live in harmony with one another. Do not be proud, but be willing to associate with people of low position.*

Music can be extremely enjoyable. There's something about a blend of sounds that pleases our hearts.

In the midst of my usual morning rush, something uniquely odd happened. As always, when I finish my oatmeal, I rinse out the bowl (I found that oatmeal turns into concrete if left to dry). Afterwards, I was turning to make my mad dash out of the door when I heard this amazing sound. It was so incredible that it stopped me in my tracks. I thought it must have been a cell phone setting, but it was coming from the sink.

The water was dripping down and hitting the side of my bowl in such a way that it made a wonderful tone. It truly took my thoughts from preparing for the rush hour traffic to suddenly having curious thoughts about God and His "inventions." In fact, that "musical bowl" changed my entire ride to work.

When we live in harmony with one another, we are a beautiful tone to God. It's the "harmony" of getting along instead of backbiting, and the beauty of looking to respect those "of lower position" rather than degrading them.

PRAYER: *Father, You are amazing and give me amazing things. Help me to forgive and get along with others. I want to honor You with sweet sounds to Your ears.*

CJ

CULTIVATING CIRCUMSTANCES

James 1:4 – *Let perseverance finish its work so that you may be mature and complete, not lacking anything.*

As a member of the Class of 2020, my daughter Maddie missed out on all the good stuff that normally accompanies the end of a student's senior year of high school. Prom, senior trip, a normal graduation service, and her final track season are just a few of the meaningful extracurricular activities that Maddie lost because of the COVID-19.

Additionally, as a freshman in college, she lost her cross country season and much of the campus life she had expected to experience. Obviously, Maddie was not alone in all of this. Millions of students who were members of the Class of 2020 dealt with the same challenges.

Interestingly enough, I watched my daughter and her friends develop a remarkable sense of determination and a great deal of perseverance as a result of these circumstances. To be candid with you, I couldn't be more proud.

Adversity cultivates growth. James 1:1-4 reminds us that trials test our faith, and tested faith produces perseverance. James goes on to tell us that perseverance creates maturity. Moving forward, begin facing your challenges head-on, knowing that God is using them to mold and shape your heart.

PRAYER: *God, help me face my trials today. Build spiritual maturity in my heart and soul.*

SP

SLEEP IS GOOD

Genesis 2:7; 22 – *Then the Lord God formed a man from the dust of the ground and breathed into his nostrils the breath of life… Then the Lord God made a woman from the rib he had taken out of the man, and he brought her to the man.*

On the sixth day of Creation, God formed Adam from dust. Adam woke up and the first thing he saw was God! His Creator! Then, God led Adam through the process of naming the animals only for Adam to discover he was missing a partner.

So, God put Adam back to sleep, and God took a rib and formed Eve. When Adam woke up the second time, the first thing that he saw was naked Eve. His pre-fall, unaffected-by-sin wife!

Adam's conclusion? Sleep is good.

What is even more interesting is that because God created Adam on the sixth day of Creation, Adam only got in one good day's work before he had a mandated day off on the seventh day. God is making a point here early in Adam's life about the necessity of Sabbath and rest.

How are you doing with resting? God built this principle of rest into His calendar from the beginning, and not because He needed it—we need it. We need a Sabbath each week…rest, renew, and reflect.

PRAYER: *God, thank You that You care enough to call me to rest. I know that Jesus is my ultimate, eternal rest, and I want to reflect that in my life currently and according to Your plan.*

DF

NO CUTTING IN

Galatians 5:7 – *You were running a good race. Who cut in on you to keep you from obeying the truth?*

I know of a young man who earned a scholarship to play basketball in college, and this young man had high morals, ethics, and faith. Unfortunately, the other players did not, to say the least.

Not surprisingly, the young man was teased and left out by the others because heavy partiers usually want everyone to join them in their youthful immorality and lifestyle in order to justify it. If one is "staying clean," then an uncomfortable guilt can filter in, and they'll do anything to avoid that, including leaving others out.

Needless to say, the young man started wanting to throw in the towel and go to the strip clubs, get drunk, and pick up girls because he wanted to fit in and have some friends. Nevertheless, he managed to stand firm, and in God's strength, he continued *"running a good race."*

Over time, the other guys started to look up to him. Before long, they were even going to him for advice and help. Most importantly, he kept his inner peace and joy.

PRAYER: *Father, help me to start over when I allow others to negatively influence me. Give me the strength to run a good race, especially when there is strong resistance. Thank You that the benefits and prize are well worth it.*

CJ

I CANNOT STOP

Romans 10:15 – *As it is written: How beautiful are the feet of those who bring good news!*

At the age of 18, Amar became a follower of Jesus Christ in a part of the world where there was a genuine resistance to Christianity. Soon after his conversion, Amar felt called by God to preach the Gospel and start a church. Within a year, he saw twenty-one men and women come to faith in Jesus Christ and join his secret house church.

While walking home from the market one evening, Amar was attacked by three men who demanded that he disband his church. They left him lying in a heap, but it was there that Amar determined in his heart that he would never stop preaching the Gospel. Over the course of the next month, Amar was attacked on two more occasions. As the severity of each beating increased, so did Amar's resolve to follow his convictions and share his faith.

Out of fear for his safety, Amar's church family asked him to consider taking a short break from his evangelism efforts and church work—at least until the target was removed from his back. While he understood their concern, he simply replied, "I cannot stop. The people here are lost, and they need Jesus. My feet were made to carry the Gospel."

PRAYER: *God, help me today to be more passionate about the Gospel. Give me courage and provide me with opportunities to speak with others about Jesus Christ.*

SP

SPIES LIKE US

Numbers 13:33 – *We saw the Nephilim there (the descendants of Anak come from the Nephilim). We seemed like grasshoppers in our own eyes, and we looked the same to them.*

My favorite line from the movie that also bears the title of today's devotion goes like this:

> *Keyes: By your actions, sir, you are risking the future of the human race!*
> *General Sline: To guarantee the American way of life, I'm willing to take that risk.*

When we think of spies, we tend to think of Jason Bourne or *007*— crafty and brave. Twelve spies once went into Palestine and saw the amazing things that God had prepared. What's interesting is that two of the spies almost did not even notice the giants because of the lush vegetation. The other ten spies, however, could not see the providence of God, because they were fixated on the giants of man.

Sometimes, we are too much like General Sline—we are more interested in guaranteeing our way of life than trusting God's way of life.

We will all face down our own giants, no matter what land we choose. Our giants are IN us, just as much as they are AROUND us. Our giants are things such as addiction, comfort, control, selfishness, and so on. They may not look as formidable, but they are every bit as deadly.

You will have an opportunity today to trust or run. Choose wisely.

PRAYER: *God, I want to trust You today. In the next day or the next week or the next month, I will be faced with a choice between Your provision and my desire for a guarantee. Help me to recognize and choose wisely.*

DF

ME AND MY SHADOW

2 Timothy 3:1-4 – *There will be terrible times in the last days. People will be lovers of themselves… without self-control…lovers of pleasure rather than lovers of God—*

Our minds always seem to go to, "What can I do that will be fun?" or "What will make me feel good?" Believe me, I desire fun, but it's like chasing a shadow. Try to catch up to it, and the shadow moves farther away from us. Walk away from it, and the shadow pursues us!

In the same way, when we are constantly seeking pleasure, life becomes shallow, and we seem to lose fulfillment and enjoyment. But when we are making better efforts to have times of prayer, checking out the Scriptures, and serving others, then life's enjoyment and fulfillment seems to find us.

For example, the best date I was ever on entailed six couples walking around a Colorado park. Our goal was to help out and encourage random people. Then, we met back together and shared funny and emotional stories. It was a blast, and interestingly, our focus wasn't just fun, even though fun chased us down.

PRAYER: *Heavenly Father, remind me to seek times with You. Remind me to think of other people's needs, not just my own. I know I can trust You for life's fulfillment, pleasures, and enjoyment.*

CJ

SNAP AND TAP

John 10:10 – *I have come that they may have life, and have it to the full.*

Standing outside a surf shack in Hawaii, I overheard an instructor encourage his surfing class by saying, "Maximize every moment in the water and enjoy the exhilaration of each wave."

The devil wants you to believe that the Christian life should be a drag—an ordinary existence defined by the mundane. Unfortunately, too many believers have accepted this lie and walk around planet Earth with their shoulders slumped and their heads down.

Snap out of it! As a Christ-follower, you have the opportunity to pursue purpose, experience joy, and live in fullness. In addition to receiving unconditional forgiveness and the promise of an eternal home in Heaven, your salvation also provides you with the opportunity to experience an abundant life here on earth.

Tap into it! Because of your faith, you have a relationship with Jesus Christ and the Holy Spirit lives in you. There is nothing ordinary or mundane about their presence in your life. Supercharge your life! Find a unique way to serve Jesus and allow the Holy Spirit to speak to you through God's Word.

Grab your board, jump in, and enjoy the exhilaration of each wave.

PRAYER: *God, remind me of Your goodness today. Show me Your abundance and fill me with purpose and joy.*

SP

OFFICIAL TALK

Psalm 115:2-3 – *Why do the nations say, "Where is their God?" Our God is in Heaven; He does whatever pleases him.*

I enjoy coaching basketball. I have coached my kids' teams throughout their elementary years. I have coached my daughters' teams in middle school (mainly because no one else would). And I have coached one of my daughters at the junior varsity level.

An important nuance of coaching is relating to officials. Prior to games, coaches and officials seem like best of friends. You would think they vacation together at the beach.

Then, the game begins.

And. The. Talk. Changes.

On one occasion, an official had lost control of the game. He knew that, because I'd casually mentioned it to him as he passed by my bench.

With joyful exuberance, he gave me my first and only technical foul as a coach, which I received well in my opinion. However, the church members who were present enjoyed it much more.

When I confessed it to the church on the following Sunday, a new family was attending for the first time. The husband (who may be one of the other authors of this book) later told me that he looked at his wife and said, "This is our new church."

Talking to God is not "official talk." You cannot butter Him up or work Him to give you the best calls. He is interested in you—He is not impressed by your record.

PRAYER: *God, thank You that You want time with me more than You want something from me. You are not like other gods who demand service in exchange for blessing. You have already blessed me before I ever come to You.*

DF

LITTLE PICTURE OF THE SUN

Romans 2:13 – *It is not those who just hear the law who are righteous in God's sight, but it is those who obey the law who will be declared righteous.*

One time, I was on a certain medication that had to be taken for ten days. I read the warning on the side of the little bottle that said, "avoid direct sunlight while taking this medication," and the bottle even included a picture of a small sun beside the warning.

For nine days, I followed that "sun law" and was feeling pretty good. However, on day ten I spent the afternoon outside…in the sun.

The next morning I woke up to a splitting headache and an extremely tired body. I can just imagine the person who is responsible for those warnings watching me outside in the sun and saying, "What is this idiot thinking? I tried to protect him. I even had an artist put a little picture of the sun beside my advice."

In today's verse, Paul is basically writing to plead with his readers to not just read God's Word but to also follow what it is saying. God's law is there for our own protection!

PRAYER: *Father, I don't want to settle with just knowing and reading about You. Help me attempt to follow Your law, so You can protect and provide for me.*

CJ

DEAR ADDICTED

Deuteronomy 20:4 – *For the Lord your God is the one who goes with you to fight for you against your enemies to give you victory.*

Dear Addicted,

I remember when things were different, and your struggles were light. I know you are in a battle now. Keep fighting, my friend.

Finding victory will take time and determination. More than that, it will take a work of the Holy Spirit. Remember that God loves you. I love you. He hasn't turned His back on you, and neither have I.

I'm here to help you. Let me know what I can do. If there is someone else you need to speak to about all of this, I can arrange for it. Is it time for something like that? I'm not pushing. I'm just asking.

You are not alone. God is fighting with you, and I am fighting for you. He wants you to triumph. I'm standing with you now, and I'll be standing with you when you claim victory.

PRAYER: *God, help me take steps today to begin breaking this stronghold in my life. Give me strength, determination, wisdom, and grace.*

SP

DIAMONDS ARE FOREVER

Proverbs 3:11-12 – *My son, do not despise the Lord's discipline, and do not resent his rebuke, because the Lord disciplines those he loves, as a father the son he delights in.*

My mom grew up on a farm where coal was discovered. Eventually, it became a secondary source of income for her family during the Great Depression. Every time I see or feel coal, I'm amazed to think about how that lump of carbon becomes a diamond.

If you laid an average lump of coal beside my wife's ring, you might wonder what is the difference between the two? (My close friends would enjoy answering that question with sarcasm: "Maybe $10?").

The only difference is that the coal has experienced enough pressure over enough time to become something beautiful. A diamond is just a lump of coal that wouldn't quit.

What pressure are you under today? What has been going on in your life so long, that you think it will never change; it'll never go away? God is using those things to forge beauty in your soul.

PRAYER: *Father, help me to embrace the pressure today, instead of wishing my life were something different, instead of living in self-pity. I receive the pressure, because You are with me. You are doing something beautiful.*

DF

MOM, THANKS FOR CHANGING MY DIAPER

Luke 17:15-17 – *One of them, when he saw he was healed, came back, praising God in a loud voice. He threw himself at Jesus' feet and thanked Him. Jesus asked, "Were not all ten cleansed? Where are the other nine?*

Jesus healed ten men of a horrible, flesh-eating disease called leprosy. While all ten were thrilled with the results, only one came back to thank Jesus.

Now, I'm sure Jesus didn't heal these guys just for a "Thank you, Pal." However, He wants us to understand the importance of having a thankful heart.

I always get a kick out of the parents who drag their children up to another adult who did something for them and say, "What do you say to Mr. Joseph?" Then, I hear the "heartfelt" and obligatory, "Thank you," as the kids look down at their feet.

When our children were little, my wife and I never expected a thank you. We took care of them regardless. Yet, as they grew older, we saw their maturity develop and, along with it, a sense of thankfulness. When we hear, "Thanks Mom for the ride," it still isn't expected. We don't need their affirmation, but instead we are thrilled to see they are developing the vital trait of gratitude.

PRAYER: *Lord, teach me to thank others, especially those I can take for granted. Help me to recognize the things You do for me and truly thank You.*

CJ

BADMINTON BEATDOWN

John 14:11 – *For all those who exalt themselves will be humbled, and those who humble themselves will be exalted.*

As a senior in high school, I took a boys advanced physical education course. Like most P.E. classes, it was fun and offered great competition for a group of high school athletes who thought much too highly of themselves.

Halfway through the course, our teacher Mr. Grimley introduced us to the game of badminton and challenged us to try and beat him. As he threw down the gauntlet, we literally laughed out loud. There was no way old Mr. Grimley would even win a match.

For the next three days, he wiped the floor with all of us. No one scored more than three points against him, and we were all athletically humbled by a teacher older than our parents. Little did we know, Mr. Grimley had played competitively as a younger man.

It's easy to think more highly of ourselves than we should. We often forget that God is the Author of all our achievements and accolades. Failing to give Him credit fills our heart with pride and arrogance. The Bible calls us to walk in humility and consider others better than ourselves. Put God in the driver's seat, place others on the passenger's side, and you take the back seat.

PRAYER: *God, help me today to give You glory and lift up the people around me.*

SP

THE HARD WAY

Hebrews 12:3 – *Consider him who endured such opposition from sinners, so that you will not grow weary and lose heart.*

A few years ago, my wife and I were engaged in the kind of flirtatious behavior that makes our children want to throw up in their mouths a little bit. In the middle of the exchange, I believe I said something sarcastic (because sarcasm is my love language), and my wife whacked me on my backside.

She immediately recoiled her hand in pain and said, "Ouch!" She shook her hand for a few seconds and said, "I think I just broke a blood vessel in my finger, when I tagged your behind."

I immediately responded, "You better think twice about what you are hitting."

The reality is that her finger perfectly hit one of the steel rivets in my Levi's.

Sometimes, we run into something tough. Life has its fair share of hard moments, hard seasons, and difficulties. They can grow us or inhibit us. The Bible encourages us to consider Jesus, the perfect man, the powerful Savior, and remember how He suffered on our behalf.

PRAYER: *Father, help me to endure whatever comes my way today or this week. I don't want to merely go through tough times. I want to grow through them.*

DF

MANSION NAILS

Colossians 1:17 – *He is before all things, and in Him all things hold together.*

Do you ever think about the huge mansions that sit back from the road?

While mansions are very expensive, the major item that holds those gigantic structures together are very small, very inexpensive nails. Take these little pieces of metal away, and the building collapses!

Similarly, we all have our personalities, responsibilities, and appearances, but something has to hold us together as well. Many times I'll hear of people who appear to have it all together having emotional breakdowns or being unable to cope with normal living. Such a downfall tends to shock people because we tend to see the "outer building" of people. But what is truly holding us together?

God can strengthen our own inner nails—our hearts and our minds. He longs for us to turn to Him and ask Him to change us from the inside out. We need to open ourselves up in intimate prayer with God, read His Word, and make efforts to grow our faith daily. As this becomes more and more of our focus, then the nails of our inner-being develop and multiply so that we can hold together a mansion.

PRAYER: *Father, I need You to invade my life, my thoughts, and my very being. Harden the nails of my insides, so I can support a mansion of fulfilled living.*

CJ

AARON'S AWKWARD ABSURDITY

Proverbs 21:23 – *Those who guard their mouths and their tongues keep themselves from calamity.*

Like a scene from an absurd sitcom, every time Aaron spoke, he put his foot in his mouth. From congratulating an UN-expectant woman for her pregnancy to asking a dinner party host about the cost of their new home, Aaron's words often resulted in an icy stare from his conversation companion.

Because the impact of his words was relatively benign, it's easy to smile at Aaron's verbal gaffes and cringe-worthy moments. The Bible, on the other hand, has serious words to say about the genuine trouble our words can cause.

Scripture teaches that it's hard to control our words. From unwarranted opinions and harsh disagreements to gossip and corrupt talk, our sin nature craves verbal engagement. The testimony of God's Word and the wisdom gained from life experience remind us that the more we give in to the tongue, the more we can expect trouble.

I once heard a friend say that difficulty, disorder, and drama follow the unbridled tongue. I agree and encourage you to practice the fine art of purging your words. Resist the urge to chime in. Measure your words and recognize that sometimes the best course of action is to say nothing at all.

PRAYER: *God, help me today to have control over my words.*

SP

WEIRD NAMES

Colossians 4:7 – *Tychicus will tell you all the news about me. He is a dear brother, a faithful minister and fellow servant in the Lord.*

The last chapters of Paul's New Testament letters read like a weird Hebrew phone book—Epaphras, Onesimus, and Aristarchus. None of those are on the list of the 100 Hottest Baby Names. They are like the names at the end of the movie credits.

Here's a name from today's verse: Tychicus. His name means "fortunate," regardless of the fact that very few know it, and even fewer can pronounce it.

Every time he's mentioned, it's in relation to two things: care and delivery. Tychicus delivered Paul's letters to the Colossians and the Ephesians. So, even though you don't know his name, without Tychicus, we don't have Ephesians and Colossians.

His ministry? He could *walk*. No paparazzi lined up around Tychicus' house. He was just faithful to do his part. He had what didn't seem like an important job then, but it was incredibly important in light of history.

Who wants to be the person who loses a book of the Bible? "I'm not really sure!?! I was taking the book of *Daytonians* to Lexington, but there was this Jimmy Buffet concert in Cincinnati, so I stopped and looked down and *Daytonians* was gone."

A huge part of following Christ is learning to be faithful in the little things—when no one but you and God are watching.

PRAYER: *Spirit, help me to both understand my role and be faithful to it today. You are the leading character, and I'm in the background. Thank You that my small acts can make an eternal difference in Your bigger story.*

DF

NEVER, EVER WORTH IT

Hebrews 2:18 – *He is able to help those who are being tempted.*

One time I was watching the TV series *SpongeBob SquarePants*, and SpongeBob and his best friend, Patrick, stole a balloon. They were excited about the fun they would have and believed it really didn't matter that they stole because they planned on returning the balloon later. However, in the midst of their excitement, the balloon popped. Their plan of returning the balloon literally blew up in their faces.

We have all found ways to "justify" our sin with excuses such as, "Everyone else is doing it", "My friends do worse things than this", and "God's not really real anyway." These are just a few of the mental missiles that battle in our heads.

God realizes that temptations can overpower us, resulting in damaging choices.

So, an important sentence to commit to memory to help us fight this fleshly war zone brewing in our brains is this: "Sin is *never* worth it!"

To put it another way, before the football is snapped on the "temptation line of a scrimmage," be convinced that bad choices are not worth it. Don't try to fight through the onslaught of justifying a poor decision. Instead, just say, "Sin is never, ever worth it. Help me, Lord."

PRAYER: *Father, program "sin is never worth it" into my heart and mind. Give me the ability to ask for Your strength to turn away.*

CJ

BIBLE SCRAP

Revelation 19:16 – *On his robe and on his thigh he has this name written: King of Kings and Lord of Lords.*

Back in the 1990s, I borrowed a Bible from the lost and found box at a camp in Michigan. I needed to consult a different version of Scripture as I made a last-minute adjustment to the message I'd prepared. In the days before smartphones and Bible apps, this was my only recourse. As I thumbed through the Bible, a scrap of paper fell to the floor. Picking it up, I read the following words:

> Jesus was born as a baby and preached as a child.
> He was killed as a man and rose as a conqueror.
> HE WILL RETURN AS A KING!

As a reminder of Jesus' ultimate authority, I jotted the words down in the margin of my personal Bible next to Revelation 19:16. If the way of the world has you down and discouraged, take heart! The return of Jesus is imminent. Until then, live with confidence and know that one day He will right every wrong.

PRAYER: *God, thank You for Your power and authority. You are my King. Give me boldness to live for You today.*

SP

April 12th

JUST A JOB

Psalm 37:4a – *Take delight in the Lord.*

We don't want to be married to somebody who just goes through the motions; we want heart! When my wife and I had been married for four years, I was invited to speak at a retreat in Toledo Bend, LA, and we worked it out where Angie could go with me.

I covertly called ahead to the spa.

> "What kind of massage would she like? Therapeutic?"
>
> "Sure? Sounds great," I responded.
>
> "Thank you, Mr. Fulks. Now we have two masseuses—Greg and Wendy."
>
> "We don't want Greg—how about Wendy? Yes, we will take Wendy."

And I bought her flowers, and not just flowers—ROSES!

What if my wife had said to me, "Why did you do all of this?" and I responded, "Well, it's what I am supposed to do. I made those vows, so it's my job, I guess." For all of you younger husbands, that is the wrong answer. My answer was something like, "If I've learned anything in four years, you are the best thing that's ever happened to me in this world. This is just what I can do right now. You deserve a lot more."

Sometimes, I wonder if God is any more pleased with our empty, mechanical religious rituals? Our Christian duty?

PRAYER: *God, I want to see You and serve You today and not because I have to or because I think I can leverage You to get what I want. I want to walk in step with You today. When my emotion starts to fade, encourage my spirit in Your goodness.*

DF

NO WAY, JOSE

Philippians 2:5 – *Your attitude should be the same as that of Christ Jesus.*

One time I was challenged to make a "hate list." This meant I had to list all of the people I didn't like.

I did it, but what happened after several days is that I started to look at these people with a newfound compassion. Somehow, I found forgiveness in my heart (thinking about the incredible degree that God has forgiven me made it a whole lot easier). To be honest, I did notice that the hardest people to forgive were those who I knew didn't like me. Still, not only did forgiving these individuals help my relationships, but it also gave me a feeling of freedom.

Today's verse makes me think about how Jesus forgave those who hated Him, lied about Him, made fun of Him, and even beat Him. He sets the forgiveness bar very high for us. In order for us to have "the same attitude of Christ," it must be an act of God working in our lives.

The idea of the "hate list," where we pour out our hearts about who we are struggling to love and forgive, can give God a chance to become real to us because there is no way to conjure up this type of forgiveness on our own.

PRAYER: *Lord, help me forgive others, especially those who seem "unforgivable." Thank You the freedom that will follow.*

CJ

SUPREME COMMANDER AND PRESIDENT

Philippians 2:3 – *Do nothing out of selfish ambition or vain conceit. Rather, in humility value others above yourselves...*

A handful of years ago, I found myself sitting in a boardroom with a group of colleagues. The man in charge of the meeting was notorious for being pretentious and smug. On this day, he managed to live up to his reputation. I remember thinking, "I'm not following him anywhere."

Dwight D. Eisenhower was one of our country's most honored and decorated leaders. He served as Supreme Commander of the Allied Expeditionary Force during World War II and became the 34th President of the United States. Foundational to his leadership was his understanding of how to treat people. Eisenhower once placed a string on a table and said, "Pull it, and it will follow wherever you wish. Push it, and it will go nowhere."

We've all been around leaders who attempt to influence others from a "Push" posture. When they don't receive their desired results, they turn to demeaning words and harsh actions. This technique may work for the short term, but it will ultimately fail and lead to resentment.

How much better would it be to engage people from a "Pull" posture? Leading and influencing is a difficult task. While we should always set standards and levy expectations, we should also learn to season everything we say and do with humility and kindness.

PRAYER: *God, help me lead and influence people in a way that challenges, encourages, and inspires.*

SP

GOLIATH NEVER HAD A CHANCE

1 Samuel 17:50 – *So David triumphed over the Philistine with a sling and a stone...*

In sports, the underdogs steal the show: the 1980 US Men's Hockey Team, Buster Douglas, and Rudy. Many times, those moments are described as "David vs. Goliath" battles.

In these battles, the champion with the impressive resume faces the challenger without a chance in the Valley of Elah. That's the David and Goliath story that many of us (most of us) believe.

However, in Malcolm Gladwell's *David and Goliath*, he describes David very differently. He discusses clues that lead us to believe that David was an expert marksman with a sling. He describes how these Hebrew snipers could hit a very small target from a long distance. And David was certainly a warrior, if he had killed bears and lions.

Maybe this knowledge takes away the underdog aspect, but it certainly enhances the importance of preparation. Gladwell premise begs a question. What if David had not spent all of those years training? Answer: David would have missed his moment.

What if all of the steps God has asked you take—from years ago to yesterday—have been in preparation for today? If your Valley of Elah is today, are you ready? All you need is all that God has already given to you.

PRAYER: *Father, help me to be ready today. I believe that I have everything I really need, because I have You. If today is another day of preparation, I receive the training You have for me this day.*

DF

PLAY TO WIN

Galatians 5:13 – *You, my brothers, were called to be free. But do not use your freedom to indulge the sinful nature; rather, serve one another in love.*

My sister played on an amazing high school volleyball team. The team's key players were all juniors when they surprised everyone by winning a state championship. The following year those players all returned as seniors. However, this time, the season started off slow. They were barely winning games, enthusiasm was down, and morale was low.

After losing some matches in the middle of their season, something seemed to change. They managed to turn it around and went on to dominate the rest of their opponents, easily winning a second straight state title.

What made the change was their perspective—they stopped playing not to lose and instead started playing to win.

Just as with our relationship with God, we can't just walk around trying not to sin. Instead, we need to ask Him for direction, seek out opportunities to love others, and live with the understanding that we are "free" to live life to its fullest.

PRAYER: *Father, help me to enjoy the freedom and blessings You have to offer. Help me to avoid and confess sin, yet let my focus be more on You, Your power, and Your hope of a great future.*

CJ

TWENTY-TWO YEARS INSIDE

2 Timothy 3:16 – *All Scripture is God-breathed and is useful for teaching, rebuking, correcting, and training in righteousness...*

I met Jesse in 2011 while speaking at a men's conference outside of Chicago. He was an imposing figure at 6'4" tall and 240 pounds. At the conclusion of the event, Jesse made his way forward and introduced himself.

For the next twenty minutes or so, he told me of his life behind bars, and the stories he shared were enough to make my skin crawl.

At the age of twenty-four, Jesse was sentenced to twenty-two years in prison. Early in his incarceration, he came to faith in Jesus Christ. Though his faith was real, Jesse's life inside a maximum-security prison was no picnic. When I asked him how he kept his sanity, he pointed to his Bible and said, "God's Word. It was my correction, protection, and direction."

People usually smile when I tell them Jesse's story. During his imprisonment, he devoured Scripture. He read the Bible and memorized portions of it every day. Jesse was committed to God's Word, and it changed his life. Choosing to do the same could change your life too.

PRAYER: *God, help me today to become a man or woman of Your Word. Help me receive the correction, protection, and direction it provides.*

SP

FAMILY BUSINESS

Ephesians 6:4 – *Fathers, do not provoke your children to anger, but bring them up in the discipline and instruction of the Lord.*

Comedian Brian Regan once said, "My wife and I have two wonderful kids." When the audience stopped cheering, he said, "But we actually have three children."

The Bible is full of people who struggled with parenting. For example, David wrote at least 78 Psalms filled with words such as, "As a deer pants for the water, so my soul pants for you," and yet as passionate as he was, he struggled as a dad.

At one point, David's son, Absalom, led a rebellion against David. Just so everyone knows where Absalom stood, he publicly had sexual relations with David's concubines on the roof of his house.

Eventually, David's army regrouped and battled Absalom's forces, and Absalom was killed. When the first soldier returned, David asked, "How is it with the young man Absalom—is the young man Absalom safe?"

What's interesting is that nowhere while Absalom was alive does David ever use a really important word: "son." It's always "Absalom—young man Absalom." So, it's ironic that when David found out Absalom had been killed, he responded, "Oh Absalom, my son, my son, my son, would that I died today instead of you" and wept for days.

From the time a child is born, parents have 6,570 days until a child turns eighteen. You won't be a perfect parent. But don't waste a day.

PRAYER: *Spirit, thank You for my opportunity to impact the next generation today as a parent, teacher, coach, mentor, or grandparent. Help me to invest today and not waste it.*

DF

April 19th

LEARN FROM SIMBA

Ephesians 2:10 – *We are God's workmanship, created in Christ Jesus to do good works...*

My family watched *The Lion King* one evening. In the film, the king's son, Simba, was so riddled with the guilt of his father's death that he decided to quit, even though he was heir to the throne.

So, Simba ran away and found some friends who taught him about "Hakuna Matata," which means living a lifestyle of no worries, where nothing really matters, where we avoid responsibility, where we seek pleasure and escape stress....Sound familiar?

In the end, Simba realized he was needed as the king of a failing kingdom. His people needed him to do what he was created to do. Although he debated the work and responsibility it would entail, Simba eventually went back to fulfill his calling.

Gratification, personal blessing, and a sense of worth came over the young heir of the throne. He realized that "Hakuna Matata" sounded good, but it just didn't work.

We were created by God to do good works. If we ask God to use us, He will put opportunities in our path to help others. Then, that all-important sense of significance will manifest itself in our hearts.

PRAYER: *Father, don't allow my guilt to stop me from doing good works. Thank You that I can confess and start over. Bring opportunities my way to help others.*

CJ

FUEL MATTERS

Philippians 4:8 – *Finally, brothers and sisters, whatever is true, whatever is noble, whatever is right, whatever is pure, whatever is lovely, whatever is admirable—if anything is excellent or praiseworthy—think about such things.*

There we were, stranded on the side of the road in Lyon, France. One of our team members inadvertently put diesel fuel into the gasoline tank of our passenger van. It was time to call a tow truck.

I'm not a car guy by any stretch of the imagination, but what I discovered that night is that gasoline engines cannot combust diesel fuel. Quite simply, if you want your vehicle to run, you have to give it the right fuel.

In the same way, if you want your life to reflect the person of Jesus Christ, you must be willing to fill it with relationships, influences, and media that honor Him. Who we spend time with, who we listen to, what we watch, and what we pay attention to directly impacts the fruit our life produces.

The Bible calls us to fill our hearts and minds with beautiful, righteous, and praiseworthy things. At the same time, we are instructed to let go of that which causes us to sin. Take time to evaluate and consider how you feed your soul. Giving it the right fuel will draw you closer to Jesus and help you make a difference in others.

PRAYER: *God, help me discipline my heart and mind today as I endeavor to fill my life with Your people, Your thoughts, and Your Words.*

SP

CALVIN AND COVID

Proverbs 23:7 – *For as he thinks in his heart, so is he.* **(NKJV)**

Most people struggled during the CV-19 pandemic in 2020. People are passionate about their beliefs and opinions in the middle of a crisis.

During COVID, I had the opportunity to meet Cal, a ninety-five-year-old veteran of World War II, and he was incredibly sharp. He served in military reconnaissance in the war. At night, he led a battalion as close as possible to enemy territory to acquire critical information.

I asked Cal about COVID. His response was, "Yes, yes, it's kind of like the Cholera outbreak we had when I was younger. Or the Polio crisis that we had. You know, my wife had some of that." I think Cal was sending me a message that we were not the first people to face a crisis, and we certainly will not be the last.

"What's your secret," my wife asked him. He replied, "It's simple really, just be positive—you know, you've got a lot to live for, really."

God has given you a lot to live for today. Your attitude determines how you will handle most of it. For God's sake, be positive.

PRAYER: *Father, help my attitude today to reflect what You have given for me and to me. Please help people to see my life and believe in the value of following You.*

DF

LIGHT SHOWS THE CHAIN

Psalm 119:105 – *Your word is a lamp to my feet and a light for my path.*

I think God invented light and darkness to show us our need for His guidance and insights.

One dark, summer night when I was a kid, I was cruising around on my bicycle. I decided to turn off the road toward my favorite park. Before I knew it, my Huffy bike abruptly stopped on a dime. I still can recall the shocked and baffled feeling that I experienced as I catapulted over my handlebars and into a face-plant.

I got up to see that some genius had decided to put a large chain across the path entrance. The chain was thick, brown, and nearly impossible to see at night.

Looking back on that event made me think. It seems as though the more we talk to God and think about His Word, the more light shines onto our paths. Mistakes get avoided, and casualties and obstacles get sidestepped. Of course, there will always be mistakes and unavoidable tragedies in life. However, those are the times when God's light allows things to make more sense.

PRAYER: *Father, draw me close to You through prayer and Your principles, so that I can have more and more light on my path. Direct my daily decisions and choices.*

CJ

A QUESTION WORTH ASKING

John 14:6 – *Jesus answered, "I am the way and the truth and the life. No one comes to the Father except through me."*

Pulling up to the rural hospital, I noticed a man lying on the ground. Getting out of the truck, my translator said, "He's deceased. They have placed him outside until his family can claim the body." A million questions went through my head. Chief among them was whether or not this man had ever come to faith in Jesus.

The question is worth asking today. Do you know Jesus? Have you put your trust in Him as the Forgiver of your sins and Savior of your soul?

The Bible teaches that everyone is born a sinner and must be forgiven if they long for a home in Heaven. Likewise, the Scriptures teach that because Jesus is the Son of God and because He died on the cross and rose from the grave, He (Jesus) is the only One with the power and authority to forgive you. Lastly, the Bible tells us that we must turn from our sin and put our faith in Jesus to receive His forgiveness.

Do you remember a time in your life when you asked Jesus to forgive you of your sin and be the Savior of your soul? If not, ask Him to do so today (see Appendix).

PRAYER: *Jesus, I put my faith in You today. I turn from my sins, and I ask You to forgive me. Become the Savior of my soul.*

SP

SCARY CLOSE

Psalm 145:18 – *The Lord is near to all who call on him, to all who call on him in truth.*

When our oldest child was four years old, she quietly snuck into our bedroom around 2:00am. She was sleeping with this old baby doll that could only open one eye. Upon entering the room, she bent down three inches from her mother's sleeping face with the creepy doll and loudly whispered, "Mom!" My wife awoke frightened out of a dead sleep and swung a Miyagi-Do karate and struck me in the chest. "Mom, I'm thirsty. Can I get a drink of water?"

The Bible has a fair amount to say about sleep. When we are fighting worry, sleep can be difficult. Your angry moments cause you regret. Your medical test results are delayed. Your prodigal children have not yet returned home. Your aging parents concern you. Maybe temptation is wearing you out. Perhaps you've lost someone you love.

Tonight, when you lay your head on your pillow, there's good news— God is right there in your face. You won't take a breath of which He is not aware. He is always with us. King David said, "If I ascend to the heights of Heaven you are there…if I go to the depth of Sheol you are there…where can I go?"

Answer: "Nowhere." So what? David finishes, "I will lie down and sleep in peace…for you, O Lord, make me dwell in safety."

PRAYER: *Lord, I will rest in You today and tonight. You are always with me, even when I do not recognize Your Presence. Spirit, help my awareness of Your awareness of me to grow!*

DF

LIQUID GUTS

Ephesians 5:18 – *Do not get drunk on wine, which leads to debauchery. Instead, be filled with the Spirit...*

When a person is drunk, the individual is influenced by the effects of the alcohol buzz. Back in my college days, we called it "liquid guts" because it gave us the confidence to ask attractive girls to dance.

Back in those days, my consistent drinking lifestyle led me into destructive relationships, troubles from bad choices, and just a feeling of inner blah (which, of course, led to more drinking).

In the midst of my college binges, I actually prayed to God and invited Jesus into my heart to change me. I was scared because I saw firsthand what drinking did to my family growing up.

Well, God did a miracle in me. I learned to be "filled" (empowered and directed) by the Holy Spirit instead of alcohol. My inner blah somehow turned into inner peace, and I liked the new, refreshing feeling of calm.

The word "filled" in today's Scripture is that of a boat sail being filled with moving air. This filling is what drove the massive ships of old to advance powerfully across the sea. In the same way, God's Spirit can move powerfully in us.

PRAYER: *I can't live this life productively, wisely, or pleasingly to You, God, but You can. Live through me, moment by moment. Remind me to ask for Your power and direction. Fill me.*

CJ

I DON'T WANT THE SPECIAL

I John 4:1 – *Dear friends, do not believe every spirit, but test the spirits to see whether they are from God, because many false prophets have gone out into the world.*

Recently, I met a good friend for lunch. When the server came to the table, she asked if we wanted to hear about the specials. My friend politely said, "No, thank you." After the server left, he channeled his best Jerry Seinfeld impression and said, "If the specials were so special, they would already be on the menu. I'm not ordering a meal that is auditioning to get on the team."

Spiritually speaking, there is an ever-increasing amount of counterfeit truth "auditioning" to make its way in mainstream Christianity. False teachers are attempting to add and take away from the Gospel message of Jesus Christ.

In response, we have to vigorously guard the truth. In today's verse, John the Apostle instructs the church to authenticate new teaching and be willing to regard it as truth or falsehood. Furthermore, he states that the litmus test for Gospel truth is found in what someone teaches about Jesus Christ.

Let's make it simple. If someone's teaching and instruction do not line up with the words of Jesus Christ or the New Testament Apostles, it's false. If it were true, Jesus or one of the Apostles would have already said it. Know the truth. Speak the Gospel. Defend the truth.

PRAYER: *God, help me today to be discerning. Help me to know and defend the truth of the Gospel.*

SP

THE SOUND OF SIRENS

2 Corinthians 5:14 – *For Christ's love compels us, because we are convinced that one died for all, and therefore all died.*

In Greek mythology, Ulysses (on his way home after the Trojan War) was tested at the island of the Sirens. The beautiful Sirens would sing to tempt a man to his doom. In order to avoid such a fate, Ulysses had his sailors tie him to the mast, so he wouldn't do something in the *moment* that he would regret for a *lifetime*. He knew there would be a moment of temporary insanity that would "leave his corpse to rot away…rags of skin shriveling on his bones."

What will keep you tied to the mast in moments of temporary temptation?

You need a love that is stronger than any other love in your life, stronger than your passion for the approval of others, tougher than your desire for control, and more significant than your entitlement to comfort. Jesus stayed on the mast for us—He was crucified to a cross. Paul says that Jesus' love "compels," or "controls" us.

Don't do something in a moment that you will regret for a lifetime. God will forgive any sin, but its consequences may be hard to carry. Let His love guide your life.

PRAYER: *God, I need to rely on Your love today. Strengthen my inner man towards You and grow my love for Your sacrifice in my life. Thank You for staying on the Cross for me.*

DF

LOATHE COMPLAINING, NOT LIFE

Job 10:1 – *I loathe my very life; therefore I will give free rein to my complaint and speak out in the bitterness of my soul.*

When I was growing up, I saw hints that my parents loved each other, but I knew for a fact that they also hated each other. The only time I can remember them not barking back and forth at each other was when they were either asleep or found something to mutually complain about.

As a result, I was thoroughly trained in the art of complaining. It wasn't until I gave my heart to Christ that I started to slowly change.

I learned that God does not like complaining, and it is detrimental to my inner well-being and my relationships. But that didn't end my complaining as I began to complain about people who complained. Clearly, I needed spiritual surgery to fight this complaining disease that was eating me up.

When we complain, we "speak out in the bitterness of the soul." Look around this week and listen to all of the complaining that goes on at work, sporting events, school, home, on TV, with friends, and so on. When we catch ourselves complaining, allow God to do surgery.

PRAYER: *Father, when I complain, remind me to admit it and quit it. I am depending on You to change me. I don't want to be balled up in bitterness.*

CJ

LOVE IS A VERB

1 John 3:18 – *Dear children, let us not love with words or speech but with actions and in truth.*

Damon loved playing hoops at the outdoor basketball court in the city park. Since he was an exceptionally talented high school junior, the fierce competition brought out the best of his basketball abilities. Likewise, Damon's summers spent on the court and at the park created within his heart a deep love for the people in his neighborhood.

One summer evening, shots rang out from a car as it sped past the park. As people scattered, Damon saw a seven-year-old boy paralyzed with fear standing alone in the middle of the park. Without hesitating, he ran toward the boy just as the gunmen circled back around and sprayed bullets into the dispersing crowd. Reaching the boy in time to shield him from another attack, Damon was hit in the leg twice.

Ultimately, the little boy's life was saved, and Damon recovered from his injuries. Days later, when asked about the incident, Damon said, "I didn't think much about it. I love that little guy—known him his whole life. I just snapped into action."

Talking about love and demonstrating love are two different things. One involves words, and the other requires action. Love is a verb.

PRAYER: *God, help me to practically and tangibly demonstrate love toward someone who needs it today.*

SP

MILLIONS OF VILLIONS

Mark 10:18 – *"Why do you call me good?" Jesus answered. "No one is good—except God alone."*

We've all done some things of which we are not proud. One Monday morning, we arrived at our church to discover that some teenage gang members had painted graffiti onto some surrounding buildings and our church van.

Using red spray paint, they originally painted the word "Villions" onto the back of the van. So, they corrected the spelling with extra red pant to "Villains." Lucky us! We got the gang who finished well in the elementary spelling bee!

I shared about what had happened with our church, because I did not want them to think that we had decided to give our student ministry an edgy new name.

So, I think we can all agree that painting someone else's property falls into the sin category, correct? But, how bad is that in the "bad" category? I mean, are the young people who did that going to Hell? Actually, yes they are—just kidding.

My point is that we are all "villions." None of us is good is comparison to God's standard of perfection. We all need a salvation that is only provided by a perfect Savior.

PRAYER: *Jesus, thank You that Your death removes the stains of my sin. Thank You for the reminder today that I cannot meet Your standard, so You met it for me. I am grateful for my salvation!*

DF

MAKE ME A GOOD MEMORY

Psalm 49:10 – *For all can see the wise die, that the foolish and the senseless perish, leaving their wealth to others.*

When it comes to life and death, most of us are familiar with the old adage, "we can't take it with us." However, the good news is that there is much that we can leave behind.

When I was in high school, I vividly remember an older lady pulling me aside to tell me how she could tell my bad knee slowed me down, yet she saw my great effort on the basketball court in spite of it.

I also remember my father praising me for a certain skill I had, the family friend who gave a huge gift to help in a time of need, and the young man who saw my desire to please God and told me that he wanted to do the same.

We have the ability to leave behind a good memory for others. We can be the so-and-so for someone else. We can be the "I'll never forget when so-and-so did this for me" or "when so-and-so gave me words of great encouragement" or "when so-and-so lived a life for others and God, and it made me want that for myself."

While we will leave our material things behind, we also can leave an impact behind as well.

PRAYER: *Lord, make me a "good memory" for others when I am gone from this place. Help me to make and see opportunities to help others.*

CJ

CRIMSON-COLORED GLASSES

Romans 8:1 – *Therefore, there is now no condemnation for those who are in Christ Jesus…*

The first time I put them on, I couldn't believe my eyes. My new ski goggles helped me see everything in a different light. The rose-colored lenses literally changed my view of the slopes. In an instant, everything looked beautiful.

As a Christian, God views you as one who has received His grace and mercy. At the moment you choose to accept Jesus Christ as your Lord and Savior, His blood covers your sin. From that point forward, it's as though He puts on crimson-colored glasses and only sees your life through the lens of the Cross. As a result, you are forgiven, and your failures no longer condemn you to an eternity separated from Him in hell.

This remarkable truth is worth shouting from the rooftops. At the same time, it should cause us to live in a state of endless gratitude toward the One who gave His life for us. Crimson-colored glasses don't exist without the willing sacrifice of Jesus. He chose to die for you. Choose to live for Him.

PRAYER: *Jesus, help me live today with a spirit of absolute gratitude for Your work on the Cross.*

SP

HIDE AND SEEK

Jeremiah 29:13 – *You will seek me and find me when you seek me with all your heart.*

As a kid, I was the neighborhood sports doormat: chubby with two cowlicks in the front of my hair that stood up like devil's horns (which my mom called "prophetic"). While I was not a sports all-star, I WAS the king of hide-and-go-seek.

I could leave other kids searching for hours and before finally quitting—it was beautiful. Naturally, when my two-year-old daughter began to play the game, I was excited. She wanted me to hide first, so I jumped under the clean laundry pile my wife had been folding.

My little princess looked forever. I even waited until she was around the corner, so I wouldn't give away my spot. When it was my turn to count, she just stood right in front of me. I looked over her head like she was invisible.

So, I gave her some lessons—she hid behind a floor lamp. When I started to "pretend-look" for her, she immediately jumped out and said, "Here I am!" What I learned is that for her, the joy is not in hiding; it's the fun of being found.

Some of us think God is trying to "All-e-all-e-in-free" us into submission. But Jeremiah says that God wants to be found. He is jumping out into the open saying, "Here I am!"

PRAYER: *God, I want to seek You today and search for You with all of my heart. I am flawed and imperfect, but I want to engage my mind, body, and spirit to see You at work.*

DF

INSIDE OUT

Ephesians 3:16 – *I pray that out of His glorious riches He may strengthen you with power through His Spirit in your inner being.*

A true believer in Jesus has the indwelling Holy Spirit. That's where we get our inner strength. As we go throughout our day, God loves when we ask the Holy Spirit to empower and direct us.

Back in my Christian college days, most students bowed their heads to say a quick prayer of thanks for their cafeteria food, but I was usually so hungry that I would pray while waiting in line!

Still, after getting my food and sitting down to eat, I felt the need to say a quick prayer purely out of peer pressure. That was stupid, so I started legitimately using that time to ask God to help me interact with those around me (especially if there was a cute girl at the table).

That experience taught me a valuable lesson. I learned that God heard those consistent prayers and actually developed my social skills. The Spirit was working in me.

PRAYER: *Lord, I need Your inner strength in all I do and say. Work in and through me to make me the fulfilled person I was created to be.*

CJ

SAID AND DONE

Ecclesiastes 5:5 – *It is better not to make a vow than to make one and not fulfill it.*

Shannon consistently made promises she couldn't keep. With her boss, she would guarantee the on time completion of a project. To her parents, she routinely vowed to stop by and visit. With her young children, she agreed to sleepovers and camping trips. Unfortunately, Shannon rarely kept her word.

My good friend, Craig Peters often says, "When all is said and done, will more have been said, or will more have been done?" It's a fair question to ask Shannon. Don't get me wrong; she wasn't mean-spirited about breaking her promises. She had a huge heart, but her ability to follow through was just severely lacking.

It is easy to overextend yourself and make commitments you can't keep. Most people have the best intentions and make promises in an effort to help someone. They don't realize that in their failure to follow through, they end up hurting the people they hoped to help.

God wants you to keep our word. To do so, you may need to limit the number of commitments you make over the course of a week. It's better to come through for a few people than to disappoint many. Get into the habit of keeping your word.

PRAYER: *God, help me today to keep my word and follow through on my commitments.*

SP

PRISONER OF THE MOMENT

Ephesians 3:1 – *For this reason I, Paul, a prisoner of Christ Jesus on behalf of you Gentiles.*

At one point in my early ministry, I led a prison ministry. One week, while awaiting the inmates, there was a breach in the prison—a riot in a cell block close to the chapel. Needless to say, the leaders began praying intensely; it wasn't a normal prayer meeting.

While I haven't done anything worthy of a maximum-security sentence in my life, I was afraid in that moment of being behind bars. Paul, the Apostle, knew the feeling. However, instead of calling himself Rome's prisoner, he chose to refer to himself as Christ's prisoner. He was chained to a Roman guard all day and night, but he could say that because he knew a simple principle:

Your faith grows in the fight.

It's difficult that bad things occur WHEN you love God, but it's discouraging that bad things happen BECAUSE you love God. Remember, it's not just that Paul was in prison. Paul was there because he was trying to obey God. The truth is, the more consistently you walk *with* Christ, the more likely you are to suffer *for* Christ.

That's not great Gospel marketing. We don't put that on a Christian mug. However, everyone lives in some type of prison. Maybe it's the prison of other people's approval, a prison of anger, or one of regret. So, whose prisoner are you?

PRAYER: *Right now, Father, I dethrone anything that's above You in my life. In this moment, I say again that I am Yours and You are mine.*

DF

INDULGENCE BINDS UP FREEDOM

Galatians 5:13 – *You, my brothers, were called to be free. But do not use your freedom to indulge the sinful nature; rather, serve one another in love.*

When we hear that we have freedom, it lends itself to the thinking that we can do whatever we feel like doing. However, that kind of thinking leads to a restricted and unfulfilled existence.

Back in the ol' college days, a group of eight of us guys rented a condo in Florida. I remember looking around the place after just two days and realizing that we exercised our "freedom." In other words, the whole living area was a junk pile.

The kitchen was so filled with trash that we couldn't cook, and we had to hurdle objects just to get around the family room. Our "freedom" made it an annoying hassle to exist in that messy living space, and we couldn't relax until we cleaned up.

It's the same in our own lives. God wants us to be free, but freedom doesn't work well with indulgence. An out of control area of our personal lives can actually place bondage and restrictions on us. True freedom comes from attempting to follow God's principles, confessing our troubled areas, and serving one another.

PRAYER: *Father, I want freedom and enjoyment. Help me to make good choices. Show me how to depend on Your guidance.*

CJ

May 8th

FIVE DOLLARS AND FIFTY CENTS

Matthew 6:7 – *And when you pray, do not keep babbling like pagans, for they think they will be heard because of their many words.*

In college, I became friends with a guy who hailed from a highly refined family in the Northeast. In his home, if you used a one-syllable word when you could have used a two-syllable word, his parents would say that you just weren't trying hard enough.

On the other hand, Mark Twain once said, "Don't use a five-dollar word when a fifty-cent word will do." I couldn't agree more.

Spiritually speaking, we can feel comfortable using fifty-cent words when we pray, as opposed to the five-dollar variety. The Lord is seeking authenticity and sincerity when we pray. Furthermore, He prefers concise and simple language (Matthew 6:7).

Because of our faith in Jesus Christ, we can pray to the Father in His (Jesus) name. We can approach Him as regular people with regular language. We can offer praise for who He is and thanks for all He has done. At the same time, we can speak candidly about our failures and seek His help for our personal needs and the needs of others. Talk to Him today. The simplicity of your words and sincerity of your heart is music to His ears.

PRAYER: *God, help me today to develop a habit of simple and straight-forward conversations with You.*

SP

BOOT PEOPLE AND PILLOW PEOPLE

John 11:25-26; 35 – *I am the resurrection and the life. He who believes in me will live, even though he dies and whoever lives and believes in me will never die. Do you believe this…Jesus wept.*

When Lazarus dies, Jesus shows up late to the funeral. Lazarus' two sisters make virtually identical statements to Jesus, but He responds differently, almost schizophrenically, to the pair. The first sister, Martha, says, "If you had been here, my brother would not have died," and Jesus responds, "I'm the resurrection and the life." Martha is suffering, and He is going to teach her a Sunday School lesson. It's literally, *"Can't you see that as long as I'm here, I trump death. Can you handle this teaching?"*

Then Mary, the second sister, says the exact same words, and what is Jesus' response? He just cries with her. Wait! How is that fair? One sister gets a sermon, and the other gets sympathy. It's an incredible reminder that ONLY God knows exactly what we need and when we need it.

The reality is that we don't merely need a sermon or sympathy—we need both. God uses other people to minister both to us at just the right time. I refer to them as boot people and pillow people.

Sometimes, you need someone who is softer like a pillow. And sometimes, you need someone who kicks you in the rear end (not literally) like a boot.

Boot people. Pillow people. And Jesus, full of grace and truth, sends the right person at just the right time.

PRAYER: *Father, help me to see right now that You are bringing people into my life to make me a better disciple. Help me to look for and receive them today.*

DF

I WILL PUNCH YOUR LIGHTS OUT!

Psalm 37:8 – *Refrain from anger and turn from wrath; do not fret—it leads only to evil.*

I looked up "fret" in the dictionary, and it means "to cause corrosion; gnaw into something."

God issues us this warning about fretting for our own protection. In essence, He's saying, "If we live in anger, it will corrode and gnaw away at our very core."

Here are some suggested prayers that I have used:

- "Lord, I want to tear my teenage son's ears out of the sockets right now. Help me to calm down and realize I was once an idiot adolescent."
- "Lord, my dad is driving me crazy with his continual nagging. Help me to forgive him and realize he really does care."
- "Lord, my wife gets upset with me for doing the exact same thing that she does. Please take away my anger and help me to look past her hurtful words."
- "Lord, that ref is costing us the game. Help me to stop imagining myself strangling him and enable me to forgive him so I can enjoy this game."

Refraining from anger is difficult, but as a friend once said, "Blessed are the flexible, for they shalt not break."

PRAYER: *Father, I get bothered. Please don't allow me to camp out on my gnawing anger. Help me to hand it over to You even when it's a legitimate reason.*

CJ

MY TOP FIVE

Psalm 62:8 – *Trust in him at all times, you people; pour out your hearts to him, for God is our refuge.*

The other day, I had a dear friend tell me that he was discouraged in his faith. As a follower of Jesus, he didn't doubt his salvation or feel far from God because of a sin issue. Instead, he was genuinely exhausted by the energy it took to navigate his life and lead his family in our spiritually bankrupt culture.

As a result, my friend's trust in God's purpose and plan began to waiver. He wondered where God was in all the chaos of our world. At that moment, I had the opportunity to encourage him to fight the good fight and finish the race—to keep the faith. Furthermore, I had the chance to remind him why he could trust God's purpose and plan.

Today, I share what I reminded him of with you. Below are my top five reasons you can trust God:

He knows you by name.
Isaiah 43:1

He has plans for you.
Jeremiah 29:11

He is your refuge.
Psalms 62:8

He will fight for you.
Exodus 14:14

He will never leave you.
Matthew 28:20

PRAYER: *God, remind me today of Your love for me. Remind me that I can trust You during moments of chaos and doubt.*

SP

WHERE ARE MY GLASSES?

Deuteronomy 6:6-8 – *These commandments that I give you today are to be on your hearts. Impress them on your children. Talk about them when you sit at home and when you walk along the road, when you lie down and when you get up. Tie them as symbols on your hands and bind them on your foreheads.*

It finally happened to me. Two things that I swore to myself as a younger man: 1) I will never own a minivan and 2) I will never be that guy who constantly loses his glasses.

I have failed on both counts.

And it's not just that I failed in losing my sunglasses. It's "where" I lost my sunglasses and "who" discovered them.

I'm in a hurry; I need to leave, because I'm running late. I sprint back into the house and declare, "Has anyone borrowed my sunglasses?" I know, as if my teenage daughters want to wear their dad's sunglasses.

Everyone should spring into action and help me locate them, but all I get are weird looks and chuckles.

Finally, my wife says (those of you 40+ know what is coming), "They are on your head."

Moses told the Hebrews to tie God's Word to their foreheads because you cannot forget what is on your head, right? Wrong—I (and many others before me) have proven that to be wrong.

I think God wants His Word at the front of our minds. The Hebrews took that literally, which is a beautiful picture. We should take that to heart spiritually. God's Word needs to be our grid for "Just Thinking."

PRAYER: *God, I want to meditate on Your Word today. Let it feed my soul. I want it to be my lamp, my light. Spirit, use the Word to guide me into truth.*

DF

HOWDY NEIGHBOR

2 Corinthians 9:7-8 – *for God loves a cheerful giver. And God is able to bless you abundantly, so that in all things at all times, having all that you need, you will abound in every good work.*

When something good comes our way, we tend to keep it for ourselves. All of us have the ability to help and encourage others, but we tend to get too caught up in our own needs being met.

I had a roommate in college who complained that when he walked through campus, "Nobody ever says hi to me." I was shocked because I felt as though the students on campus were amazingly friendly.

But knowing how cold and impersonal he was, I asked, "Do you say hello to anyone?" He bitterly retorted, "No way! If they won't acknowledge me, then I won't acknowledge them." I quickly realized the problem.

To have friends, we need to be a friend. To be blessed, we need to bless. To "get" we have to "give."

PRAYER: *Heavenly Father, thank You for wanting to bless me abundantly. Give me the strength and awareness to give of myself so that You can take care of me. In Jesus' name. Amen.*

CJ

PHOTOSHOP

1 Peter 3:3-4 – *Your beauty should not come from outward adorn-ment...it should be that of your inner self, the unfading beauty of a gentle and quiet spirit, which is of great worth in God's sight.*

Scrolling through my social media feed, I spotted an interesting photo of someone I knew well. However, the photograph didn't look entirely like the person I knew. Don't get me wrong; there was a resemblance. But the picture had been edited to such a degree that I had to do a double take.

Like magic, the individual's skin appeared to be perfect, the eyes were vibrant, and the teeth were as white as the sand on Marco Island. Wrinkles were gone, and smile lines had faded away. What a transformation!

Okay, so I may be exaggerating a little for the sake of effect. On the other hand, a gentle reminder concerning our culture's emphasis on outward appearance may be in order.

As Christ-followers, our beauty should stem from something far more significant than temporary trends and fashion. Charm and beauty connected to the world's influence are deceptive and fleeting. Instead, beauty should derive from something eternal—reverence for the Lord, a gentle spirit, and a joyful heart. In other words, the inward spirit of a person is far more important than the outward appearance.

PRAYER: *God, help me today to let go of my pursuit of the world's standard for beauty. Help me develop an inward beauty that comes from You.*

SP

WHEN HEAVEN HURLS

Revelation 3:16 – *So, because you are lukewarm – neither hot nor cold – I am about to spit you out of my mouth.*

Spiritual indifference is the reality that we don't want to fully say, "Yes" to God because we don't really want to change. But we also don't want to say, "No" to God because we are afraid of the consequences.

A few years ago, somebody in our house clogged up a commode by dropping a cleaning object into it. I don't want to throw anyone under the bus, but it wasn't me or the kids. I put out an APB to the family that we could not use that commode until it was unclogged. Well, the kids evidently didn't get the message, so we ended up with a mess in the clogged toilet.

So, somebody had to go in there and fix it. Somebody has to be a big boy, put on the rubber gloves, take a deep breath, and remove the refuse to provide a solution.

In our house that somebody was my wife. I kid, I kid! While I was cleaning that toilet out by hand, my gag reflex started working. Were these kids my idea?

Do you ever wonder what makes God sick? Spiritual indifference, spiritual apathy, and the idea of having just enough of God to give us a false sense of security are the things that turn Heaven's stomach. You can say a full "Yes" to Him today.

PRAYER: *Father, I am giving you my best "Yes" right now. I want Your leadership and Your Spirit's guidance, comfort, and conviction in my life. No partial obedience, no delayed obedience. I am Yours.*

DF

CRASH LANDINGS

Psalm 37:23-24 – *If the Lord delights in a man's way, He makes his steps firm; though he stumble, he will not fall, for the Lord upholds him with His hand.*

Seeing someone trip usually makes me laugh. It's weird that I find humor in others' misfortune of going to the ground unexpectedly, but what can I say? It makes me laugh.

No matter if the fall is generated from slipping on ice or running into others, they are always good for a chuckle. Still, my personal favorite has to be bicycle falls.

I remember biking with my 6′6″ high school buddy. He pulled alongside me, and I kicked his front tire. His front brakes locked up, and this threw him over his handlebars in what seemed to be in slow motion. He quickly jumped up from this hilarious tumble and began an all-out sprint, trying to kill me.

Now, I have also fallen off a bike, and I certainly wasn't laughing. In fact, I was hurt and frustrated. But here's what I realized: falling isn't so bad; it's the landing that hurts.

As Christians, we should remember that God can hold us up and turn a fall into just a stumble.

PRAYER: *Father, teach me to place my steps on Your firm footing by depending on You daily. Help me to confess and recover from my wrongful choices.*

CJ

CROCODILE BRIDGE

Colossians 3:2 – *Set your minds on things above, not on earthly things.*

My heart raced as I reached the halfway point of the 200-foot-long train trestle. My equilibrium was off, and I couldn't take another step. I was having a panic attack sixty feet above a crocodile-infested river in Malawi. To steady myself, I crouched down onto a railroad tie. I was paralyzed with fear.

After what felt like an eternity, I remembered a mentor's words about Christ's calling in my life. Reliving the conversation helped me to take my eyes off of my surroundings and recalibrate a little. Slowly, I stood to my feet and moved forward. With each step, I repeated my friend's words until I made it across.

During my time of fear and panic on the bridge, I lost focus. My mind became distracted, and I allowed fear and anxiety to slow my movements. As a result, there was a time on the bridge when I forgot why I was in Africa in the first place—to reach people for Jesus Christ.

Stay fixated on God's purpose, plans, and promises. Limit your distractions and let go of earthly doubts and fears. Don't get stuck in the middle of the bridge.

PRAYER: *God, help me today to begin retraining my mind. Help me to focus on You and let go of distractions, doubts, and fears.*

SP

THE PRESEASON

Hebrews 11:27 – *By faith he (Moses) left Egypt, not fearing the king's anger; he persevered because he saw him who is invisible.*

> "*The secret of success in life is for a man to be ready for his time when it comes.*"
>
> – Benjamin Disraeli

Leadership has a preseason. Coaches have a saying that the offseason makes the season. Christian leaders are not all that different. Moses is the best test case. At the age of forty, Moses is young, attractive, well-educated, and on the fast track to become the next king of Egypt.

However, after murdering an Egyptian for his treatment of a Hebrew slave, Moses chooses a forty-year preseason in the desert. He went from the Oval Office to a desert cave in one fell swoop.

At age eighty, Moses stood before the burning bush and asked this question: "I am not a great man! How can I go to the king and lead the Israelites out of Egypt?" I agree *with* Moses *about* Moses—and about me.

I don't like spiritual training any more than Moses did. So, what did eighty-year-old Moses know that forty-year-old Moses didn't? Think of it this way. If you are going to lead a couple million Hebrew people through the desert, it would be a bonus if you had spent some time there.

Eighty-year-old Moses had graduated from Desert 101. And he was ready, when his time came.

PRAYER: *God, help me to see that You are preparing me in this circumstance for my next step. Help me to glorify You today and in the coming days.*

DF

DEER FEET

Habakkuk 3:19 – *The Lord is my strength; He makes my feet like the feet of a deer, He enables me to tread on the heights.*

Today's verse was written to people who were going through really hard times. The word "strength" here stands for "personal bravery" or an "invincible army." The verse also mentions having "the feet of a deer." Think about the deer-like animals that manage to maneuver around the unstable footing of mountains. Their little hooves are hard and flat enough to handle the rocks and yet pointed enough to dig into the loose terrain for stability.

When I think about this verse, it reminds me of a saying I kept with me as a teenager: "Do not pray for an easy task; pray to be stronger." Back in those days, my life was easy, so this saying only applied to things such as praying to play well in a golf match instead of hoping my opponent sliced his shot into the woods or a sand trap.

Now, life is a lot more difficult with a job, wife, kids, bills, health concerns…. However, instead of praying for God to flatten the mountain and lay an outdoor carpet over the cragged rocks for us, we need to ask Him for "deer feet."

PRAYER: *Lord, I need Your strength. I need You to make my feet like those of a deer, especially when times get tough.*

CJ

I'LL GO WITH YOU

1 Thessalonians 5:11 – *Therefore encourage one another and build each other up, just as in fact you are doing.*

The atmosphere was toxic inside the cafeteria of Memorial High School. For the past two weeks, the "cool girls" had done everything in their power to embarrass and belittle Riley, and their plan to sadden the heart of the new girl had worked. With tears rolling down her face, Riley whimpered, "I'm leaving," and walked toward the exit doors.

Jenna's heart was uneasy. Just one year ago, she was in Riley's shoes—heartbroken and despondent. But she also knew the power of a gentle smile, a word of hope, and what it meant to have someone on her side. Wanting to help, she made her way toward Riley and simply said, "I'll go with you."

At that moment, kindness and compassion won the day. Friendship was offered and accepted. Jesus was pleased.

As followers of Christ, we have an amazing opportunity to encourage those around us who are down and discouraged. I can think of no better way to demonstrate the love of Jesus than to walk with others through their dark and desperate times. They need you.

PRAYER: *God, help me to recognize the people around me who are hurting. Give me the words to say as I stand with those who need a friend.*

SP

TEXTS FROM BEYOND THE GRAVE

John 14:18 – *I will not leave you as orphans; I will come to you.*

Chastity Patterson, a 23-year-old from Arkansas, texted her father, Jason, the night before the fourth anniversary of his death. She often texted her father the happenings in her dating life, educational pursuits, and other events, even though he had been dead for some time. Jason was not her biological father, but a kind of surrogate father who had adopted her.

So, on the fourth anniversary of Jason's death, she received the unthinkable—a return text!

The text read, "My name is Brad, and somehow your texts to Jason have been coming to me for the last few years, after I purchased a new phone." Then Brad followed up to Chastity, "My daughter died in a car accident three years ago, and your texts have kept me alive. When you text me, it's like a message from God."

Brad continued, "For what it's worth, I think your dad would be proud of you. Congratulations on graduating, getting that new job, and dumping that guy you were dating. You were too good for him."

Chastity recounted to a local media member, "It was like I knew that everything was going to be okay."

What if you could receive messages from beyond the grave? Well, you can—you have! They are in God's Word in the resurrection of Jesus, which both feed your soul and remind you that Jesus makes all things new.

PRAYER: *Father, thank You for Your Word that You have given to remind me that I'm never alone. I look forward to the day when I will be with You in eternity!*

DF

DRY TIMES AND DESERT SAND

Hebrews 3:8 – *Do not harden your hearts as you did in the rebellion, during the time of testing in the desert.*

Many times we don't **feel** God's presence. Many times we don't **feel** like He cares. And sometimes, we don't even **feel** like there is a God at all. Thankfully, these **dry times** come and go. However, some **dry times** stay longer than others, and we can **feel** as though we're in a **spiritual desert**.

We simply can't base our faith and communication with God on our **feelings**. Our faith has to be based on the **facts** laid out in the Bible, history, and all of the evidence that reveals Jesus walked on earth (By the way, here are two great faith building books: <u>Evidence That Demands a Verdict</u> and <u>More Than a Carpenter</u> by Josh McDowell).

So, how do we experience great growth in our faith during those desert times? We must **stay the course**, just as the great athletes who choose to train even on those days when they didn't **feel** like it. As the great boxer Jack Dempsey once stated, "A champion is someone who gets up when he can't."

PRAYER: *Father, I know my **feelings** and emotions vary. Please help me to keep walking with You, especially in those **dry times**.*

CJ

PRIVATE GEORGE KESSLER

Romans 12:21 – *Do not be overcome by evil, but overcome evil with good.*

Private George Kessler and his two buddies were hunkered down in a foxhole. A momentary break in the fighting opened the door for one of them to pass along a message to their unit commander forty yards away. George volunteered.

Twenty yards into his army crawl, bullets began to fly. George was in no man's land, and his only option was to return to his foxhole. Two steps into a sprint, an artillery shell burst nearby. The enemy shell hit the foxhole and killed his buddies. Miraculously, George survived.

Months later, George was assigned to a POW camp where he oversaw the intake of enemy prisoners. Everything in him wanted to exact revenge. At the same time, he knew the only way to avoid being personally overcome by evil was to treat each enemy prisoner with dignity.

As Christians, we are not immune to the brokenness of this world. When we are on the receiving end of other people's cruelty and unkindness, our flesh cries out for retribution. The Bible, however, calls us to respond with goodness. Here's a thought: leave the reprisal up to God. Instead of revenge, follow His Word, choose kindness, and refuse to be overcome by evil.

PRAYER: *Father, help me today to follow the example of Your Son and repay evil with good.*

SP

CSI: LAS VEGAS

Psalm 139:23 – *Search me, God, and know my heart.*

I once spoke at a marriage conference in Las Vegas. Because that's where all the best marriage conferences are—Vegas. A really good friend of mine from Alabama planted a church in Vegas, and I have heard him say on a number of occasions, "People from Alabama don't think that Las Vegas is Hell, but they do think you can smell it from there."

At the conference, I sat at one of the discussion tables, and there was an extremely quiet couple at my table as well. In conversation, I asked the husband what he did professionally. He sheepishly said, "I'm a crime scene investigator." That statement took a minute to sink in. "Wait a minute," I said. "You are like the real CSI Las Vegas?!?!"

His wife jumped in, "He's actually the lead investigator at CSI Las Vegas and a consultant for the TV show." Naturally, I couldn't stop asking questions for the next twenty minutes. The next morning, he brought me a badge that had been used on the show. In my mind, I'm now a CSI investigator. So, if there's a crime committed at your house, you know where to come.

What if you asked God to CSI your heart right now, to search your heart and clean out anything that doesn't reflect Him? And then you turned away from relying on that comfort to relying on him?

PRAYER: *Holy Spirit, search my heart today just like You did for David's heart thousands of years ago. I repent of anything in my life that's not of You. I want to begin today clean.*

DF

DEVELOPING OVERLOOK MUSCLES

Proverbs 19:11 – *A man's wisdom gives him patience; it is to his glory to overlook an offense.*

Benjamin Franklin once stated, "Keep your eyes wide open before marriage and half-shut afterwards." In other words, there are many chances throughout each day to choose patience over frustration with ourselves, others, and our circumstances.

As a golfer, I know that by choosing frustration over patience, your round can quickly fall apart. Even more, I've witnessed much frustration on the golf course: a thrown putter that was lost in a tree, a 3-wood catapulted farther than the hit ball, strings of vulgar exclamations that made no sense, a grown man beating up a fir tree with his pitching wedge, and a friend proclaiming his resignation from golf "forever" (for the 50th time) while throwing his entire bag of clubs into a pond.

Frustration can also snowball our emotions. We are wired to respond in a negative way when something goes wrong or when we're offended. It's as though we need an "overlook muscle" to cope, which is simply possessing the ability to overlook offenses and frustrations.

PRAYER: *Father, help me call on Your supernatural "overlook abilities" of not getting even, angry, or running to gossip buddies.*

CJ

FIGHTING WORDS

Romans 7:19 – *For I do not do the good I want to do, but the evil I do not want to do—this I keep on doing.*

From an outsider's perspective, it must have looked like the scene in Rocky IV when Ivan Drago towered over Rocky Balboa before the big fight. Though we were both in the seventh grade, the barbarian in front of me was taller, meaner, and stronger. I didn't stand a chance.

A playground argument had escalated, and now I found myself standing in the center of a pack of rowdy middle schoolers. I set my jaw, clenched my fist, and prepared for the worst. Just as my adversary prepared to throw the first punch, a whistle blew, and the recess monitor stepped in and saved the day. There is a God!

In life, there is a fight between doubt, disobedience, commitment, and dedication that rages in our hearts. Thomas the Apostle is remembered most for doubting the resurrection of Jesus. However, he also demonstrated extraordinary commitment and dedication when he encouraged the Disciples to return to Judea with Jesus, even if it meant they would die there.

Let's face it; sometimes, we are doubtful and disobedient, and other times we are committed and dedicated. Create consistency in your walk with God by diving into His Word and developing an accountability relationship with someone. Fight for your faith!

PRAYER: *God, help me take steps today to build a consistent walk with You.*

SP

SMOKIN' JOE

Genesis 39:12 – *She caught him by his cloak and said, "Come to bed with me!" But he left his cloak in her hand and ran out of the house.*

I once asked a mentor about temptation, "Well, is this a sin? If that's a sin, could someone do this?" You know, I certainly wasn't asking for myself…just asking for a friend.

My wife and I had three young children around that same time. So, my friend said to me, "Let's say one of your kids had to be driven to a preschool at the top of a mountain with a winding, narrow road and very steep drop-offs. Would you want the driver to see how close he could drive to the edge or how close he could stay to the mountain?"

I replied, "Which kid are we talking about here?"

His point was clear. If you love God, focus on staying close to Him, instead of seeing how close you can get to the edge without cliff-jumping.

Joseph was a young man, full of hormones, being tempted by what we can assume was a very attractive woman in Genesis 39. No one would have ever known what transpired between them—except Joseph and the One whom he loved. Joseph chose to run from temptation because he believed that he was running to Someone better. To what or whom are you running today?

PRAYER: *God, You are better than life itself. Right now, I'm running to You. Nothing compares to You.*

DF

COBBLER

2 Corinthians 9:8-9 – *God loves a cheerful giver. And is able to make all grace abound to you…*

There once was a cobbler who was so busy fixing shoes that he didn't have time for his own. A lady noticed his tattered footwear, so she placed a good, used pair at his door. The next day, the lady saw those shoes on her doorstep, and they were completely cleaned and repaired along with a note that read, "No charge."

The lady told others in the small town. One man was so touched that he dropped off an old horse and buggy for the cobbler to use. The next day, the man looked out his front window to see a young horse with a reupholstered buggy. The note attached said, "No charge."

Curiosity moved the folks to look into the cobbler's history: he once was a wealthy king and had chosen to live in their town amongst the commoners.

We have a Heavenly Father Who made that move through Jesus— from living as royalty to living amongst the common people. To this day, like the cobbler, He takes our giving and blesses it.

PRAYER: *Lord, make me a giver. Thank You that all my needs, inner and outer, will be met.*

CJ

LOYALTY'S FINEST HOUR

Ecclesiastes 4:10 – *If either of them falls down, one can help the other up. But pity anyone who falls and has no one to help them up.*

Jack stared at the map in disbelief. He knew his lifelong friend was behind enemy lines, injured, and on his own. Over the course of the next ten hours, Jack managed to create a rescue operation, airdrop behind enemy lines, and rendezvous with his buddy in a hastily dug foxhole.

Risking life and limb, Jack brought food, water, and first aid to his wounded friend. All that was left now was getting back safely, and it would take one thing: dedication!

In Paul's second letter to Timothy, he writes from prison about the loyalty of a man named Onesiphorus. At this point in his prison sentence, Paul had been abandoned by nearly everyone for fear of persecution—everyone except Onesiphorus. With complete disregard for his safety or reputation, this devoted man visited Paul and ministered to his needs while he was in chains. Loyalty!

When the people you love most find themselves with their backs against the wall, stand with them. When they fall, pick them back up. And when they need to be rescued, put on your cape and go to work.

PRAYER: *God, help me today to show unconditional love, loyalty, and devotion to my family and friends.*

SP

WHEN BIGGER ISN'T BETTER

Job 38:4 – *Where were you when I laid the earth's foundation? Tell me, if you understand.*

People don't aspire to make "okay" movies. Nobody dreams about being the sixth man or woman on a basketball team—it's number one or number none.

Job was the wealthiest, healthiest, most God-blessed man of his generation. However, within hours, he loses everything: his health, his wealth, and his children. He's left with a wife who seems more interested in collecting his life insurance policy than his healing.

That's the first two chapters of this amazing narrative. The rest of the story (with a nod to Paul Harvey) is Job talking out his thoughts about suffering with his buddies. Job has this profound sense that God is silent during this painful season. So, Job accuses and criticizes God.

At the end of the book in chapter 38, God finally speaks to Job. Depending on how you count, God asks Job 66 consecutive questions, and Job cannot answer any of them. God starts by asking for the architectural measurements of the earth and progresses onward.

Through His questioning, God is being kind, not sarcastic. We need a God who is transcendent—so much bigger than we are or could even imagine. If not, then we don't have a God. We only have a better version of us. Just like teenagers, we do not have everything figured out.

PRAYER: *God, please help me to understand that I don't understand everything right now. You graciously reveal some things to me, but there are other things I won't understand until eternity. Either way, I choose to trust You today.*

DF

BRIDGE OVER TROUBLED WATERS

John 14:27 – *My peace I give you…Do not let your hearts be troubled and do not be afraid.*

The word "troubled" makes me think of Paul Simon's song, "Bridge Over Troubled Waters." I picture a cold river with choppy waves crashing into the walled banks, and a troubled heart can feel like this type of angry current.

I once learned a lesson from my sixth grade teacher about what to do when we experience troubles. This teacher was a young, lanky man who didn't seem very motivated as I recall having to fetch his two cups of coffee from the office. After seeing the spills of coffee running down the sides of his cup, he explained to me that if I looked at the coffee while walking, it would spill. However, if I looked ahead, it wouldn't. Don't ask me why, but it worked!

This principle is also one that God is encouraging us to use. If we keep our eyes up on Him in the midst of hard times, then He will calm the waters of our hearts. Peace is available there for us. We can (and should) ask for His calm and peace, for He says, "My peace I give you."

PRAYER: *Father, remind me to look to You instead of down at the problems. Give me Your peace.*

CJ

A LOPSIDED CONVERSATION

Proverbs 18:2 – *Fools find no pleasure in understanding but delight in airing their own opinions.*

Waiting to board a flight to Washington, I noticed a group of senior adults gathering in the gate area. As the size of the group increased in number, I found myself standing near a couple who were conversing with a rather self-important gentleman from their tour group.

Intrigued by their interaction, I immediately noticed how the couple could not get a single word into the conversation. Whenever the husband or wife attempted to make a point, the verbose gentleman cut them off and offered even greater dialogue of his own. It was exhausting to watch. And though they tried to mask their annoyance, both the husband and the wife let out a sigh of relief when the conversation finally came to an end. I couldn't help but chuckle inside when I heard the wife say to her husband, "I guess we know where to go if we want someone's opinion."

As you build and develop relationships, be sure to do so in an environment of equal exchange. Share your insights, but temper your opinions. Open the door for others to engage in the conversation—their words may be full of wisdom and understanding.

PRAYER: *God, help me today to be slow to speak my opinion and quick to hear the wisdom of others.*

SP

BONKISTRY

John 8:32 – *Then you will know the truth, and the truth will set you free.*

Dr. James Bonk taught Intro to Chemistry at Duke University for fifty-three years—long enough that the students began referring to the class as "Bonkistry." One semester, a couple of smart guys did well in the class and had A's heading into the final exam.

So, the two students blew off studying for their Monday final and went to the University of Virginia to party with friends over the weekend. The students were so hungover that they didn't get back in town until early Monday morning. Instead of taking the final, they went to Professor Bonk and created a lie about having a flat tire.

When they asked if they could take the final on Tuesday morning, Dr. Bonk agreed. Their ruse seemed effective. On Tuesday morning, Dr. Bonk gave them their exams and put them in separate rooms. Page one had a simple 5-point problem about molarity. The young men thought, "Sweet! This is going to be easy."

However, they were unprepared as they turned to the second page that simply read, "95 points—which tire?"

Jesus offers us a choice of truth and freedom over lies and pretense. Live in the light today. You can repent and restart again today.

PRAYER: *Holy Spirit, reveal truth to me from Your Word and in me from my life patterns today. I want to live according to Your truth and not my version of the truth.*

DF

"GOOD EFFORT, WILLIE. GREAT HUSTLE, PHIL."

Proverbs 11:25 – *He who refreshes others will himself be refreshed.*

It was a cruel, ninety-plus-degree day, and I stood at the second base position on an all dirt infield (Old age had removed me from shortstop). Just as I was feeling sorry for myself and starting to question why I was still playing in softball tournaments, the Bible verse I was studying flashed into my thoughts. So, I decided to put it into practice.

I verbally began *"refreshing"* my teammates with words of encouragement and motivation. Our team ended up playing six games that day, as we fought our way through the loser bracket to win the championship. What a day!

As I reflected on the day's events, I realized my words that were meant to give life to others were returned to me as I had plenty of energy to finish the games. While vicious leg cramps and exhaustion settled in after I got home, I will never forget how God kept His promise to *refresh* me when I *refreshed others.*

PRAYER: *Father, remind me to say words of encouragement to those around me. I want You to take care of me more than my taking care of myself.*

CJ

THE SCALES OF JUSTICE

1 Peter 1:3 – *In his great mercy he has given us new birth into a living hope through the resurrection of Jesus Christ from the dead.*

I watched with curiosity as my professor scooped a handful of sand into one of two pans hanging from an oversized balance scale. Allowing the sand to sift through his fingers, he asked us to imagine each grain of sand as an act of disobedience or sin. "The scales of justice," he exclaimed as he repeated this process until the pan overflowed.

With the scale entirely out of balance and thoroughly leaning in the direction of the sand, he picked up a small, steel cube and placed it in the opposite pan. Immediately the scale reacted to the weight of the steel and tilted in the direction of the cube. My professor then looked up at all of us and said, "Christ's mercy."

Richard Sibbes, an Anglican theologian in the early 1600s, is credited with saying, "There is more mercy in Christ than sin in us." In short, mercy takes hold in our lives at the moment of salvation, and the volume and severity of our past sin become inconsequential. Our decision to follow Christ removes the weight of sin and tips the scales of justice toward mercy and forgiveness. Have you experienced His mercy today?

PRAYER: *Father, today I call upon Your mercy and ask Your Son Jesus to forgive me of my sin. I invite Him into my life as my Lord and Savior.*

SP

THE LITTLE BANOS

Ephesians 2:14 – *For he himself is our peace, who has made the two groups one and has destroyed the barrier, the dividing wall of hostility.*

The Bible clearly teaches that there's a spiritual barrier between people in their natural state and God in His perfect state. We all understand barriers.

I once took a group of mainly young, single adults on a mission trip to Central America. If you have ever traveled internationally, you have experienced language barriers.

That week, our group ministered to children through a medical/dental clinic, a pharmacy, and various children's ministries. One of our team members set up an audiology clinic, and for the first two days of our trip, she saw over fifty children.

One of the main Spanish words for "child" is "niño." However, at the end of the second day, we heard her refer to a child with a completely different Spanish word: "baño," which means—bathroom. For two days, she called all of the village children "bathrooms!"

Jesus came to live as an example for us and to suffer and die on a cross for us, so that we could know God. To put it another way, He gave us a way to speak God's language; He was our translator. It's not surprising, then, that the Apostle John called Jesus the Word of God. Jesus was God's communication to us in human form.

PRAYER: *God, today I'm grateful for the sacrifice of Jesus. Thank You that, even though I was far away because of my sin, You have brought me close to You.*

DF

DEATH PUTS LIFE INTO PERSPECTIVE

Hebrews 9:27-28 – *Just as man is destined to die once,… Christ was sacrificed once to take away the sins of many…*

Actor and comedian Woody Allen once stated, "I'm very proud of my gold pocket watch. My grandfather, on his deathbed, sold it to me." Death is one of those issues we avoid thinking about, yet death actually puts life into perspective.

In school, I was the math student who understood the process better if I started with the answer and worked my way backwards. In the same way, realizing the fact that our lives will be over some day should help us to make better choices, not take things for granted, and appreciate the people in our lives.

There are those who take another approach and say, "If I'm going to die, then why not party my life away?" Because death isn't the end for those who have accepted Christ. My goal in life is to have people be encouraged at my funeral after seeing my faith in Jesus that resulted in helping others and living rightly.

PRAYER: *Jesus, thank You that I can go to heaven when I die because I placed my faith in You. Help me to make good decisions and appreciate my time here.*

CJ

CORRUPTIONS CASUALTY

I Corinthians 15:33 – *Do not be misled: "Bad company corrupts good character."*

Daniel was in over his head. Decisions he'd made over the previous five years had finally caught up with him, and now he found himself sitting in the back of a police car while detectives raided his office. With his head buried in his hands, he said to himself, "How did this happen to me?"

I once heard it said, "Corruption of the best is the worst." In Daniel's case, the sentiment rings true. For most of his adult life, Daniel was a man of faith and integrity. He loved God and lived his life in a way that honored Him. And then, Daniel changed.

It all started when he entered into a business relationship with some questionable people. Daniel surrounded himself with dubious partners who impacted his thinking and darkened his heart. Ultimately Daniel compromised his principles, made terrible decisions, and broke the law.

The people we spend time with have a direct influence on our lives. Choose your friends and business associates wisely. Surround yourself with people who seek God and demonstrate His character—honesty, virtue, kindness, and goodness. Embrace people who encourage your soul and inspire you to follow Jesus Christ.

PRAYER: *God, help me surround myself with people today who know and love You. Give me wisdom as I embrace those who will influence my life.*

SP

CLYDE THE GLIDE

Nehemiah 8:10b – *...the joy of the Lord is your strength.*

Today is not about Clyde "the Glide" Drexler, whose nickname matched his smooth basketball play on the Dream Team. It's about a different Clyde. Have you ever met someone with spiritual poise? Someone who seemed to live counter-culturally? Someone who did not get rattled at the first sight of adversity? For me, that person was Clyde Cranford.

Clyde had very little use for the things that others thought were important. He lived in a very small home, drove an old vehicle, and never wore trendy clothes. Yet, every time I was around him, I wanted more time with him. And he was gracious to give that to me.

He met with me weekly for two years. It took me a while to learn his secret. His spiritual poise was the result of walking with a spiritual Presence.

Clyde died way too early, only 43 years old. But he wasn't made for this planet. My father-in-law preached his funeral and asked for the men whom Clyde had discipled to stand. One group of men stood. Then, he asked for the men who had been disciplined by the already-standing group of men to stand as well (a 2nd generation). In the end, there were 100-plus men standing—at a funeral the world would disregard, but Heaven could not ignore. Clyde's life demonstrated that Christianity is meant to be enjoyed—not merely endured—because God's joy is your strength.

PRAYER: *Father, help me to live in, live from, and enjoy Your Presence today. I believe that You are with me all day today. I have Your favor and blessing, even when circumstances say otherwise.*

DF

PERSONAL FITNESS TRAINER OF MY SOUL

2 Corinthians 4:16 – *Therefore we do not lose heart. Though outwardly we are wasting away, yet inwardly we are being renewed day by day.*

Like it or not, we are all getting older. I remember long summers as a child when the biggest decision I had to make was whom I was going to play with. As an adult, the only reason I even know it's summer is because I hear guys talking about baseball.

Time marches on! We go from teaching our kids how to take those first steps to their running by us in the backyard while saying, "Come on, Dad. See if you can catch me." "No, son. Maybe tomorrow. I think my back went out after sitting on the couch and reaching too far for the bag of chips."

The Bible is clear that, physically, we are *wasting away*. It's as the famous comedian Jackie Mason once said: "It's no longer a question of staying healthy. It's a question of finding a sickness you like."

Despites what's happening on the outside, our "insides" don't have to waste away! Bible reading, praying, and thinking about God is like our Fountain of Youth for the mind and soul. We just need to drink from it often and watch God renew.

PRAYER: *Lord, give me the strength to exercise my body both outwardly and inwardly. Be the personal fitness Trainer of my soul.*

CJ

FEAR IS CLOSING IN

Psalm 56:3 – *When I am afraid, I put my trust in you.*

Sawyer Simpson was pinned down by enemy fire. One of his buddies was hit in the shoulder, and the other had taken shrapnel from a grenade. Their attackers were closing in, and fear gripped Sawyer's heart.

Air support was thirty seconds out. If he could hang on for half a minute, he might just survive. At that moment, he remembered his mother's words on the day he deployed: "When you are afraid, put your trust in Jesus."

Fear is real, and it can stop us in our tracks. It can manifest itself physically, emotionally, or spiritually. The key to overcoming fear is to replace it with a genuine trust in the Lord's presence. God's presence in our lives provides protection, offers strength, and gives us the grace to endure hardship.

In the same way that we trust God for salvation, we can also trust Him when we are afraid. Refuse to give in to doubt and fear. God is present in the firefight—know that He is there. Regardless of what happens, trust God's absolute goodness, mighty power, and sovereign plan.

PRAYER: *God, help me feel Your presence and trust You today. Give me courage and strength.*

SP

THE COMEBACK

1 Corinthians 15:22 – *For as in Adam all die, so in Christ all will be made alive.*

Woody Allen is famous for his work in comedy. He once said, "You're born…you don't know why. You're here…you don't know why. You go…you die…your family dies…your friends die…people suffer. People live in constant terror. The world is full of poverty and corruption and war and Nazis and tsunamis…the net result, the final count is, you lose…you don't beat the house." And we call him a comedian?

If all we see is all there is, then Woody is right.

Ted Williams is most famously known as being the last guy to hit .400. However, a close second is that he is also known for being connected to the Alcor Life Extension Program. His family paid $136,000 to cryogenically freeze The Splendid Splinter postmortem by shooting his corpse full of human anti-freeze and placing him in a liquid nitrogen canister at minus 196 degrees Celsius, so he can have "Life Cycle #2." Why does Woody Allen despair, while the Williams family is so determined?

Christian or not, we'd all like a mulligan at the end of our lives. But only Christians have the hope that because Christ was raised, we will be raised as well. We will see our loved ones in Christ and everything restored to its original design.

PRAYER: *Lord, thank You that You have not only given me life in this current world, but You have also given me eternal life forever with You. I look forward to seeing everyone in Christ who is already with You and seeing everything restored under Your leadership.*

DF

SHADOW OF THE ALMIGHTY

Psalm 91:1 – *He who dwells in the shelter of the Most High will rest in the shadow of the Almighty.*

When I got a new bike for Father's Day, I started riding it for exercise. Even though there were some days of intense summer heat, I stayed committed to pedaling off the pounds (actually, all of this new exercise just made me hungrier. I think I possibly gained weight).

Most of my bike trail was directly under the rays of the brutal sun, but there was a stretch I always looked forward to—about 100 yards of shade provided by a line of large trees.

That stretch of shade was the first thing that popped into my mind when I read today's verse. Even though I was actively exercising while biking through the shade, I was, in a sense, still "resting" in the shadows of those trees. They were a much-needed break from the heat.

For believers, dwelling with the Almighty, having a relationship with God, and attempting to walk with Him will supply us with the rest, relief, protection, and help we need from the intense heat of daily pressures.

PRAYER: *Lord, help me to walk with You so I can experience the "shadow of the Almighty." Thank You that I can call on You for a break from the heat.*

CJ

June 13th

BY YOUR LOVE

John 13:35 – *By this everyone will know that you are my disciples, if you love one another.*

It used to be hard to share your thoughts with the masses. Not anymore. Technology has simplified the process. With nothing more than a mouse click or a screen tap, anyone can get his or her message to the world.

With this in mind, consider for a moment the impact of your words. You have at your disposal the power to reach a multitude of people. When the rest of the world reads your post or listens to your voice, make sure they recognize you as a disciple of Jesus Christ.

Will they know you're a Christian by your political putdowns or unkind commentary? Probably not.

Will they know you're a Christian by your vulgar memes or insensitive talk? Of course not.

How will they know you are a Christian? By your love.

PRAYER: *God, today I ask for Your help. Help me reflect Your love with the words I choose to write and the words I choose to say.*

SP

MY GOD SUPPLEMENT

Matthew 6:33 – *But seek first his kingdom and his righteousness, and all these things will be given to you as well.*

Growing up in my family, we were not big vitamin/supplement people. My wife's family is a little different. After getting married, I began to see a trend of using supplements in our home.

So, I put my foot down as the man in the house, the one who wears the pants (I wear whatever pants my wife lays out for me). My confession is that we have become full-on self-diagnosing, homeopathic, supplement-taking, essential oil diffusing hippies.

Whenever we see our doctor, he looks at us funny, as though we are running some medicinal moonshining still in our basement.

Here's the spiritual reality—God is not a supplement.

We cannot just show up at church once a week to take a God-vitamin. If God created the universe, the trillions of stars and billions of galaxies, either He's at the center and you do everything in reference to Him, or you are just worshipping a god of your own making.

You don't just have God *at times.* He's not that little something extra to get you over the hump. There's no other way to relate to God other than complete devotion.

PRAYER: *Jesus, I want You at the center of my life—the One thing that I pursue. You are the reference point for everything else in my world.*

DF

SLOWTOWN'S DOSES OF JOY

Philippians 1:3-4 – *I thank my God every time I remember you. In all my prayers for all of you, I always pray with joy.*

It seems that Paul took breaks during his extremely busy schedule to sit back and pray for old friends. While he prayed, he also reminisced, which, in turn, put joy in his heart, his gut, his inner being.

There are many times I could have used a dose of joy in the midst of the daily hustle and bustle. Paul is a great example to us, showing us the joy that's available if we take the time to STOP, PRAY, and REMINISCE.

The band Twenty One Pilots has a song titled "Slowtown," and it was written about a group of senior high school guys who got together at a campfire several times in the spring and summer of their graduating year. The young men just wanted to sit around the fire, talk, laugh, and reminisce.

I urge you to Google the song and listen to the words: "Hey, hey. Wouldn't it be great, great? If we could just lay down and wake up in Slowtown…." There is much to be found when we take the time to slow down and pray.

PRAYER: *Lord, help me to take the time to stop, pray, and reminisce. Thank You for the doses of joy that I so desperately need.*

CJ

UNIQUELY QUALIFIED

Psalm 139:16 – *Your eyes saw my unformed body; all the days ordained for me were written in your book before one of them came to be.*

Standing in the concert hall, I can still hear the voice of one of my favorite artists. In the 1980s, Michael W. Smith helped raise the banner of Christian Contemporary Music by writing thought-provoking music and playing amazing live shows across the country.

On this particular night, during a pause in the music, Michael took a moment to say a few words and encourage the crowd. For the next several minutes, he recited a Psalm that I was unfamiliar with at that point in my life. I was captivated, and to this day, Psalm 139 is my favorite passage of Scripture.

The following day, I read and reread Psalm 139. At that moment, I understood God's role in my creation. I realized how familiar He was with the intricate details of my life. And, for the first time in my life, I understood my uniqueness.

God doesn't make mistakes. He created you with a specific purpose and plan in mind. Be encouraged. Your uniqueness qualifies you for a specific job. I love the old saying, "God gave you a fingerprint that no one else has, so you can leave an imprint no one else can."

PRAYER: *God, I thank You today for how You created me. Give me the courage to use my uniqueness and serve You today.*

SP

GREED FIGHTING

2 Corinthians 9:7b – *God loves a cheerful giver.*

When our kids were younger, I kind of felt badly for them when they opened their Christmas gifts—not because of how *much* they received but about how *slowly* they had to receive their gifts. But my wife is a greed fighter.

The scenario: it's Christmas morning with extended family, and the gifts from grandparents, aunts/uncles (really just aunts), and cousins have been distributed. Let's say there are twenty-five of us there, and half are younger than twenty years old. The little ones are licking their chops. It's Christmas chaos!

But not for my kids. My wife makes every one of our children stop after every opened gift, look the gift-givers in the eye (after getting their attention which can take some time), and thank them for that specific gift.

Why did my wife do that? She's more concerned about them developing the right kind of heart than just receiving the right kind gift.

Our Heavenly Father loves to give, but He doesn't want you and me to become entitled brats. The only way we can fight that is to give—cheerfully. We can become the generous people that God has designed us to be.

PRAYER: *Spirit, I want to be generous with my resources today. I want to know the joy of giving just as much as I know the joy getting. I am not entitled to anything You give, but I want to be grateful for everything You give.*

DF

STREAM ME

Psalm 1:3 – *He is like a tree planted by streams of water, which yields its fruit in season and whose leaf does not wither. Whatever he does prospers.*

I like the picture that God paints in today's verse. Even the driest times of summer won't affect a tree planted at the bank of a lively stream—it remains very healthy.

Once I watched an episode of the TV cartoon *SpongeBob SquarePants*, and the cartoon's underwater sponge (SpongeBob) was put on dry land. This caused the sponge to slowly shrivel up, making him on the verge of death, but he managed to get back to water just in time to save his life.

In today's verse, God uses the idea of being planted by a stream of water to symbolize someone who depends on God and His principles. Like SpongeBob, our inner joy, peace, and character start to dry out when we stop depending on God. We become harsh and ineffective. We are depressed, stressed, and lacking in our social abilities.

The Bible is clear that we need to continue to confess our wrongs, ask God for strength, look to Him for guidance, and seek to learn and apply His principles. When we do so, our roots tap into the "Great Stream of Life" that affects every area of our being, both inside and out.

PRAYER: *Father, I need You. Redirect me when I am being selfish and self-dependent.*

CJ

BLAMELESS AND BOLD

Daniel 6:10b – *"Three times a day he got down on his knees and prayed, giving thanks to his God, just as he had done before."*

My friend Jerry (not his real name) recently retired from the CIA. As I talked with him, I was intrigued by the vetting process he went through to secure his job in the intelligence community. Jerry told me, "They left no stone unturned in the examination of my conduct, and they expected me to be a person without compromise."

Interestingly enough, Daniel demonstrated similar character qualities in the book that shares his name. In Daniel 6, he is portrayed as a man of blameless testimony and bold conviction—a man who served God continually. When King Darius' men examined Daniel's life, they discovered that his conduct was exceptional, trustworthy, and incorruptible. Later, he exercised his convictions and purposefully ignored the king's edict that restricted his prayer life. Consequently, he was thrown into the lion's den and left for dead.

Daniel's uncompromising obedience and courage inspire me. He had no foreknowledge or expectation of the rescue that would ultimately come his way. He simply endeavored to honor God and understood that his faith required him to pursue obedience, regardless of the consequences. As a result, Daniel's blameless testimony put him in position to make a difference, and his bold conviction ended up impacting the heart of the king.

PRAYER: *God, I know I'm not going to be perfect, but help me pursue obedience today. Give me courage.*

SP

SHE'S SHOWING

Ephesians 1:13-14 – *When you believed, you were marked in him with a seal, the promised Holy Spirit, who is a deposit guaranteeing our inheritance until the redemption of those who are God's possession.*

In this verse, the word "sealed" is "sphragizo," which means to stamp. The word describes the process of a king's sealing a letter by putting candle wax where the folds came together. Then, the king would stamp the wax with his ring as proof of authenticity.

The word reminds us that when we place our faith in Christ, we are signed, sealed, and delivered (with all deference to the incomparable Stevie Wonder).

The second idea is that a king's seal was public—anyone could see it. It was obvious. God's Spirit should also become obvious in us. God's sealing means our faith should be showing.

We use the word "showing" when a lady is obviously pregnant (when a guy eats an entire pizza, why don't we say, "Oh, he's really showing."). What we mean is the amazing biology that a young, pregnant woman has seen on the ultrasound and heard in her child's heartbeat has become public.

This verse also says that the Holy Spirit is a "guarantee" or a down payment—a clear reminder that someday there's a payoff coming. When God completes His resurrection promise, you will be free of cancer, poverty, loneliness, and racism. The people of God will gather…every tribe, nation, and tongue surrounding the throne of God…signed, sealed, delivered.

PRAYER: *Holy Spirit, I want Your clear Presence guiding and guarding my life. I look forward to the day when we will be together for eternity.*

DF

WISE OLD BIRD

James 1:19 – *Everyone should be quick to listen, slow to speak and slow to become angry.*

God advises us to stop thinking of just ourselves and to stop reacting too quickly. Instead, we should learn to *listen to others* and ask good questions rather than simply doling out our answers.

Sometimes our "listening" is really us just waiting for our turn to talk. When this happens, we can't completely hear the feelings and intent behind what others are saying. If we desire to encourage someone, we must *listen to the individual.* True friendship and true conversation can't exist without it!

I once heard a poem that goes a little something like this…

> *A wise old owl sat on an oak;*
> *The more he saw the less he spoke;*
> *The less he spoke the more he heard;*
> *Why aren't we like that wise old bird?*

This poem offers some fantastic, practical advice. We need to dwell daily on the importance of listening.

PRAYER: *Heavenly Father, help me to develop my listening ear. I desire to bless others by learning to be quick to listen and slow to speak. In Jesus' name. Amen.*

CJ

LETTER TO MY FRIEND

1 John 1:9 – *If we confess our sins, he is faithful and just and will forgive us our sins and purify us from all unrighteousness.*

Dear Friend,

Please return home.

I remember when there was a fire in your soul. Your faith was real, you pursued holiness, and you hungered for truth. Goodness poured out from you. The light of Jesus shined through you.

Something happened. I don't know when or how. But your eyes are dim, and your soul seems lost. You move in dark circles, without purpose or plan. Your heart has changed.

In my mind's eye, I see flashes from another time and place. You made us laugh and inspired our minds. Your faith stirred our hearts. I miss the way you used to be.

If you are broke and desperate, you can return home. If you believe you are outside of God's grace and mercy, you can still return home. You are never outside the reach of the One who loves you most.

Come home. Claim the truth of I John 1:9. Rest and restoration await you. All is forgiven, and you are loved. We're waiting for you.

PRAYER: *God, help me let go of the sin that has captured my soul. Help me take the first step today and seek Your forgiveness. Help me return home and rekindle my faith.*

SP

GOD-FATHER

Luke 15:20 – *But while he was still a long way off, his father saw him and was filled with compassion for him; he ran to his son, threw his arms around him and kissed him.*

Depending on our upbringing, our views of God can range from a soft, grandpa-like Kris Kringle character to a bullish, Bobby Knight-type figure.

In the Gospels, Jesus most often addresses God as "Father," which speaks to how God wants to be known. Whether your parents were wonderful, terrible, or something in between, God is a greater Father.

Earthly parents often see themselves in their children's successes. Consider when a child learns to walk. Little Tommy pulls up to a standing position against a piece of furniture. And God has made little Tommy's head so big and heavy that eventually that weight gets out in front of him. So, he can stick a foot out or face plant.

What follows that step? Cheers, video cameras, phone calls, praise, clapping, smiling! Inevitably, children fall on the second step. However, I have never witnessed a dad say, "Tommy, you stink at walking; one foot in front of the other…even the dog can do it!"

Some of us think God is that kind of father—displeased, cruel, impatient—but today's verse says that God is looking for His children to return. So, no matter how far away from God you are, you can come home today.

PRAYER: *God, I failed yesterday. So, right now, I'm coming home to You. I want to start over in my relationship with You today. Thank You for the forgiveness that comes in Jesus Christ.*

DF

WEIGHT ROOM OR HATE ROOM?

Romans 5:3 – *We know that suffering produces perseverance.*

The word "perseverance" means the strength to keep going in the midst of adversity. The athlete understands this well, and that growing physically stronger takes training. One key to weight room strength training is realizing that the mind will tell the body it can't go on much sooner than the body will tell it.

Hall of Fame NFL coach Tom Landry once stated, "Leadership is getting someone to do what they don't want to do, to achieve what they want to achieve." God is the ultimate Leader and Coach. He can help us achieve when we continually rely on His energy. He will use the "weight room" training sessions of life—the difficulties, the hard times, the hurtful experiences—to make us stronger if we depend upon Him to teach us and pull us through.

Just as the athlete seeks enhanced performance through rigorous training, we can achieve better relationships, direction, and inner peace by embracing God's training. So, when difficulty comes, we can choose the weight room or the hate room.

PRAYER: *Father, remind me that my sufferings build my inner perseverance. Help me to talk to You when I am hurting, especially when I don't feel like it. Thank You that You will take care of me.*

CJ

DIRTY AND DILAPIDATED

Matthew 23:28 – *In the same way, on the outside you appear to people as righteous but on the inside you are full of hypocrisy and wickedness.*

The lobby of the roadside lodge appeared nice and tidy. A fresh coat of paint covered the rustic block walls, and ceramic tiles adorned the handcrafted check-in counter. I remember thinking, "Staying the night in Mozambique might work out after all."

As I left the waiting area and made my way toward my room, the conditions quickly turned dirty and dilapidated. At this point, it occurred to me that there may be a considerable step down in cleanliness from the lobby to my sleeping quarters. Opening the door to my room only confirmed my suspicion. It was going to be a long night.

By creating a beautiful lobby, the innkeeper had tried to make me believe his entire establishment was well-kept. However, by neglecting to keep the actual rooms clean, he had failed in his most important responsibility. Often, we are guilty of the same. We work hard to present a clean and righteous appearance, when, in reality, our inner self is dirty and wicked.

Don't spend your life trying to fake people out. Allow God to work on your soul. Get into His Word and onto your knees. Create a version of you that is beautiful on the inside, and the outside will take care of itself.

PRAYER: *God, help me today to tear down the facade and build a genuine relationship with You.*

SP

POTTY TRAINING

1 Corinthians 11:1 – *And you should imitate me, just as I imitate Christ* (NLT)

Christianity is not a divine set of rules to be followed. It's a relationship to be applied, yet so many believers settle for "information intake." We don't treat information that way in other areas of our lives. Take potty training, for example.

If you're a parent or teacher, this training information is CRUCIAL.

As parents, we stand outside the door of the bathroom, "C'mon. Push. You can do it. Woo-hoo!" Once, my wife was in the bathroom, and one of our small children sat outside the bathroom, "C'mon, Mom. You can do it! You'll get a gold star on your chart!"

Now, our child wasn't applying the training, yet she was encouraging others to follow. A lot of us know all the information, and we can even tell others the information. However, the reality is that we aren't applying it ourselves. Jesus reminds us of the importance of application when He said, "*Who hears My words and does them…*"

When you are going to remodel a room, you go to Home Depot, get paint swatches, buy the paint, and then…paint! You don't go to all the trouble of comparing the paint, thinking about the colors, and then buy the paint just to let it sit on a shelf.

In today's verse, Paul makes a bold ask, "Imitate me." What if everyone applied Christianity just like you?

PRAYER: *God, help me today to live in ways so that others could follow my example all the way into a relationship with You.*

DF

COOKIES AND VITAMINS

Ephesians 2:8-9 – *For it is by grace you are saved through faith—and this is not of yourselves, it is the gift of God—not by works, so that no one can boast.*

Someone brought cookies to work and I "tried" to have one. That "one" turned into nine, so I decided that would be my lunch.

I always take vitamins after meals, so I had to chuckle after my lunch of cookies and thought, "What the heck am I doing!?"

Many times, we think God is keeping track of the good and bad things we do. We foolishly believe that if we are being more good than bad, then He loves us a little more on that day. Then we wrongly believe there's a grand tally at the end of our lives: if we were good enough, then we can earn heaven.

The Bible is clear that we do not earn our salvation. It is a gift from God. In fact, God wants us to be less concerned about our ledger of good and bad and concern ourselves with delving into a deeper relationship with Him.

Our salvation is not a dietary contest of cookies versus vitamins.

PRAYER: *Father, teach me how to know You more. Thank You that only faith in Christ puts You on my side.*

CJ

LOOK IN THE MIRROR

Galatians 6:8 – *Whoever sows to please their flesh, from the flesh will reap destruction; whoever sows to please the Spirit, from the Spirit will reap eternal life.*

Mr. Johnson welcomed his class to the first day of middle school. Sitting on each student's desk was a handheld mirror. Understanding that the students would experience greater freedom as a middle schooler, he also wanted to make sure they understood their new-found responsibilities.

Asking his students to hold their mirror in front of their face, he said to the class, "Meet the person responsible for your choices, grades, success, words, and actions."

More and more, it seems as though we have all taken a masterclass on the art of avoiding personal responsibility. While it may be more prevalent today, don't forget that within the first three chapters of Genesis, Adam attempted to blame Eve for his sin in the Garden. Blame-shifting was around then, it's here now, and it will be here until Jesus returns.

Nevertheless, the Bible clearly teaches that we are accountable for our actions. Personal responsibility is tied to the principle of reaping and sowing—a hallmark teaching of our Christian faith. So, from the everyday choices of life to choosing whether or not to make Jesus the Lord of your life, you are responsible for your decisions. Choose wisely.

PRAYER: *God, help me today to embrace personal responsibility. Forgive me for shifting blame and help me to make wise decisions.*

SP

ROCKY BALBOA AND BILLY JOEL

Philippians 2:14-15 – *Do all things without grumbling or disputing, that you may be blameless and innocent, children of God without blemish in the midst of a crooked and twisted generation, among whom you shine as lights in the world.*

When I was introducing my wife to the five greatest movies of all time (Rocky I – Rocky V), we got to the scene in Rocky III, where Rocky has the charity match against Thunder Lips (a.k.a. Hulk Hogan). Both of them had these enormous, rippling muscles.

My wife looked at them and looked at me, back at them and back at me, and then said, "I haven't ever really liked big muscles." I looked for the compliment underneath the surface, but it was tough to find. Obviously, they had been training more than me.

I grew up in a musical family, so I tried to play a few instruments. I even tried singing. But I actually gave those things up because of my love for music. Music deserved better than what I had to offer. Billy Joel would remain unchallenged.

What I eventually learned is that muscles and music have something in common. Training wins over trying. It turns out that growing muscle and musical perfection both take practice. Effort and desire are only the beginning.

Great skill comes from great habits. What are your Christian habits? If we want to grow, we have to approach God in prayer, read His Word, and stay connected to His people.

PRAYER: *Jesus, help me to imitate Your habits, while You were here on the Earth. I want to pray like You prayed, know the Word like You did, and be part of a Kingdom movement.*

DF

DIVINE THINK TIMES

Proverbs 14:15 – *A simple man believes anything, but a prudent man gives thought to his steps.*

I grew up golfing and became a pretty good player. Often, what happens to good golfers is they are asked for tips from less competent players. While I didn't mind giving advice on the practice range, I don't desire to do so in the middle of a match.

One day I was playing with a guy who kept badgering and badgering me for advice, so on one hole, I told him to set up in his stance and then proceeded to give him tips that he followed to a tee (no pun intended).

I intentionally adjusted his grip and his swing to be completely wrong, so he hit his next drive sideways and into a cornfield. I can still picture the look on his face as the rest of our foursome hit the ground in laughter (I have since asked forgiveness).

The moral of the story? We all tend to blindly believe anyone who is successful. Instead, we need to have what I call "Divine think times." These are times when we think things through as we ask God to guide our thoughts.

PRAYER: *Lord, help me to be a thinker. Give me times alone with You to ponder all facets of living.*

CJ

KIND OF A BIG DEAL

Luke 10:42 – *Mary has chosen what is better, and it will not be taken away from her.*

The most famous person on the planet was coming to her house, and Martha wanted everything to be perfect. I'm not exactly sure what needed to be accomplished, but I do know that it must have been an enormous honor for Martha to have Jesus in her home.

Martha was service-oriented. No doubt, she wanted to provide Jesus with a clean home, good food, and comfortable surroundings. On the other hand, her sister Mary seemed less interested in rolling out the red carpet and more interested in spending time with Jesus. When Martha complained about Mary's lack of service, Jesus informed her that Mary had chosen that which was better.

Too often, we allow our Christian life to be defined by our acts of service while we fail to develop our relationship with Jesus. As Jesus' words reveal, we need to flip the script and create a lifestyle that builds our relationship with Jesus first before launching into active service for Him.

Know the One you serve. Spend time in prayer and in His Word. Build your relationship with the Savior of your soul and the Creator of the universe. Then, serve Him well—in your church, in your community, and on the mission field.

PRAYER: *God, create in my heart a rich desire to know You and serve You well.*

SP

WHATEVER WORKS

Exodus 20:8 – *Remember the Sabbath day by keeping it holy.*

My dad grew up as one of eleven children during the Great Depression. Because things were so tight financially, my grandfather started a dairy, and my dad grew up daily milking cows three times a day. My parents both lived and instilled in my siblings and me a strong work ethic. As humans, God has wired us to work. Work is good. But work makes a really bad god.

Americans are the most overworked employees in the Industrialized World. Eighty-six percent of American workers put in more than 40 hours/week. Americans work 137 hours more annually than Japanese workers, 260 hours more than British workers, and 500 hours more than French workers.

Regardless of what you think about those statistics—right or wrong—they reveal that our hearts need to be rearranged regarding work.

Instead of working to live, we are living to work. If you've lied, stolen, or committed adultery, you've felt some guilt about breaking those commandments. However, you've never gone to a counselor about breaking the fourth commandment even though it gets more words than any other commandment!

You have to love the God who says, "Thou shalt take a day off!" Why is it so important? The Sabbath reminds us that God is our source.

PRAYER: *Father, I'm relying on You as my Source of joy, wisdom, and providence today. I'm grateful for my work, but I don't have to have it—I must have You.*

DF

FEELING TOSSED AROUND

James 1:6 – *...the one who doubts is like a wave of the sea, blown and tossed by the wind.*

When we are children, our parents guide us in our decision-making: what we have for dinner, when is our bedtime, and so on. So, for a kid, a "major decision" is deciding which cartoon to watch on Saturday morning.

However with age, the burden of choices begins to fall on our shoulders. Often, we allow our culture to be the basis of our choices, or we simply go with our gut (I don't know about you, but I don't want tacos to influence my life's major decisions).

As we make these grownup decisions, there are times when we just do what we feel like doing, even though we know it's against the grain of our relationship with God. Other times, we don't even think before acting. It's important to remember our feelings and emotions are a terrible gauge for decision-making.

Professor Howard Hendricks once saw a bumper sticker that stated, "If it feels good, do it." Aware of the flaw in that philosophy, he so badly wanted to ram into that car. When the person asked, "What did you do that for?" He would simply say, "Because it felt good."

A prayed-over decision may not always feel good, but it pays off in the long run.

PRAYER: *Father, don't let my feelings and peer pressure toss me around. Help me not to doubt You.*

CJ

UNDYING RESPECT

John 15:13 – *Greater love has no one than this: to lay down one's life for one's friends.*

As a junior in high school, my son earned an invitation to the U.S. Army National Combine. The event was designed for underclassmen and brought together the nation's top football talent for two days of competition, showcase, and coaching.

Emerson worked hard to earn his invitation, so I was thrilled to accompany him to San Antonio for the combine. For two days, he had a blast competing in the Alamodome with top-tier athletes from across the country.

While the coaching and competition were extraordinary, Emerson was equally impacted by the words of challenge and encouragement from U.S. Army officers and enlisted personnel. The advice offered by these brave men and women made an impression on his heart.

Members of our armed forces make tremendous sacrifices to serve the land and people they love. Here at home and around the world, they consistently consider others more important than themselves. Daily, they exhibit strength and courage so that we can sleep in peace. In the protection of our freedoms and liberty, they are willing to lay down their lives. These brave men and women deserve our undying respect. To all past and present members of our military, I say thank you!

PRAYER: *God, help me today to go out of my way and express my sincere gratitude to those who serve our country.*

SP

YOU'RE A SAINT

1 Corinthians 6:11 – *And such were some of you. But you were washed, you were sanctified, you were justified in the name of the Lord Jesus Christ and by the Spirit of our God.*

The small words are some of the most important words in today's verse. Case in point, WERE. It reveals that certain things that *used* to define you *no longer* make up your identity.

Take St. Augustine of the early church. He was quite a womanizer before he became a believer, and he slept with lots of women. Yet, he traveled abroad in the summer of 386 AD and was converted to Christianity. Almost a year later, he returned to Hippo, his home city in Africa.

One night, he found himself alone on the streets of Hippo. A former lady friend noticed him walking down the street and said, "Augustine, it's so good to have you home," and invited him to spend the night. Augustine totally ignored her, so she ran ahead and stood squarely in front of him and said, "Augustine, don't you recognize me—it's me!"

Augustine looked at her and said, "But it's no longer me." His identity had changed. Remember, he was alone. Who would've known? But he no longer needed her acceptance, because God's acceptance was enough for him. You are just as much a saint as Augustine. It's possible to change and to have joy instead of just fleeting comfort.

PRAYER: *Father, thank You for accepting me in grace just like I was and making me new. Thank You that Your salvation has re-made me. Help me to remember that when I sin, that doesn't define me. I can start over again.*

DF

DIVINE MULLIGANS

James 4:10 – *Humble yourselves before the Lord, and He will lift you up.*

We all desire to indulge in pleasures that feel good. They are those times when we want to turn off our conscience and plunge ourselves into what just feels good.

One time I polished off two large chocolate chip cookies topped with whip cream. Then, I ate a Kit Kat and afterwards found an ice cream sandwich that died a fast death during my feeding frenzy. I was actually on an effective diet and had lost twenty-five pounds in two months. Yet, it was one of those difficult days, and I chose to turn off my brain and let my desires lead the way.

Needless to say, I feel sick to my stomach, guilty, and angry. But, I also could start over! I could *"humble myself before the Lord"* and confess that I need Him for willpower and strength. Humbling entails our admitting that we can't do it on our own, and thankfully, God knows we need "divine mulligans" (FYI to non-golfers: mulligan's are basically a "do-over" shot in golf).

PRAYER: *Father, thank You that You are the God of the do over, start over, and second chance. Please lift me up when I am down!*

CJ

THE I-MONSTER

Galatians 6:14 – *May I never boast except in the cross of our Lord Jesus Christ...*

A few years ago, I played in a golf tournament and was paired with a gentleman who loved to talk about himself and his accomplishments. In addition to having a doctorate in braggadocio, he had mastered the fine art of always having a better story. If I ran a 5K, then he ran a half-marathon. If I met Sugar Ray Leonard, then he met Mohammed Ali. Needless to say, it was a long afternoon.

From time to time, we all give in to the I-Monster, and our favorite words become me, myself, and I. As our insecurity kicks in, we feel compelled to tell the world about our accomplishments. It makes us feel good, but in doing so, we make ourselves the star of the show and reduce God to a background player.

If our goal is to impress people with who we are and what we have accomplished, then bragging about ourselves might be the way to go. But, if our goal is to leave people with an impression of who Christ is, then boasting of *His* love, grace, and mercy would be in order. Imagine what would happen if we stopped speaking so highly about ourselves and started bragging about Jesus and His work on the cross.

PRAYER: *God, help me to take my eyes off of myself. Remind me today that people need to see You. Give me opportunities to boast of Your son Jesus.*

SP

GOD OF THE CHAOS

John 16:33 – *I have told you these things, so that in me you may have peace. In this world you will have trouble. But take heart! I have overcome the world.*

My first international mission trip was to Honduras, which at that time was the poorest country in the Western Hemisphere. So, it was not only my first experience outside the US but also my first experience in a third world country. I was a young pastor; however, my father-in-law was on the trip, so I felt "comfortable-ish."

I was the first team member to speak on Monday morning to the Hondurans, as they came into a medical/dental clinic we had established. I was speaking about the Prodigal Son, and after a few minutes, a woman on the front row began unbuttoning her blouse.

My only thought was, "What is happening right now?" She proceeded to peel back the right side of her shirt, while seeming to listen intently. Suddenly, I was not only preaching on the prodigal son, but I felt like the prodigal son!

Then, the young woman began nursing her child, which was completely culturally appropriate. My father-in-law knew it would happen and intentionally didn't tell me. He came up to me afterwards and said, "Great job—really—breast sermon ever."

There are moments in our lives where we ask, "What is happening right now?" If God is the God of the calm moments, He is also God of the chaotic moments. Nothing surprises Him.

PRAYER: *Father, nothing happened yesterday that You were surprised by, and nothing will happen tomorrow that You don't know is coming. I trust in Your sovereign power over my limited abilities.*

DF

CHIGGERS

Proverbs 14:29 – *A patient man has great understanding, but a quick-tempered man displays folly.*

I have learned in my sixty plus years of life that people will bother other people. It's hard to control that feeling of being bothered. However, we **can** control our response.

Many times, while gritting my teeth, I find myself pleading with God to help me not let certain people bother me, to help me forgive, or to help me understand how to get beyond my anger. The more I attack these issues through prayer, the more I find myself able to endure and understand.

Speaking of irritating encounters, one day I came home with chiggers, which are little bugs that burrow under the skin and leave a trail of small bumps. In order to get rid of them, they have to be suffocated. I found that nail polish works great to coat the skin and deprive these chiggers of their much-needed oxygen.

My experience with chiggers helps me to understand that when we pray to God, He can toughen us to keep irritating people from penetrating our skin. When we ask God for the strength to forgive and understand our offenders, it will, like nail polish, suffocate the intruders.

PRAYER: *Lord, I need Your strength to forgive and be patient with those who get under my skin. Thank You that You promise to give me great understanding if I work on this.*

CJ

TAKE MY MASK

John 8:36 – *So if the Son sets you free, you will be free indeed.*

It's 2020, and wearing a mask is part of the standard operating procedure. To be perfectly candid, wearing a mask is uncomfortable for me—my face gets hot, my glasses fog up, and I feel claustrophobic. Needless to say, I am praying for an end to this madness.

Though literal masks cover millions of faces every day, people have been wearing figurative masks since the beginning of time. We have donned our masks to cover up what is really going on inside our hearts—our struggles, insecurities, and anxieties.

The world is broken and has created a structure that encourages mask-wearing behavior. There is stress to fit in socially and economically, there is pressure to hide vulnerabilities and weaknesses, and the list could go on indefinitely. When people realize they cannot meet the steep criteria of the world's expectations, they hide behind their mask.

Here is the good news. Jesus sees behind your mask and desires to help. He knows everything about you and still chooses to love you. In this promise, you can begin to let go of the world's opinion and pressure. In this promise, you can take off the mask and experience freedom.

PRAYER: *Jesus, help me release my struggles, insecurities, and anxieties today. Help me experience freedom.*

SP

July 11th

THE HUMAN RACE

Revelation 5:13 – *Then I heard every creature in heaven and on earth and under the earth and in the sea, and all that is in them, saying, "To him who sits on the throne and to the Lamb be praise and honor and glory and power, forever and ever!"*

The world is waiting for something to unite us. Until then, we will struggle for power in political parties and middle school cliques. Racism exists ethnically, financially, along gender lines, and even among siblings in families. Racism exists any time that we pre-judge someone based on our own assumptions.

The good news is that there's a finishline to this human race. The last book of the Bible tells the story of the future in John's Revelation. The scene reveals people of every race gathered in Heaven worshipping the same God.

Finally, there will be unity. What *should* be, ultimately *will* be. But how does the Gospel help us today? We can bring those Heavenly values into an earthly context. The Gospel teaches us that we are ALL imperfect—different races, different genders, different financial strata—ALL flawed.

That destroys superiority and any presuppositions. No one has the claim to be better than anyone else. None of us is what we ought to be. But if we are in Christ, someday we will all be everything God has designed us to be: a restored people gathered around God's throne forever.

PRAYER: *Father, help me today to see myself the way You see me. Help me bring Heaven to earth in the way that I love others, particularly those who are different from me.*

DF

GREEN BANANAS

Philippians 1:21 – *For to me, to live is Christ and to die is gain.*

I was sitting in a room chatting with two elderly men. Both had that scruffy, slightly slurred voice that seems to develop after turning eighty. Still, both gentlemen were so full of life and vigor. I could see the evidence of walking with God for years exuding through their cheerful countenance.

One of the wrinkly-faced men poked at the other by saying, "Ol' Earl here doesn't buy green bananas anymore." They both laughed hysterically because such bananas take several days to become edible, and Earl was acknowledging that his days on earth were numbered. However, this reality just didn't seem to bother them at all.

As believers in Christ, they had the mentality that they can't lose, even if they lose. While hard times come, God uses them as a growing tool in the lives of believers. And when death comes, they'll celebrate an amazing existence in paradise.

PRAYER: *Heavenly Father, thank You that as I walk with You, I can't lose, even if I lose. In Jesus' Name. Amen.*

CJ

COMING IN TOO HOT

Hebrews 4:16 – *Let us then approach God's throne of grace with confidence, so that we may receive mercy and find grace to help us in our time of need.*

Sitting in the aisle seat of the front row, I could see into the cockpit of our Boeing 737. Because our flight from Blantyre, Malawi to Johannesburg, South Africa was technically a charter, the flight crew decided to leave the cockpit door open.

Making our approach, the copilot was in control of the airplane. Everything appeared fine until our altitude reached about five hundred feet. At that point, the plane abruptly pulled up and aborted the landing. As passengers gasped, I heard the copilot say to the pilot, "We were too hot. I couldn't put it down safely."

As we circled and prepared for another attempt, I could hear the one-sided conversation between the flight crew and air traffic control. Though it seemed as if an error had been made, I was impressed by the pilot and copilot's calm demeanor. The flight crew and air traffic controllers appeared unfazed and content to recalibrate and try again. They didn't care about the past mistake; they just wanted to land the plane safely.

As Christians, we can confidently approach the Lord when we fail. His grace awaits us. He simply desires that we own up to our sin, recalibrate, and try again.

PRAYER: *God, help me today to live in obedience and remind me to lean on You when I fail.*

SP

YOUR BARNEY UNDERWEAR

Ephesians 3:16 – *that according to the riches of his glory he may grant you to be strengthened with power through his Spirit in your inner being.*

In her *Best Devotions* book, Barbara Johnson wrote about a little girl with influenza who went to the doctor's office. The pediatrician (like a lot of pediatricians) liked to keep the mood light and fun with children. So, the doctor was doing just that with this particular young lady who was not happy to be at the doctor's office.

He checked out her ears and said, "I wonder if I'll find Big Bird in there." The little girl replied, "No." He checked out her nose. "I wonder if Cookie Monster is in there." She again said, "No." He pulled out his stethoscope to check her heart. "I wonder if Barney is in your heart." Her reply was priceless: "No, Jesus is in my heart. Barney is on my underwear."

Some of us tolerate being part of a spiritual community like we tolerate going to the doctor. We will answer the questions when necessary, sing on cue, and smile at others as we leave.

But we also have a question, one we don't like to admit, "Where is God?" He's hard to find sometimes. The Bible suggests that God is "in your innermost being." Most times, that's where we need to look, and it's the last place we check.

PRAYER: *God, help me today to listen for Your voice to speak. Grant me the grace to not only look for You in the big, miraculous events, but to hear Your still, small voice, as well.*

DF

July 15th

MY '72 OLDSMOBILE CUTLASS SUPREME

James 1:22 – *Do not merely listen to the Word, and so deceive your-selves. Do what it says.*

When I was a young high schooler armed with a driver's license and an orange '72 Oldsmobile, I met a really cute young lady who asked me to come over to her house to visit. This occurred before the days of GPS, so she had to explain to me the directions to her home.

Believe me, I didn't merely listen to her words! I pulled out a pen and paper and confirmed that I understood every single turn, street name, and landmark along the way. I didn't just hope I would maybe find her house; I HAD to find it!

This is how we need to approach God's Word. When we read the Bible, hear a sermon, or receive today's daily verse, our encounters with the things of God should make us think and pray. We should pray questions such as, "How can I pull this off?", "How does this apply to my daily routine?", and "What are the situations that I must go through to make this work?"

PRAYER: *Father, tap me on the shoulder and remind me of the things I have learned about You as I go through my day. Give me the strength and determination to be a doer of Your Word. Thank You for the blessings that will follow.*

CJ

PROFOUNDLY SCRIBBLED WORDS

Proverbs 14:12 – *There is a way that appears to be right, but in the end leads to death.*

Over the years, I have seen my share of hastily written notes on the covers of camp devotionals and conference journals. Most often, the scribbled words were the work of a student who had jotted down a quote or sentiment that was particularly helpful during the week.

Below is one of my all-time favorites:

<u>Choose Wisely</u>

The World Says: Be true to yourself.
Jesus Says: Be true to me.

The World Says: Treat yourself.
Jesus Says: Deny yourself.

The World Says: Keep everything you earn.
Jesus Says: Give to those in need.

The World Says: Believe in yourself.
Jesus Says: Believe in me.

The World Says: Follow your heart.
Jesus Says: Follow me.

The words of Jesus rarely coincide with popular opinion. The world's formula for purpose, happiness, and achievement is self-centered and temporary, while Jesus' formula is soul-centered and eternal. To be clear, one is wrong and leads to death, while the other is right and leads to life. Choose wisely.

PRAYER: *Father, help me today to let go of the world's prescription for joy, contentment, and success. Help me pursue the way of Your Son, Jesus.*

SP

DUMB PEOPLE

1 Peter 2:9 – *But you are a chosen people, a royal priesthood, a holy nation, God's special possession, that you may declare the praises of him who called you out of darkness into his wonderful light.*

When I was younger, I would begin asking inquiries with the phrase, "This could be a dumb question, but…." One teacher consistently responded, "There are no dumb questions—just dumb people." However, *different* doesn't equal *dumb*.

I have friends who lead a ministry in Florida, and their vision is to empower people. A college student from UCF revealed to them that she had been date-raped two years earlier. After receiving counseling, she had taken some big steps forward.

She also shared that she received this spark of joy from "hula hoop dancing." So, she asked her leaders (my friends) if she could go all over the world sharing both the Gospel and joy by teaching hula hoop dancing.

So, my friend says to me, "What would you say? I thought it was a dumb idea. but I told her, 'If you sense God calling you, and your closest friends believe in it, go for it.' That was seven years ago."

Just Google hoolaforhappiness.org—it's amazing. This young lady has given away over 50,000 hula hoops with offices in seven different countries. She was invited to do a TED talk, and it's all because someone said, "If it's from God and lines up with His Word and other believers, go for it."

What is God calling you to do?

PRAYER: *God, I'm listening for Your calling today. You haven't designed me to merely receive but to give back to the world. My "yes" is on the table!*

DF

TURTLE ON A FENCEPOST

Ephesians 3:20 – *Now to Him who is able to do immeasurably more than all we ask or imagine, according to His power that is at work within us.*

There are situations in life that seem overwhelming. There are also times when we encounter circumstances that seem to have us trapped. We can come face-to-face with our biggest fears and just want to run away.

During those wretched times, we can hear our inside voice tell us things such as, "There is no way out," "It will never work," "I can't get over this," "There is no escape," "I will never get any relief," "I am doomed, stuck, destined to fail," "I'll never catch a break."

In those times of gloom, we need to think "BUT GOD." While it seems there is possibly no way out of our troublesome situation, "BUT GOD." While we can't do it on our own, "BUT GOD."

It's just like the old country preacher who told me to think about the turtle he saw on a fencepost. He realized that the only way that ol' turtle got up there was by an outside force—he couldn't get there on his own.

PRAYER: *Lord, thank You that You can do more than I can even think, ask, or imagine. I can't, but You can. Make me a "turtle on the fencepost."*

CJ

A HUMBLE HIKE

Proverbs 11:2 – *When pride comes, then comes disgrace, but with humility comes wisdom.*

Hiking Arizona's Camelback Mountain is a daunting task for a novice hiker. The trail is 1.23 miles long and ascends 1,280 feet. To get to the top, you have to navigate treacherous mountain terrain and climb through a steep canyon of enormous boulders.

Having made the trek before, I warned my sister's family of the challenge they faced in making the climb for the first time. Without throwing anyone under the bus, one member of her family proudly referenced their personal hiking resume and indicated that Camelback would not pose a problem. The following day, I watched this particular member of my sister's family fail to make it to the top.

While this humorous, benign anecdote is something we can all relate to, pride can be a serious struggle for some. Pride causes us to think more highly of ourselves than we should. It causes us to boast of our success. And most egregious, pride diverts glory from God and points it toward us.

If God gives you a special gift or skill set, glorify Him. If you find victory, praise His name. Honor God, choose humility, and become wise.

PRAYER: *God, help me today to choose humility. Help me abandon my pride and credit You for every good thing.*

SP

FROM THE BENCH

Isaiah 33:22 – *For the Lord is our judge, the Lord is our lawgiver, the Lord is our king; it is he who will save us.*

Fiorello La Guardia was the mayor of New York during the Great Depression. Sometimes (just for the fun) he would preside over the police court in New York. One bitterly cold day, a trembling older man was brought before him. He had been charged with stealing a loaf of bread, and the man explained that his family was starving because of the Depression.

La Guardia was moved but said, "I have to punish you. The law makes no exception. I sentence you to a fine of $10." Of course, the man did not have $10, so La Guardia reached into his pocket and said, "Now, here's $10 to pay your fine."

Then La Guardia said, "And now I charge everybody in this courtroom fifty cents for living in a town where a man has to steal bread to feed his family. Mr. Bailiff, collect the fines and give them to the defendant." A hat was passed and the trembling old man who was waiting to be taken to jail was given $47.50!

That's you and me. Not only does God save us through His grace because there's nothing we can do to earn it, but He also gives us all of these extra blessings on top of salvation!

PRAYER: *God, today I'm grateful for how You paid my fine. You paid for the sins that I committed. Not only have You given me salvation, but You also have given me life.*

DF

UNFAIR ROCKS TO HIGHER GROUND

Jeremiah 17:11 – *Like a partridge that hatches eggs it did not lay is the man who gains riches by unjust means. When his life is half gone, they will desert him, and in the end he will prove to be a fool.*

From being overlooked for a job for which I was probably overqualified to being "politically" cut from a middle school baseball team, I have experienced several disappointing and unfair situations in life.

Now that I'm older, I realize this is very common. The key question isn't, "How can I avoid this happening to me?" The truth is that life happens. So, the question then becomes, "How do I handle this when it happens to me?"

Anger, frustration, disappointment, feeling like a failure. These are all natural responses to the challenges of life. On the other hand, recovering strong is supernatural.

Unfair situations are like a rock. If we stay angry and discouraged, slander, gossip, hate, or become depressed, the rock will crush us. However, if we give our natural responses and unfair situations over to God, as we pour out our hearts to Him in prayer, then the rock becomes a stepping stone to a higher ground.

PRAYER: *Father, help me to get past my natural responses when (not if) I experience unfair situations. Raise me to higher ground so that I can comfort others..*

CJ

IT'S DARK IN HERE

Matthew 5:16 – *In the same way, let your light shine before others, that they may see your good deeds and glorify your Father in heaven.*

Several years ago, I was on a group tour of Mammoth Cave in Kentucky. Partway through the tour, our guide asked everyone to gather together in a large space within the cave system. He then proceeded to turn off all the lights, and for several minutes, we were face to face with absolute darkness. After a short while, he turned on his lantern. The light pierced the darkness, and once again, we could see.

For the rest of the day, all I could think about was the fact that we live in a dark world in desperate need of light.

As the church, we have an opportunity in front of us. Theologically, the idea of shining our light in a darkened world is not a complicated truth; it just requires more than lip service. To be clear, shining our light calls for followers of Jesus to demonstrate love, joy, peace, patience, and kindness in every circumstance—to extend grace, mercy, and help to everyone around us.

If we choose to allow our attitude and actions to reflect God's goodness, we will shine in the darkness. We will stand out, people will notice, and they will be drawn to Him.

PRAYER: *God, help me today to speak and interact with people in a way that draws them to You. Help me reflect Your goodness. Help me to shine.*

SP

TAKING THE "ME" OUT OF MARRIAGE

Ephesians 5:21 – *Submit to one another out of reverence for Christ.*

The Bible gives instruction about marriage, but it's remarkably unsentimental. You won't find The Hallmark Channel, *The Notebook*, and Jerry McGuire's, "You had me from 'hello,'" in the Scriptures. Think about biblical marriages: Abraham called Sarah his sister (instead of his wife) to save his life, not once but twice.

How about Moses and his wife, Zipporah? When Moses refused to circumcise his son (in accordance with God's Law), Zipporah stepped in—she not only circumcised their son, she threw the foreskin on Moses' feet, and called Moses "a bloody bridegroom." Someone should put that in a Valentine's Day card!

The myth we have is that marriage is about me—*my* fulfillment. Forget the "we" in marriage, because it's more about "me."

I think the unconscious question most of us ask about marriage is, "How can I get what I want?"

Early in our marriage when I would arrive home, my wife and I would generally ask the question, "How was your day?" Underneath whatever words we used was a kind of subtext that went, "My day was harder than your day, so you really ought to take care of me."

Instead of a "Me-centered" marriage, let's serve our spouses the way that God has served us.

PRAYER: *Father, thank You so much for my spouse. Help me to serve my spouse today without reservations or conditions.*

DF

UNDELIVERED CARDS

Romans 8:15 – *You received the Spirit of sonship. And by Him we cry, Abba, Father.*

In our school's teacher meeting, one of the staff asked if she could mention something that had just happened. She began by saying she was thinking about her four-year-old granddaughter who had passed away from cancer.

She then told us that her son (the father of the little girl) was going through some items in a closet and a card fluttered down from a shelf. He discovered it was an undelivered birthday card that his little daughter had made by hand for Grandma.

On the card was a big picture of a spider. The granddaughter revealed that she loved her grandma so much that she wished she were a spider. That way, when she hugs Grandma, she has eight arms to do it with—two arms just aren't enough!

It's almost as if this grandmother was delivered a card from God through the little girl.

I firmly believe that God will meet us in those heartbreaking times if we cry out to Him to show us His love and understanding. Watch for those "undelivered cards" because having God as our "Abba Father" means we have an intimate and loving daddy.

PRAYER: *Lord, when I'm down, remind me to seek You even more. Give me those undelivered cards that show Your care for me.*

CJ

GRANDPA'S WISE WORDS

Matthew 6:20 – *But store up for yourselves treasures in heaven, where moths and vermin do not destroy, and where thieves do not break in and steal.*

Doug's grandfather was a faithful man of God who lived an uncomplicated life. He had a knack for making everything simple—including his faith.

Three years ago, Doug's grandfather passed away unexpectedly. A day or two before the memorial service, Doug found himself leafing through his grandfather's Bible. Taped to the inside cover, he found the following handwritten list:

Store Up Treasure In Heaven

Give Your Heart to Jesus
Read the Bible and Talk to God
Serve People and Serve the Church
Obey the Instructions
Tell People About Jesus
Give and Forgive
Laugh and Smile

Growing in your walk with God doesn't have to be complicated. Endeavor to store up treasure in Heaven, and the formula for simple faith creates itself.

PRAYER: *God, help me today to strengthen my walk with You. Help me create a simple pattern of faith that pleases You.*

SP

EAT YOUR VEGETABLES

Colossians 4:2 – *Devote yourselves to prayer.*

Unfortunately, our attitudes about praying and dieting are similar. We've got an, "Eat your vegetables" attitude towards prayer: "You should pray. It's good for you." However, prayer is not like broccoli.

Our perception is that the most spiritual among us think you're a failure if you aren't praying at 5:00am. However, God is awake at 8:00am too (and 8:00pm for that matter). Maybe you're like me and you love vegetables—with lots of butter and cheese on them. My mom used to say, "You won't even try them. You can't even taste them." My reply was, "Then leave them out if I won't taste them." Savoring your steak is a joy. Nobody savors beets.

So, why do we treat prayer the same way we treat vegetables? Prayer was the joy of Jesus. What if prayer is life's main course and the rest of life is just vegetables?

We all know it wouldn't be acceptable if I said to my wife, "I want you to know that I am making a commitment to talk to you for five minutes every day. I am going to tell you what I need…my requests." (Some guys are saying, "What's wrong with that? I don't get it.") Remember, prayer is the entrée, not the neglected side dish. And while prayer may not change my circumstances, prayer does change me.

PRAYER: *God, thank You that You have made a way for me to communicate, to talk with You. Help me to see the necessity of prayer for me and to lean into You more and more.*

DF

WASH YOUR HANDS

Psalm 18:20 – *The Lord has dealt with me according to my righteousness; according to the cleanness of my hands He has rewarded me.*

As a young boy, I remember smelling the aroma of my mother's home cooking drifting throughout our house. I would be watching Superman or Bugs Bunny and anticipating that magical call of "Come and get it!"

Salivating and with a growling stomach, I'd plop down in my kitchen chair. Then the dreaded question was always asked: "Did you wash your hands?"

I could have lied and probably did at times, and my whine during my reply of "Why?" probably made my mother want to slug me. At the time, her question about the cleanliness of my hands just didn't make sense to me. I wasn't handling kryptonite (though I did come to the table wearing my superhero towel-cape).

Studies show how important it is to wash our hands because they pick up so many germs that can bring illness. Spiritually speaking, if we "wash our hands" through admitting our wrongs to God, He can help us grab ahold of His blessings. In addition, if we "keep our hands clean" by living a life of obedience, He also promises to "reward" us.

PRAYER: *Father, give me the strength to make right choices and the wisdom to admit my wrongs to You. Thank You for the rewards that will follow.*

CJ

LANE JUMPING 101

Proverbs 4:23 – *Above all else, guard your heart, for everything you do flows from it.*

You know The Lane Jumper—the driver who aggressively seeks the fastest route in a traffic jam by changing lanes ten times within a half-mile stretch of brake lights and gridlock.

My experience tells me that most people take pride in impeding The Lane Jumper's progress. And by tailgating the car in front of them, they can close the gap—making it impossible for him to weave in and out of traffic.

Everyone knows The Lane Jumper needs one thing to be successful: space. If you give him an inch, he will take a mile.

Satan operates in the same manner. He tries desperately to maneuver his way into your lane. He is relentless in his pursuit to take up space in your life. And the moment you let your guard down, he stands ready to capture your heart and mind.

A word of advice: Don't let the devil in. Set up safeguards and boundaries related to whom you associate with, where you go, what you see, and what you hear. In other words, avoid making choices that give the devil a foothold in your life. Guard your heart.

PRAYER: *Father, help me keep my guard up today. Help me surround myself with people who will keep me accountable for the boundaries I set in place.*

SP

July 29th

A BITTER PILL

Ephesians 4:26-27 – *"In your anger do not sin." Do not let the sun go down while you are still angry, and do not give the devil a foothold.*

Anger doesn't ALWAYS equal sin. Did Jesus ever sin? No. Did Jesus ever get angry? Yes.

However, most of the time, we get angry, because we do not get our way. Paul gives us an admonition here to process our anger when he says, "Don't let the sun go down on your anger." As humans, we are weak, so we need to reflect on the source of our anger daily to navigate whether or not we are angry for the right or wrong reasons.

Someone once suggested that my wife and I should never go to bed in argument. Angie and I have sought to practice this principle. Once we stayed awake for 2.5 weeks, but we did it!

Verse twenty-seven says, "Don't give the Devil a foothold." Climbers know that footholds are essential. Cracks and crevices in the rock become footholds that propel climbers up a mountain. What does this mean for us? Bitterness is a foothold to propel the enemy's activity in your life.

Bitterness is unprocessed anger that hangs around your soul and signs a long-term lease. Bitterness hurts you more than the person who wounded you. We forgive because we have been forgiven (Jesus forgave even His crucifiers) and because offering forgiveness allows us to heal.

PRAYER: *Father, thank You for forgiving me. Thank You for modeling how to forgive others. Thank You that I can trust You to hold others accountable for their actions.*

DF

WHAT IN THE WORLD IS A HAGRITE?

1 Chronicles 5:20 – *and God delivered the Hagrites into their hands, because they cried out to Him during the battle. He answered their prayers, because they trusted in Him.*

I received a plea for prayer from the parents of a Marine who was home on leave but missing in the wilderness of Montana. The authorities decided to go on one last search for the man, and the prayer request was for the search team to have wisdom and also for a miracle. While the missing Marine was not found, there was a miracle.

A father and son were hiking on the trail and passed the searchers. Later that same day, the father and son came back toward the searchers in need of help themselves. The son is a severe diabetic with an insulin pump that had stopped working, so the search team flew the boy out on their helicopter to the hospital in Helena.

He would have died had the search team not been there with helicopter access! God used that team to save the life of another son. While I'm not exactly sure about all of the mechanics and behind the scenes of how prayer works, I do know that God works through prayers.

PRAYER: *Lord, convince me that You hear my prayers. Thank You that You care and that You actually want to hear from me.*

CJ

START STRONG AND FINISH STRONGER

2 Chronicles 15:7 – *But as for you, be strong and do not give up, for your work will be rewarded.*

On November 8, 2014, a University of Utah football player did the unthinkable. In a nationally televised game against a highly ranked opponent, a Utah receiver celebrated his 79-yard touchdown too early and let go of the football one yard short of the endzone. To make matters worse, while he continued to celebrate what he thought was a huge, scoring play for his team, his opponent picked up the ball and returned it the other way for a 99-yard touchdown. This blunder accurately demonstrates what it means to start strong and finish poorly. Unfortunately for Utah, the play changed the momentum, and they ended up losing the game.

Asa, king of Judah, started strong. He followed God for the first thirty-five years of his reign. Pursuing righteousness, he sought after spiritual revival for his people. Yet in the thirty-sixth year of his reign, Asa entered into an unholy pact, and from that point forward, his relationship with God changed for the worse. Ultimately, Asa died without ever fully returning to a vibrant walk with God.

Suffice it to say, a formidable start isn't enough. You have to finish well. Pursue faithfulness and chase after righteousness each day. Set your mind to start strong and finish stronger.

PRAYER: *God, help me today to finish strong. Give me strength when my faithfulness begins to fade. Help me walk closely with You each and every day.*

SP

I KNOW

James 4:10 – *Humble yourselves before the Lord, and He will lift you up.*

There's nothing worse than arguing with a Know-It-All. No matter what you say, the response is something like, "I know, but…." I wonder if we aren't that way with God sometimes?

We say, "I know how to run my family; I know how to run my marriage; I'm smart enough to run my business." But what if you're wrong?

What if you are making the same mistake that I did, when I bought my son the Dino Island playset for Christmas? It came in one million pieces, even though the box read, "*Some* assembly required."

So, I set the instructions aside. I mean, some people need them, but I'm from southern Ohio. And I have a degree from The Ohio State University, the Ivy League of the Midwest.

The reality is that if I misconfigured Dino Island (and I did—Christmas Eve was late night!), I could box it up and take it back to Wal-Mart. But you can't box up your kids and take them back to Target. You only get one shot to invest in their lives spiritually.

What if you aren't smart enough? What if you don't know? Sometimes, you don't get a mulligan.

So, humble yourself…ask God for wisdom…and apply what He says.

PRAYER: *God, instead of giving a bunch of requests today, I want to start my day by admitting that I don't know. I need Your wisdom and Your guidance, and I'm here to listen.*

DF

WHEN THE GOING GETS TOUGH...

Galatians 6:9 – *Let us not become weary in doing good, for at the proper time we will reap a harvest if we do not give up.*

As we see from today's verse, "Doing good" doesn't necessarily give us immediate results. "At the proper time" could be hours or even decades from now. So, I guess our motivation shouldn't be to get a pat on the back for our every good deed. We probably shouldn't even expect our acts of kindness to be noticed.

However, doing good impacts our very core. It shows God that we believe He is real and worth following, even when we get nothing tangible in return. It also gives Him an open door to our insides, character, and total being where God can have free reign to develop us from the inside out. It allows Him to do surgery on those flaws that hamper us.

My dad always quoted to me, "When the going gets tough, the tough get going." Those words encouraged me that I could separate myself from the pack by not giving up or giving into mediocrity, especially when many around me were caving.

PRAYER: *Lord, I need Your strength to "do good" especially when those around me don't care. Thank You that my faith grows every time I make the right choices. Also, thank You for always letting me start over.*

CJ

TWENTY-EIGHT PAINTERS

Colossians 3:17 – *And whatever you do, whether in word or deed, do it all in the name of the Lord Jesus…*

The Golden Gate Bridge is massive. At 8,981 feet long and 90 feet wide, the engineering marvel is a sight to behold. Each tower rises to 746 feet while the roadway boasts an above water clearance of 220 feet. Everyday, approximately 112,000 vehicles drive across the massive suspension bridge in San Francisco.

Painting the Golden Gate Bridge is a thankless job that most people don't even think about while driving or walking across the monstrosity. However, the rust and corrosion from the Pacific waters combined with the salt-laden fog native to the Bay Area make painting the bridge a necessary and never-ending task.

As many as twenty-eight painters work together to protect the bridge from the atmosphere's corrosive and destructive elements. Literally, the bridge's structural integrity depends upon each painter's faithfully executing his anonymous, yet critical, task.

Speaking of which, God is interested in how faithfully we perform our tasks. Whether our job is recognized by the world or goes relatively unnoticed, the Lord is attentive to our work. Quite simply, God desires that our efforts bring honor to Him. So, whatever you set out to do today, do it in a way that glorifies the Lord Jesus.

PRAYER: *Lord, help me today to honor You as I accomplish each task. Help me put forth my best effort, whether the world notices it or not.*

SP

SURPRISING THINGS JESUS NEVER SAID

Luke 5:27b – *Follow Me.*

The words that Jesus of Nazareth spoke are the most well-documented in history. More manuscripts, texts, and educational material are written from His words than from any other person. Around the world, His statements have become commonplace. What are less documented are the things He NEVER said.

"The Lord helps those who help themselves." Nope.

"God won't give you any more than you can handle." Uh-uh.

"God works in mysterious ways." Not in the Gospels.

I think I can argue that not only is Jesus the most quoted historical figure, but He's simultaneously the most misquoted.

What's a little closer to home are some of the churchy things WE (if you are a Christian) say that Jesus never said. "With every head bowed and every eye closed." "You need to go to church." Now, let me be clear. I'm all for moments of meditative prayer, and I believe the Bible calls us to gather as the church. But as much as anything else, Jesus said, "Follow Me."

He says it more than twenty times in the Gospels to different kinds of people. I think He's still saying it today. Don't overcomplicate loving God. Just follow Him.

PRAYER: *God, You are the Leader and I am the follower. Forgive me for the times that I try to take Your place. Help me to simply follow You.*

DF

WHAT'S IN YOUR BACKPACK?

Philippians 2:13 – *For it is God who works in you to will and to act according to His good purpose.*

Being a principal of a Christian school gave me plenty of unique opportunities to help young people think through how to make their faith practical.

There was a boy who was constantly getting in trouble, and one time he was sent to my office for some serious correction. I could tell there was more needed to be done than a couple after school detentions. So, I showed him how he could receive Christ into his heart, and then the student sincerely prayed with me.

I could tell he wanted more, so I explained that now that he has accepted Christ into his life, he has an amazing source of strength to tap into. I told the young man that it's like having a backpack that he can reach into for strength, forgiveness, or direction. When he feels like being ornery, unzip that backpack of God's power to change him.

Henry David Thoreau once stated, "Things do not change. We change." How blessed are we that God can change us!

PRAYER: *Father, make me aware of the "backpack" of strength, forgiveness, and direction that You have given me. Change me where needed.*

CJ

PRISON MIKE

Proverbs 15:1 – *A gentle answer turns away wrath, but a harsh word stirs up anger.*

In his teens and early twenties, Mike was known as a brawler. If there was a fight, he was probably involved. By the time he was thirty, Mike had seen his share of bar fights and street clashes. Ultimately, his combative demeanor led to an altercation that landed him in prison.

While in prison, Mike came to faith in Jesus Christ and tried desperately to get his life in order. During routine visits with the prison chaplain, he traced most of his troubles back to his inability to control his tongue. If someone said something to anger Mike, he always responded in anger, and his responses in those situations was like throwing gasoline on a fire.

We live in a broken world, and people are going to use inflammatory words. Some will purposely try to evoke an angry response from you. Arguing with people who are bent on being angry or engaging them in heated discourse will only lead to greater hostility. Life will go better for you if you choose to walk away or respond with a levelheaded and calm reply.

PRAYER: *Father, help me today to exercise self-control and respond to others in kindness.*

SP

WORKING FOR PEANUTS

2 Chronicles 16:9 – *The eyes of the Lord range throughout the earth to strengthen those whose hearts are fully committed to him…*

George Washington Carver may be the greatest scientist in American history, yet he taught at Tuskegee College for $1,500/yr. Thomas Edison once offered Carver $100,000/yr. to move to the northeast to be on Edison's team (incidentally, Carver said he often didn't even cash his checks from Tuskegee, as he had "little use for money").

Carver's greatest accomplishment came in the middle of a crisis. The boll weevil decimated the southern cotton crops in 1914. Carver encouraged southern farmers to plant peanuts. And farmers planted so many, too many, peanuts. They flooded the peanut market and crushed demand. Carver was desperate.

He prayed, "God, how did you make the universe?" He sensed God say, "Your question is too big." Carver responded, "How did you make a man?" He sensed God say, "Still too big for your small mind." Carver's third prayer, "Lord, what could You do with a peanut?" He sensed God say, "There's a prayer I can answer."

Carver found 300 uses for the peanut, most of which we still use today—shaving cream, shampoo, wood stains, plastics, peanut oils, paints, etc. George Washington Carver saved the south by asking God, "What COULD You do?" What if you asked a similar question: "God, what could You do with my life completely in Your hands?" God's eyes are still *searching, ranging* throughout the earth for someone just like you.

PRAYER: *God, what could You do with my life completely surrendered to You today? Right now, I give up my rights to my day and my future. Please fill me and use me as You see best.*

DF

VERBALLY STOP IN YOUR TRACKS

Matthew 7:4 – *How can you say to your brother, "Let me take the speck out of your eye," when all the time there is a plank in your own eye?*

Many times we find comfort in criticizing or correcting others.

The challenge is to communicate with God when this feeling or temptation comes to us. At that moment, we need to verbally stop in our tracks and breathe a quick prayer, asking Him to remind us of how much we've been forgiven. Taking this challenge will bolster our personal character and enable us to be a positive influence on those around us.

Back as an inexperienced coach, I could relate to the famous comedian, Groucho Marx, when he stated "I refuse to join any club that would have me as a member."

You see, I was once hitting ground balls to a girls' softball team. I corrected their every mistake, and they weren't enjoying it at all. I left and came back to find a less knowledgeable guy hitting the ground balls. He said nothing to them, and they got better! I could tell they were glad I had left—my criticism didn't help them but had actually deterred them.

PRAYER: *Father, help me to see the "planks" in my life. Thank You that You love me anyway. Give me victory over criticizing and correcting.*

CJ

HUGO AND KATE

Isaiah 41:10 – *So do not fear, for I am with you; do not be dismayed, for I am your God. I will strengthen you and help you; I will uphold you with my righteous right hand.*

Hugo cried out to God as he knelt next to his daughter's hospital bed. For six days, he had prayed that God would heal his little girl. On day seven, she began to improve. By day twelve, she had checked out of the hospital and was headed home.

At the age of thirty-one, Kate unexpectedly lost her husband. The love of her life and the father of her children wasn't coming home. The sudden loss shook her to the core. Though she leaned on her faith, Kate was devastated, and her heart was broken.

Followers of Christ are not immune to chaos, trouble, and hardship. Like the rest of the world, we can expect to have our lives upended from time to time. But unlike the rest of the world, we have Jesus.

Sometimes Jesus calms the storms, and at other times He allows the storm rage on—standing with us through the wind and the rain. In both cases, He is present and desires for us to lean on Him and grow in our faith. We may not understand the steps He has ordained for us, but we can always trust His presence, power, and love.

PRAYER: *Lord, remind me today that You are with me in the storm. Hear me when I call upon You and help me find peace in Your presence.*

SP

FRENCH FRIES AND FIRE

Proverbs 4:25 – *Let your eyes look straight ahead; fix your gaze directly before you.*

One year after Easter services, our kids wanted hamburgers and homemade French fries. The homemade fries were my specialty. While I love making homemade fries, I also love watching the Masters, which was on TV that Easter Sunday.

Maybe I didn't pay attention to how much oil I put into the skillet. Maybe the hot oil overflowed that skillet, because Phil Mickelson had just made birdie on #12 in the middle of the Amen Corner. And maybe we ended up with a raging fire on our stove.

Luckily, the damage level was low, but the fear level was high. In fact, the kids didn't want to come back into the house that afternoon! Not gonna lie—I watched the Master's in peace.

You and I need to beware of the spiritual distractions that come up at any given moment. Each day, our hearts have the tendency to attach to the first opportunity—a negative news headline, a weird look from your significant other, a text from a boss/coach, and so on. It's important that we tune our hearts to God and pay attention to His Word daily to fight those distractions.

PRAYER: *God, help me to fight being distracted today. Tune my heart to Your voice first. Let me hear You speak into everything that comes into my day.*

DF

TOXIC PEOPLE

Colossians 3:12 – *Therefore, as God's dearly loved, clothe yourselves with…long suffering.*

Some people just rub us the wrong way; then there are others who rub everybody the wrong way.

I once received a flyer in the mail advertising a seminar titled, *Toxic People: Living and working with high-conflict individuals.* I had to chuckle as I thought through all of those who immediately popped into my head. They are people who are always upset, complaining, angry at someone, pointing out flaws, appalled at every rule change, opinionated, can't be corrected yet are always correcting….

Toxic people are very frustrating, and they can even make us toxic. However, God wants us to be "long suffering" (patient with others). Thankfully, we can go to God with our frustrations and ask for His strength to not only put up with toxic people, but also be an encouragement to them. These people come across as if they are very strong, but they usually are filled with various needs and insecurities that make them toxic.

The next time you encounter (or get verbally attacked from) a toxic person, choose to say a quick prayer for your reaction and for them. Then watch God go to work over time.

PRAYER: *Lord, don't let toxic and irritating people ruin my day. Remind me to say a quick prayer for and forgive them.*

CJ

BENJAMIN BURKE IS PRISON BOUND

Mark 8:36 – *What good is it for someone to gain the whole world, yet forfeit their soul.*

Benjamin Burke never thought he would find himself standing before a judge in an orange jumpsuit. However, five years ago, he entered into a money-laundering scheme with a powerful drug lord in Los Angeles. Benjamin's goal was to get filthy rich. In pursuit of vast wealth, he let go of his moral compass and entered into a world of death and destruction. Now, he was about to be sentenced to life in prison.

Benjamin's decision was reprehensible and facilitated the addiction, overdose, and murder of countless people. While his particular circumstance is extreme, he is not alone. From the beginning of time, people have chosen to compromise their integrity and chase after ill-gotten wealth, fame, and power. It's nothing new.

Avoiding this pitfall is a two-step process. It begins with developing a desire to please and obey God. It ends with the belief that God has something for us in eternity that is far better than anything we could accrue by dishonest, evil, or improper schemes.

Keep the endgame in mind. The condition of your soul is far more important than anything you could accumulate on planet Earth.

PRAYER: *God, help me live a life today that pursues integrity and obedience over the temporary resources of this world.*

SP

THOUGHTS AND PRAYERS

Ephesians 1:17 – *I keep asking that the God of our Lord Jesus Christ, the glorious Father, may give you the Spirit of wisdom and revelation, so that you may know him better.*

My wife and I have been married for twenty-five years (she deserves some sort of award). When a couple gets engaged, they begin to learn more about each other—especially when choosing things for the registry.

During our registry process, my standard answer was, "Yep…love it." I didn't have a strong opinion in year one, and I still don't in year twenty-five. I didn't say recently, "I wish we had chosen the Mikasa tea cups instead of the Pfalzgraff." (We actually still have a silver serving platter in the box that's never been used. I wanted to melt it down and sell it. But it's still stored in our basement, which tells you something about how good my ideas are).

My point is that a marriage relationship doesn't stop at "I do." It's really just getting started. Now, it can stop there, but it's pretty sad when you see a stagnant marriage or one that's all about the kids.

When it comes to our relationship to God, these verses say that the purpose of prayer is "so that you may know Him better." The purpose is prayer is NOT to get stuff from God (although the Bible calls us to make requests). It's not to change our circumstances (although God is powerful). Just like marriage, our relationship with God does not stop at salvation—it's only the beginning.

PRAYER: *Jesus, I want to know You more than I want things from You. You! Your Presence is the ultimate prize. Help me today to see Your activity and know that it is You.*

DF

August 14th

THINK AND RETHINK

Colossians 3:10 – *Put on the new self, which is being renewed in knowledge…*

While there are many cut and dry issues in the Bible that need to be adhered to, there are other concepts in life that we need to be open to. For instance, there are issues such as, Ford is the only reliable truck, dinner is served only at 5:30pm, the woman does the grocery shopping, the man goes downstairs first if the wife hears an unfamiliar noise in the middle of the night (Just kidding! This is probably a biblical command that was left out).

We don't want to end up being that frustrating person who doesn't listen or that person who has to always be right just because that's the way they've always thought. Instead, we need to continually be "renewed in knowledge".

Henny Youngman once said, "I told the doctor I broke my leg in two places. He told me to quit going to those places." Youngman is poking fun at simple thinking. It sounds ridiculous, but we all have this capability to have wrong or shallow thinking. God longs to help us form good thinking and to renew our minds with His truth.

PRAYER: *Father, continually renew my thinking. Give me eyes that see the truth and a mind that understands true knowledge.*

CJ

PARANOIA

James 1:15 – *Then, after desire is conceived, it gives birth to sin; and sin, when it is full-grown, gives birth to death.*

The female Red-legged Golden Orb-weaver spider makes its home in southeast Africa and is as big as an adult human hand. The spider can trap, paralyze, and consume its insect prey in a matter of seconds. I've seen this thing in action, and I can tell you that it means business.

Several years ago, I was in Malawi, and I remember watching a butterfly flutter near one of these arachnid's massive webs. The butterfly was trying to get around the web to a flowering bush. No doubt, it was in hot pursuit of the nectar found within the bloom. I kept saying to the butterfly, "Get away. It's not worth it. You're going to get yourself killed."

As you might imagine, things did not end well. Observing the butterfly's ill-fated actions reminded me of how sin can ravage our souls if we get caught in its web. James 1:14-15 tells us that our desires often lead us to sin and those sinful choices can lead to death. Word to the wise: Develop a healthy paranoia of sin and its power to destroy.

PRAYER: *God, help me today to align my desires with Your desires and my thoughts with Your thoughts. Give me wisdom in the face of temptation and remind me of the consequences of my actions.*

SP

"I GET TO DIE FIRST"

Romans 14:8 – *If we live, we live for the Lord; and if we die, we die for the Lord. So, whether we live or die, we belong to the Lord.*

In 2007, twenty-three Korean missionaries went to Afghanistan, where they were abducted by Taliban rebels. During the ordeal, the Taliban split the Koreans into groups and took them to remote locations. However, the last time the missionaries were together, the Taliban confiscated everything except for the small Bible of one team member. He tore that Bible into twenty-three sections and handed a section to each missionary secretly.

They each said, "God, live or die, we surrender to live for Your glory. If you think it will bring You more glory if we die, we are ready." All twenty-three said that. Then, the senior pastor said, "If anyone dies, I die first. Because I'm your pastor.'" (As a pastor, I think it's a terrible strategy.)

Eventually, the team was released. Months later, the Korean pastor noticed a phenomenon, whenever he ran into team members. Team members would say, "I was afraid to die, but sometimes I wish I was back in Afghanistan. I was so close to Jesus."

Most of us will die *in* Christ before we have to die *for* Christ. Why wouldn't we make the same decision then, to live completely for Him BEFORE we die to be with Him?

PRAYER: *Father, I look forward to being with You eternally. However, I want to live for You before I get to live with You in Heaven. Help me to recognize You today.*

DF

TOUCHING MERCURY

2 Timothy 2:15 – *Do your best to present yourself to God as one approved, a workman who does not need to be ashamed and who correctly handles the word of truth.*

In today's verse, the wording "Do your best" seems to be telling us that we aren't expected to be perfect, but rather we should be trying to go in the right direction. For me, it's almost like the two steps forward, one step back idiom.

One thing that helps me "do my best" is reading the Bible while also continually trying to figure out how it's supposed to work in my daily life. But what is meant by "handling it"?

Back when I was a middle school principal, a student once brought in to school mercury from home, which is very dangerous and illegal. In fact, the school was supposed to evacuate the building because if mercury is "handled" and touched with bare hands, then it can be absorbed into the bloodstream as a fatal poison.

In the same way, we are to handle the word of truth by reading, pondering, studying, and figuring how to apply it. Then, God's Word will absorb into the bloodstream of our character and flow into our hearts.

PRAYER: *Lord, prod me to handle Your Words more and more. Penetrate Your truths into my heart and soul.*

CJ

August 18th

REAL CONVERSATIONS

Romans 1:16 – *For I am not ashamed of the gospel, because it is the power of God that brings salvation to everyone who believes.*

Driving home from work the other day, I witnessed a high-speed traffic accident that resulted in a fatality. After the smoke and debris had cleared, I couldn't help but wonder about the eternal destiny of the man who had lost his life just 100 feet away from me.

We don't talk about it a great deal, and I suppose it's because there is much more to a relationship with Jesus than just rescue from Hell. I absolutely understand this thought process and, likewise, prefer to speak more about the positives than the negatives. At the same time, I also know that one of the great truths about Jesus is that He made a way of escape for every soul that calls upon His name.

As followers of Christ, we should be willing to talk to people about the glory of Heaven and the reality of Hell. It's obviously easier to talk more about one than the other. But let's not shy away from lovingly sharing the truth of God's Word with people—it might be the conversation that points them toward faith in Jesus.

PRAYER: *Father, provide me with an opportunity to share the Gospel today. Give me courage to share the truth of Your Word.*

SP

YOU (DON'T) BE THE JUDGE

Romans 12:19 – *Do not take revenge, my dear friends, but leave room for God's wrath, for it is written: "It is mine to avenge; I will repay," says the Lord.*

Sometimes, Christians settle for choosing boundary markers instead of leaning into Christ's Presence. In other words, we talk more about what we are against than what we are actually for.

This creates a false sense of superiority, and the markers become a way to exclude people for whom we lack affinity.

Homer Simpson's fundamentalist neighbors, the Flanders, once famously quipped when coming back from a trip, "We went away to a Christian camp. We were learning how to be more judgmental."

We have this preoccupation with the appearance of spirituality, because we believe that the veneer of spirituality somehow gives us the authority to speak to anything and everything. If we can't be holy, then shouldn't we at least be weird?

There's a difference between being wise and being judgmental. Wise people learn to lean on God's Presence and His revealed truth in Scripture. Judgmental people make themselves the authority on all things. Elizabeth Barrett Browning once wrote these lines:

> *Earth's crammed with heaven,*
> *And every common bush afire with God;*
> *But only he who sees, takes off his shoes;*
> *The rest sit round it and pluck blackberries*

We need to become people who "see," instead of just becoming blackberry pickers.

PRAYER: *God, I confess my need to elevate my opinion over the opinion of others. Help me today to lean on Your convictions instead of opinions and my false sense of security and superiority.*

DF

TYPEWRITERS

Galatians 3:3 – *Are you so foolish? After beginning with the Spirit, are you now trying to attain your goal by human effort?*

I can remember the days of using the manual typewriter. Every time I pressed a key on the keyboard, it would swing a metal arm. If I didn't push hard enough, it wouldn't work. I almost needed to ice my hand down after typing a long paper.

Then the electric typewriter came out. It was like today's computer keyboard that only required a touch of the finger instead of a mighty push. What a contrast to the old ones that were so loud and exhausting!

The Spirit of God indwells us and is waiting for us to depend on Him, so He can empower all of our efforts and thoughts. It's like plugging in that old typewriter and transforming it into an electric-powered machine.

No matter what it is—your job, sports, relationships, school, figuring our your life's direction, helping someone out, getting through a hard time—these are all things that God longs to come alongside of us.

PRAYER: *Father, remind me and show me when I'm doing life through my own efforts. Empower every area of my life as I tap into Your strength.*

CJ

IF SHE CAN DO IT, SO CAN I

Mark 12:44 – *They gave out of their wealth; but she, out of her poverty, put in everything—all she had to live on.*

I'll never forget the first time I saw a congregation in Malawi take an offering. Sitting under the thatched roof of a simple mud building, I watched some of the poorest people in the world place coins in a small, hand-sewn collection bag. My heart was moved by their willingness to sacrifice and their desire to be generous.

The charity of the Malawian church reminded me of the widow who placed two small, copper coins in the temple treasury. She was among the poorest of the poor, and still, she gave her last few cents. Jesus noticed the widow's sacrifice and pointed it out to the disciples as commendable.

Many of us have far more than we need, but instead of fully realizing the beauty of benevolence, we choose to accumulate resources for ourselves. In doing so, we miss the mark.

Throughout Scripture, God calls us to give generously. His expectation is one of obedience and generosity. Allow me to encourage you to be sacrificial and open-handed. From evangelism and missions work around the world, to meeting the felt needs of people in your church or community, you might be surprised by the impact of your giving.

PRAYER: *God, place within my heart a spirit of sacrifice and generosity. Help me to be quick to use my resources for Your sake and Your work.*

SP

MILEY CYRUS AND THE TRINITY

Genesis 1:26 – *Then God said, "Let us make mankind in our image…"*

At the end of each day of Creation, God said, "It is good." In a perfect Garden with perfect people and a perfect God, there was only one thing that wasn't good. Genesis 2 tells us, "It is not good that man should be ALONE."

Adam's companionship-need wasn't a sign of imperfection but, actually, of perfection. We were created for community, and not just *for community* but *from* community. In eternity, God has existed as the Father, Son, and Spirit—the Trinity (If you find the Trinity difficult to understand, just ask my fellow author Chris to explain it).

A mom-friend of ours was trying to describe the Trinity to her four-year-old daughter and was failing miserably. Finally, her daughter responded by saying, "It's really simple, Mom. It's like Hannah Montana. Sometimes, she's Hannah, but sometimes she's Miley. It's the same person but different at the same time."

See? It's simple.

We are created in His image, so that means we need each other. For example, Paul (maybe the greatest known Christian ever) was simultaneously incredibly strong and also needed friends. In *Bowling Alone*, Robert Putnam cited research that said relationally-connected people are three times less likely to die than unconnected people in the next eighteen months.

So, here's a new motto for you: get connected or die! See? It's simple.

PRAYER: *God, thank You for the people whom You have brought into my life that care to encourage me, serve me, and tell me the truth—even when I don't want to hear it. Bless them today and give me the grace to not take them for granted.*

DF

TUMS

Psalm 103:10,12 – *He does not treat us as our sins deserve or repay us according to our iniquities. As far as the east is from the west, so far has He removed our transgressions from us.*

In the midst of another diet, I ate way too much rich and greasy food. As a result, I went to bed feeling bad and bloated, which is exactly what I deserved. I then took some Tums for the relief that I didn't deserve.

In the Scriptures, God says that He will not treat us as our sins deserve if we hand them over to Him in confession. It's like my experience with Tums: we receive a much-needed, undeserved relief.

But if we don't allow God to change our wrongful actions, we will have to live with the discomfort caused by our spiritual health issues, and it will be more than what a few "forgiveness" Tums can tame.

Comedian Phyllis Diller once said, "I'm eighteen years behind on my ironing." In other words, there was no way she could catch up. In the same way, there's no way can we catch up for all of the mistakes we've made. Only God can remove our transgressions from us.

PRAYER: *Father, thank You that I can keep starting over when I mess up and that You see me as forgiven of past sins. Thank You that they are removed. Continue to clean me of my damaging sins.*

CJ

WHAT'S IN A NAME?

2 Samuel 7:22 – *How great are you, Sovereign Lord! There is no one like you, and there is no God but you, as we have heard with our own ears.*

When you pray, remember His name. When you are worried, remember His name. When you are alone or afraid, remember His name. When you are weak or sick, remember His name. When you are ready to go your own way, remember His name. When you wonder about your future, remember His name. When you need forgiveness, remember His name. When you have any need or concern whatsoever, remember His name.

El Shaddai *Lord God Almighty*
El Elyon *The Most High God*
Adonai *Lord, Master*
Yahweh *Lord, Jehovah*
Jehovah Nissi *The Lord My Banner*
Jehovah-Raah *The Lord My Shepherd*
Jehovah Rapha *The Lord That Heals*
Jehovah Shammah *The Lord Is There*
Jehovah Tsidkenu *The Lord Our Righteousness*
Jehovah Mekoddishkem *The Lord Who Sanctifies You*
El Olam *The Everlasting God*
Elohim *God*
Qanna *Jealous*
Jehovah Jireh *The Lord Will Provide*
Jehovah Shalom *The Lord Is Peace*
Jehovah Sabaoth *The Lord Of Hosts*

PRAYER: *Father, Remind me today of Your awesome presence and power. Help me look to You as the One who can meet all of my needs.*

SP

RELAX JOHN

Ephesians 4:31 – *Get rid of all bitterness, rage and anger, brawling and slander along with every form of malice.*

John was driving home from work when out of nowhere, a silver SUV swerved into his lane and cut him off. The haphazard maneuver happened so fast that John had to slam on his brakes to avoid a collision. To make matters worse, the car then slowed to a snail's pace.

Frustrated, John pulled up next to the SUV at the red light and glared at the driver. The driver responded with a foul hand gesture, and John became enraged. When the light turned green, he put the hammer down in a show of defiance. As the cars raced side by side down the boulevard, John's anger boiled. As he pushed his new car to the limit, John's tires drifted outside his lane, and he lost control. In the blink of an eye, John suffered an accident that nearly cost him his life.

Anger can escalate quickly, and it often leads to trouble. God's Word instructs us to let go of our rage and replace it with kindness, compassion, and forgiveness (Eph. 4:31-32). Remember, there was a time when your sin deserved God's wrath. Still, God withheld His anger and forgave you. Avoid trouble and offer the same grace and mercy to others.

PRAYER: *God, help me replace my anger with kindness and forgiveness today. Transform my heart and mind.*

SP

SPRING BREAK SALVATION

Matthew 5:14 – *You are the light of the world. A town built on a hill cannot be hidden.*

There's nothing like seeing a friend or family member receive Christ. I've got a friend, Charles, who I met in the early 1990s in Florida, while on Spring Break.

Oddly enough, Charles was on his way out for a night on the town, when he happened into a church service that I led as a college student. That night was his moment. All of the light that people had shone into Charles' life illuminated the choice he would make that evening.

Charles and I have remained friends since, and he is one of the strongest Christians I know. He has family in Columbus, Ohio and has attended our church (Lifepoint) a few times.

Whenever we are together and he introduces me to someone, Charles always says, "This is the guy I told you about—he's the guy who brought me to Jesus."

For me, that's an eternal moment. It will last forever. You have a "Charles" somewhere in your life today. Maybe it's someone you already know or have yet to meet. Live in the awareness that you are God's Light!

PRAYER: *Father, please give me the opportunity to speak to someone for You today. I am asking that You would bring the Spirit's work to my family, friends, and co-workers to draw them to Yourself.*

DF

RUNAWAY TRAIN

Ephesians 5:15-16 – *Be very careful, then, how you live—not as unwise but as wise, making the most of every opportunity.*

In life, it's easy to get into a rut, and we'll tend to glaze our way through life until we reach the next event we are looking forward to. For instance, we'll grind it out until the Saturday game, the movie night, the weekend gathering, the spring break, the vacation…. As Henry Clay once said, "The time will come when winter will ask you what you were doing all summer."

In today's Scripture, God tells us to make the most of every day. We can ask Him to slow down the runaway train of our routine by reminding us to lend a hand, make a friend, and appreciate the people and things we take for granted. In other words, we shouldn't wait for a movie to laugh, cry, or enjoy life's wholesome pleasures. Those moments can be found in the everyday.

We are all getting older, or as Rodney Dangerfield stated, "Last year my birthday cake looked like a prairie fire." Weaving God into each day, asking Him to show us how to make the most of our time, and helping or encouraging others will help slow us down.

PRAYER: *Lord, help me to make the most of every opportunity and help me to see those opportunities. Thank You for the opportunities to help others.*

CJ

CAN WE GET AN ETA?

1 Peter 5:7 – *Cast all your anxiety on him because he cares for you.*

Bernie and Rose were missionaries in South America. Together, they led a team of people committed to sharing the Gospel with unreached people along the Amazon River.

Earlier in the day, three of their missionaries had set out on a jungle expedition. When the team failed to return on time, Bernie and Rose became anxious. For the better part of two hours, they paced around the compound and wrung their hands. Anxiety had officially turned to worry.

As their concerns mounted, they called the other missionaries together for prayer. As soon as they bowed their heads, the voices of the missing expedition team could be heard in the distance. Though a navigational misstep had caused them to momentarily lose their way, everyone on the team returned safely.

When fear and anxiety crouch at your door, it's easy to be over-whelmed and forget to pray. When a personal dilemma or concern for a loved one inundates your mind, resist the urge to worry and begin to pray. Worry has zero impact on circumstances. However, casting your anxiety before an all-caring, all-powerful, and all-knowing God promises to make a difference.

PRAYER: *God, help me today to be slow to worry and quick to pray.*

SP

HAMBURGERS AT MIDNIGHT

Ephesians 2:18 – *For through him we both have access to the Father by one Spirit.*

When our son was fourteen years old, he came into our bedroom and asked my wife to make him a hamburger at 12:30—AM. AND we had been asleep for over an hour.

My wife responded with something like, "There are hamburgers from dinner in the refrigerator, and you can warm one up in the microwave." My son replied with something like, "Yes, ma'am, but they are better when you warm them up on the stove."

I thought that three very different things could happen at that moment, and two of them were bad.

Per usual, my wife opted for the third option and made my son a gourmet hamburger in the wee hours of the morning. The lesson? The only person who can wake up the queen in the middle of the night is her son.

It's a reminder that we have this incredible access to the God of the universe. At any and every moment, He is with us. We can walk into His Presence night or day.

PRAYER: *God, thank You that You allow me to pray without ceasing. Not only can my life be a prayer, but I can make requests, pray Your Word back to You, and learn to hear Your voice.*

DF

I'LL FLY AWAY

Psalm 90:10 – *Our days may come to seventy years, or eighty, if our strength endures; for they quickly pass, and we fly away.*

It seems as though life goes by more quickly as we get older.

When I was a young child, summer was a long, three months of swimming, baseball, vacation, and a lot of sitting around with buddies. But now, summers slip by so fast that I need to plan out everything in advance.

Last summer I was going to read three books, build a deck, and revamp a bedroom. Before I knew it, August was here, and my reading goal turned into completing a couple crossword puzzles, my deck building turned into skimming through a magazine about decks, and the room renovation turned into my cleaning out a couple drawers.

We can slow the runaway train of life by spending time in daily prayer and giving ourselves the time to just think. Not only does it let off the acceleration pedal of busyness, but it also allows God to create in us an inner fulfillment that prepares us to one day "fly away!"

PRAYER: *Lord, help me to get the most out of my days here. Remind me to stop and talk with You daily. Thank You that You can slow life down for me, so I can think, pray, and make good decisions.*

CJ

911 PRAYERS

Psalm 71:12 – *Do not be far from me, my God; come quickly, God, to help me.*

Naomi Alpert was cautious as she drove through the night. From time to time, the wind howled, and the snow drifted across the road. Nevertheless, she felt safe in her four-wheel drive vehicle. As she approached the bridge, her vehicle started to slip and slide. Within a matter of seconds, she was in a violent spin. Naomi prayed a quick prayer, "God, save me," as she fought to regain control of her truck.

Naomi's vehicle came to a stop at the center of the bridge. Unharmed, she thanked God for His deliverance. At the same time, her adrenaline served as a reminder that none of us are promised rescue from the 911 moments we face. With tears streaming down her face, she thanked God again.

As we encounter emergencies in life, we can be certain that God hears our prayers and promises to be with us in the fight. When David feared for his life, he cried out for help and sought refuge in the Lord. He looked to God for physical rescue when times were tough. Like David, we should feel confident crying out to God when we find ourselves in desperate need of His help.

PRAYER: *God, be near to me as I face the 911 moments in life. Remind me today and every day to call out to You for help.*

SP

KARMA CHAMELEON

Matthew 6:12 – *And forgive us our debts, as we also have forgiven our debtors.*

The famous theologian Boy George, who sang "Karma Chameleon," included this lyric:

> *I'm a man without conviction*
> *I'm a man who doesn't know*
> *How to sell a contradiction?*
> *You come and go, you come and go*
> *Karma, karma, karma, karma, karma chameleon*

When asked about the meaning of the song, George said, "If you live a false life (in other words, if you cheat others, lie, etc.) you get karma justice…it's nature's way of paying you back."

In other words, nature becomes the Judge. However, if that's true, nature is a bad Judge. Think about the terrible afflictions felt around the world by some of the most vulnerable people. But if karma is *not* the answer to forgiveness and revenge, then what is?

Maybe a better question—Who is? Jesus claims that He is a righteous Judge who sacrifices. He saves us from sin, and He shows us how to forgive others of their sins against us. From the Cross, He is forgiving; that's who Jesus is. It can become who we are, as well.

PRAYER: *Lord, there are people who have offended me. Please forgive me for making myself out to be the Judge. I want to hand my gavel over to You. Help me to become a great forgiver.*

DF

I WANT WHAT I WANT, WHEN I WANT IT

Romans 8:28 – *And we know that in all things God works for the good of those who love Him.*

Not all things are "*good,*" but God can work all things *"for the good."*

Each of my four children went through the "brat" stage of growing up. It's the stage when the toddler motto seems to be, "I want what I want, when I want it!" If left up to them, life would be an all-night Captain Crunch fest in front of video games. Thankfully, maturity kicks in as they learn to cope with disappointment, TV limits, bedtimes, and so forth.

Sometimes we, adults, become "spiritual brats." When life doesn't go our way, we don't ask God what He is trying to teach us, but rather, we tend to run to Him and tell Him to just fix it. In addition, our prayer times can be a daily Christmas list of wants, instead of requests to change and mature us, and we become angry and frustrated because "I want what I want, when I want it!"

God does want to hear and meet our requested desires, but more importantly, He wants to grow and strengthen us.

PRAYER: *Father, I know You can work all things for my good. Make me and mold me into the blessed and fulfilled person I long to be.*

CJ

IT'S HARD TO TELL THE DIFFERENCE

Romans 12:2 – *Do not conform to the pattern of this world, but be transformed by the renewing of your mind.*

I remember going to the circus as a child in 1978, hoping to be shocked by the appearance of sideshow performers. I recall seeing a man with a four-foot beard, a woman covered in tattoos, and a dude with piercings on his face. Candidly, I wasn't that impressed and was only a little shocked. However, the wicked white-faced clown scared me to death with his evil smile!

Looking back, I suppose the "shocking" appearance of the sideshow performers I remember from 1978 would hardly draw a second glance today. That which was significantly uncommon then has become relatively normal now, and it's hard to tell the difference between the two.

At the same time, it has become increasingly difficult to distinguish between followers of Jesus Christ and everyone else. In many cases, standards and practices once reserved for the world have become mainstream in the body of Christ. Make no mistake, we have entered into a dangerous game.

Remember, the Bible directs Christians to dismiss the world's system, reprogram our minds, and become more like Jesus Christ. To do so requires a commitment to God's Word and a dedication to worship. Start the process today. Renew your mind and be transformed!

PRAYER: *God, begin the work of transforming me today. Help me fill my heart with worship and my mind with Your Word.*

SP

LESS FILLING, TASTES GREAT

Mark 4:41 – *They were terrified and asked each other, "Who is this? Even the wind and the waves obey him!"*

The Bible says that God is holy. That doesn't *mean* that God is *mean*. It means that everything about God is different. But at times, we want a Miller Lite version of the Almighty: less filling, tastes great.

We want a God who helps us when we are in trouble, but we don't want Him to bother us or expect too much from us. However, He is Holy. His love is different. His mercy is different. His faithfulness is different.

As Jesus and the Disciples crossed the sea, the Disciples were scared to death of the raging storm, so they awakened Jesus. They certainly were not going to allow Him to die in peace. Yet, Jesus immediately calmed the storm with a word. Prior to that, the disciples were scared to death. In fact, they even told Jesus they were going to die.

Interestingly, Mark says that *after* Jesus calmed the storm, the Disciples were even more afraid. Jesus had this quality where you didn't want to be around Him at times because He was so holy. AND you also wanted to be with Him, because He was so holy.

He is not God Lite.

PRAYER: *Lord, please help me today to not make You into something that You are not. I declare that You are my Holy King. I will follow You no matter what comes against my life.*

DF

LAMBEAU LEAP

Mark 10:43 – *Whoever wants to become great among you must be your servant.*

Green Bay Packer fans migrate many miles to a small town in Wisconsin to watch their beloved team in the stadium called Lambeau Field. My favorite tradition to watch is the "Lambeau Leap." Any time a Packer player scores a touchdown, he will "leap" over a wall and into the arms of the crazed fans.

Most touchdowns are scored by smaller players such as running backs and receivers. I always wanted to see what would happen if a 325-pound offensive lineman scored. That wall is pretty high for the average human to jump, let alone a man who could be mistaken for a mid-sized Buick.

The offensive linemen are the guys who give the quarterback time to throw a pass or give the running backs room to gain yards. Despite their important role, linemen have very limited notoriety.

When I read in the Bible about being a servant, I think of offensive linemen. They make it possible for others to excel. They do it for the team.

According to today's verse, God notices the servants, the people whom others fail to notice! He even says we are great if we help others excel and achieve.

PRAYER: *Lord, show me how to seize opportunities to serve others. I want to do it to prove that I think You are real and not to get pats on the back.*

CJ

MADE IN THE SHADE

Psalm 121:5 – *The Lord watches over you—the Lord is your shade at your right hand.*

South Carolina's beachside temperatures soared into the high nineties. To provide ample shade for our extended family, we would have to set up two tents, five large umbrellas, and ten beach chairs. The task of setting up and tearing down would be considerable, but we knew that shade would become a prized commodity during the heat of the day.

The psalmist also understood the value of shade when describing God's protection in Psalm 121. The words take on greater significance when you consider the fact that God's people resided in the Middle East and routinely contended with the relentless heat of the blazing Mediterranean sun. More than anyone, they knew that finding shade could be the difference between comfort and distress or even life and death. Certainly, the picture of God's protection in the unique form of shade and shelter resonated with His people.

In the same way, you can rest assured that God forms a protective covering over you. He offers never-ending shelter. So, whenever you seek shade under a tent or umbrella, be reminded that you can always find protection in Almighty God. He promises to watch over you.

PRAYER: *God, help me to rest in Your protection today.*

SP

APPROVAL ADDICTS

Hebrews 13:8 – *Jesus Christ is the same yesterday and today and forever.*

We tell our kids, "You can be anything you want to be," which is true—kind of. We look to spouses, kids, friends, family, and work to validate ourselves. What's the problem with that?

One of my favorite teachers says it this way. Let's say you're a young man in the early years of the United States. You have two competing emotions. One is aggression. You want to smash things and smash people. The other is sexual freedom, which means you want to sleep with whomever you want, whenever you want, and without consequence. However, the America of the 1800s says that while aggression is okay, sexual freedom is a no-no. So, you say to yourself, "I must be a warrior, but I'll put away that sexual desire."

Two hundred years later, things in the United States are completely backwards. What does the culture say to you? "Well, sexual freedom is okay, but that aggressive, warrior mentality has to go." So, modern man says, "I'll live free, but physical anger? I'll set that aside. That's not me."

What's the point? You aren't really determining who you are. You're just listening to a different voice. All you've done is found a new set of cheerleaders. But while the world constantly shifts, God never changes.

PRAYER: *God, I feel out of control in some areas of my life, but I believe that You are ultimately in control and guiding us to the restoration of all things.*

DF

"MINE!"

Philemon 1:6 – *I pray that you may be active in sharing your faith, so that you will have a full understanding of every good thing we have in Christ.*

When toddlers play together, they don't really "play together." I remember my wife's setting up playdates with other toddlers, and it always ended in a tug-of-war over toys. "Mine!" was a continual piercing shrill.

Kids at that age don't really "share" toys; at best, they play next to each other. It was amazing to see how my son would all of a sudden desire to play with a toy that had lain dormant for weeks just because this "intruder" picked it up. "Mine!"

As children mature, they can develop the ability to "share," and that's when hanging out with friends really gets fun. God also wants us to "share" our faith with others, even if it is in passing. Here are a few examples:

- "I have been praying more lately, and it has helped."
- "Our pastor talked about handing our conflicts over to God…."
- "Have you ever thought about why Jesus died for us?"

Today's verse practically guarantees that "sharing" the things of faith will not only impact others but ourselves as well.

PRAYER: *Father, bring people into my path whom I can share faith with. Thank You in advance for the great blessing that will eventually follow in my life and in those around me.*

CJ

September 9th

IS IT ME?

Haggai 1:5 – *Now this is what the Lord Almighty says: "Give careful thought to your ways."*

There have been moments in my life where I couldn't seem to get out of my own way. One semester in college really had me on the ropes. My grades were slipping, my social life was a wreck, and I was in constant trouble. No matter how hard I tried, nothing was working out.

One Friday evening, the perfect storm of academic trouble, social failure, and behavioral misstep brought my world to a standstill. With nothing to lose, I reached out to a mentor back home.

For the next twenty minutes, I found myself on one end of a payphone while listening to the wise counsel of a friend. In short, he asked me to consider my ways—to give careful thought to the way I had structured and lived my life that semester.

In the second shortest book in the Old Testament, the prophet Haggai implores those around him to consider why they were struggling. While they were working hard, they were not prospering. Their hardship was a result of their disobedience. Quite simply, their rebellion was keeping them from experiencing God's blessing.

Give careful thought to the way you live your life. Your troubles may be self-inflicted. If so, seek forgiveness and change.

PRAYER: *God, help me take stock of my life today. Help me let go of my ways and follow Your plan.*

SP

UN-PRAYED ANSWERS

Ephesians 3:20 – *Now to him who is able to do immeasurably more than all we ask or imagine, according to his power that is at work within us.*

When most of us think about praying, the first thing that pops up in our minds is the idea of unanswered prayers. "I prayed, but I didn't get the answer I asked for." In this verse, the Bible gives us an answer for why we should continue to pray—God is Able.

Everything in our prayer lives depends on this conviction. Most of us are not satisfied with our prayer lives. We feel guilty that we don't pray enough…or pray with enough faith…or pray consistently enough…or we just forget about praying.

What drives most of our concerns about prayer is the reality that God can do anything. And not just *most* of what we ask or think. He can't do just *a little more*; it's actually *exceedingly* more. Really, the verse best translates "exceedingly abundantly" more—God can do more than more!

It's so much that the writer makes up a phrase for it. Nowhere else is this phrase "immeasurably more" used in Scripture. Nothing is too big—no one is too far. God can save the unreachable. Recently, a friend texted me. This friend had been praying for another friend to begin a relationship with Christ for fifteen years. Why?

God. Is. Able.

PRAYER: *God help me to pray things right now with the belief that You are Able to accomplish them. Don't allow me to limit my prayers to my own strength.*

DF

KNOCK, KNOCK. WHO'S THERE?

Matthew 21:10 – *When Jesus entered Jerusalem, the whole town stirred and asked, "Who is this?"*

My wife and I were walking into an Ohio high school football game, and coming up to us was a long-time friend, Archie Griffin. My wife greeted him with a loud, "Kimble! How are you?" She had just mistaken the only two-time Heisman Trophy winner ever (and most famous face in Ohio) with another friend we hadn't seen in a while.

Archie and I were speechless in this most awkward moment. Most Ohioans see him and clamor or nervously ask him for an autograph because they know they are in the presence of greatness. Since we were close friends and my wife is from New Jersey, we all just acted like her blunder didn't happen.

Archie clearly isn't as famous as Jesus, but when the Jerusalem crowd saw "this Man" riding a donkey and escorted by worshippers with palm leaves, many didn't know who He was. In fact, they even asked, "Who is this?" Why? Because they knew they were in the presence of Greatness.

When we think our Lord is little, it makes our problems seem big. When we realize our Lord is big, it makes our problems seem little.

PRAYER: *When I'm reading my Bible, praying, or acknowledging You throughout the day, remind me God that I'm in the presence of Greatness.*

CJ

GUILTY AS CHARGED

Romans 5:8 – *But God demonstrates his own love for us in this: While we were still sinners, Christ died for us.*

My head was in the clouds as I cruised down the road at forty-five miles per hour. The next thing I knew, a truck flashed in front of me. I hit the brakes, but it was too late. My Toyota Camry crumpled like an accordion, and the accident was 100% my fault.

"Guilty as charged" are words no one wants to hear. Spiritually speaking, such a phrase has eternal consequences. The Bible teaches us that we are all guilty of sin. We were born into it, and we choose to participate in it. As a result, we are destined for an eternity separated from God in a place called Hell.

There is hope, however. That same Bible teaches us that Jesus was fully aware of our sin and still chose to die for us. His sacrifice on the cross and resurrection from the grave removes the guilt of our sin and unlocks the doors of Heaven.

Today, you can turn from your sin and ask Jesus to forgive you. Your guilt can be wiped away, and you can secure for yourself an eternal home in Heaven. Ask Him today to be your Forgiver, Savior, and Lord (see Appendix).

PRAYER: *Jesus, I turn from my sin and seek Your forgiveness today. I put my faith in You.*

SP

STREAKING TO GLORY

Romans 8:15 – *The Spirit you received does not make you slaves, so that you live in fear again; rather, the Spirit you received brought about your adoption to sonship. And by him we cry, "Abba, Father."*

When our kids were between the ages of two and four, they had a ritual. After the kids finished their baths, they would "make a run for it." This meant they were going to run a streaking lap through our house sans clothing and laughing wildly.

My wife is from Louisiana, so I like to say that they got it from her side of the family.

On one occasion, my three-year-old son got to the bottom of the stairs during his run. Instead of making the normal right turn, he took a left. This led him out our front door and towards the street. I sprinted to catch him in the driveway and threw him over my shoulder, as he laughed all the way…in front of our neighbors who were outside. The Beverly Hillbillies have come to the neighborhood.

I could have let my son run into the street and deal with consequences, but I'm his father. Part of the greatness of God is that He has not made us His *servants*. Rather, He has adopted us as His *sons* and *daughters*. Even when we choose to make a run for the things that would do us harm, God is always chasing after us—He's always with us like a perfect Heavenly Father.

PRAYER: *Father, help me to live today from the perspective that I'm already Your child, instead of living in the fear of never measuring up.*

DF

STOP, WAIT A MINUTE MR. POSTMAN

Philippians 3:8 – *I consider everything a loss compared to the surpassing greatness of knowing Christ Jesus my Lord...*

When I first went to college, there was a young lady I met over the summer whom I wanted to stay in touch with (It was like the movie *Grease* without the dancing and singing). Back in those days, there were no cell phones or email, so staying in touch required a bit more effort. So, every day I made my trek down to the post office to deliver and pick up my "love letters."

I would store the letters I'd received until Sunday morning, and then I'd open each one with respect and reverence. I'm just kidding! I would tear those letters open in the post office and read them over and over, all the way back to my dorm. I wanted to learn about this young lady and discover what she thought about me too. In order to really get to know her, we spent time together when I returned home from college.

In order for us to get to know God, we can tear into His "love letters" that He's given us (His Word) and not wait until Sunday to see what He has to say. We can also hang out with Him during the day, as we talk to Him in prayer.

PRAYER: *Father, show me how to know You more and more. Thanks for being my God and my Friend.*

CJ

CONSUMED BY CARDBOARD CUBES

Psalm 119:15 – *I meditate on your precepts and consider your ways.*

The last time our family moved, I was in charge of box procurement. For five weeks, my entire world revolved around securing dozens of often elusive cardboard containers. I became obsessed. I fell asleep thinking about boxes and woke up thinking about boxes. I searched grocery stores, bookstores, and outlet malls for these prized, cardboard cubes.

It's easy to find ourselves consumed with things that have little or no eternal value. I can't help but wonder what our lives would be like if we pursued the spiritually significant with the same passion and vigor that we use to chase after the less important things of life.

Let's take understanding the mind of Christ for example. It seems reasonable to think that if we are trusting Jesus for something as important as our eternal salvation, then we would be compelled to know as much about Him as possible. And quite simply, the best way to know the heart and mind of Jesus is to saturate yourself with the book that is all about Him.

Pursue the things that matter. Read the Bible and allow your thoughts to be consumed by the life and work of Jesus.

PRAYER: *God, help me prioritize time in Your Word. Help me to be consumed with the desire to know Your Son Jesus more.*

SP

WE ARE FAMILY

Ephesians 2:19b – *And members of the household of God.*

Sometimes (okay, more often than "sometimes") people struggle to love one another, and this includes Christians (okay, especially Christians). A variety of sins causes this problem. I believe the primary reason is because we forget a simple truth from the New Testament: We are family (Sister Sledge, circa 1979, had it right!).

In the New Testament, an interesting shift occurs in how the biblical authors refer to our relationship with each other. In the Gospels and the Book of Acts, Christians are often referred to as Disciples or followers of Jesus.

However, after the book of Acts, the term "disciple" disappears, and the people of God call one another "brother" and "sister." As a matter of fact, the New Testament commandment is given to *"greet one another with a holy kiss."* We can be grateful that it was cultural!

We are family. If we could express this one, simple value, there would not be enough church buildings to hold the people attempting to enter. We would never have enough seats. Family loves you, even though they know your imperfections.

We all have a family member who is different—a crazy aunt or uncle. We live with their oddity because they are family. It should be the same in the Body of Christ.

PRAYER: *Father, I won't meet anyone today whom You did not create. Nor will I see anyone today whom You do not love. Help me to see and love them the way that You do.*

DF

THE MASTER SALESMAN

Ephesians 3:20 – *Now to Him who is able to do immeasurably more than all we ask or imagine, according to His power that is at work within us.*

I once worked in an appliance store, and I started out selling the low-end, small commission stuff. My good friend was a regional manager and shocked me when he told me about the big money he'd made working in that "low-end" department. I honestly could not imagine how he could pull it off by selling mere boom boxes, typewriters, and radios.

My friend explained his strategy. After selling a CB radio or pack of batteries, he would then ask about the customer's family and kitchen appliances. The next thing you know, he's taking people who now felt cared about around the store to look at refrigerators, washers, and ranges.

I had no idea this strategy even existed.

It's the same with God. We need to realize that we don't have all the answers. There are solutions to problems, answers to prayers, hidden paths to situations working out, a person out there who will marry us, a friend to be made, if we trust the Master. He can truly do more than we can ask or imagine!

PRAYER: *Lord, thank You for Your vast abilities to make things work for my good, even when it's outside of what I can imagine. I will lean on You.*

CJ

SNORKEL LESSONS

Mark 1:35 – *Very early in the morning, while it was still dark, Jesus got up, left the house and went off to a solitary place, where he prayed.*

Looking out at the coral reef in Hanauma Bay, I couldn't wait to see the marine life that lay just beneath the surface. Sitting at the water's edge, I put on my fins and mask. For the first time in my life, I was about to go snorkeling.

Just moments into the ocean, I managed to inhale a mouthful of saltwater through my snorkel. Choking and coughing, I realized I needed to work on my breathing technique. Maximizing my snorkeling experience would require creating a new respiratory routine.

Getting into the groove of something new isn't always easy. It requires effort and determination. As Christians, the most important rhythm we can establish in our lives revolves around our communication and connection with God. If we desire to maximize our faith, we must create a pattern of dedicated time alone with God—taking time to talk to Him in prayer and allowing Him to speak to us through His Word.

Throughout the Gospels, Jesus routinely stepped away from the busyness of life to connect with the Father. Often, He left his disciples and disappeared from the masses to pray. For Jesus, communication with the Father was a priority. Let us do likewise!

PRAYER: *God, help me today to begin creating a pattern of life that prioritizes my time with You.*

SP

September 19th

ELEMENTARY, MY DEAR WATSON

2 Corinthians 5:21 – *God made him who had no sin to be sin for us, so that in him we might become the righteousness of God.*

In one of the last scenes of *A Game of Shadows*, Sherlock Holmes has foiled Professor Moriarity's plot, but the evil Moriarity threatens revenge against Holmes by harming Watson and his new wife, Mary.

Part of Holmes' genius is that he can foresee the outcomes of situations and circumstances just before they occur. Holmes "sees" the outcome of a fight with Moriarity before the battle begins. The only way Holmes can save Watson and his bride is to sacrifice himself over the edge and take Moriarity with him.

Jesus did similarly—the only way for Christ to save us was for Him to lose His life. He had to take death over the edge with Him on the cross. In the end of the movie, Holmes had an out. Our Savior was no different. Jesus, our Hero, the One who really sees everything, had an out on the third day. He took the teeth of sin's penalty in our place, only to be resurrected on the third day and beat death, while granting us the same reward.

PRAYER: *Thank You, Jesus, for giving Yourself for my sins. And not just the sins of the world but You gave Yourself for my sins personally. Thank You for being resurrected for me—for giving me hope for eternity!*

DF

PUT ME IN, COACH

Lamentations 3:22-23 – *Because of the Lord's great love we are not consumed, for His compassions never fail. They are new every morning; great is Your faithfulness.*

I've watched athletic coaches over the years. Some are very degrading, some are too laid back, and some feel as though they aren't doing their job unless they are correcting every little mistake.

I've also noticed that the most effective coaches are those who use praise and encouragement way more than correction and yelling. Athletes don't want to go through a practice or game working hard just to not "mess up." The goal and focus should be on excelling at a higher level with the freedom to fail and start over.

It's the same with God. He longs for us to excel and reach for our full potential. He desires that we tap into His power and strength to develop our abilities. He yearns to form our thinking and perspective by letting His Word invade our minds.

This can't happen unless we are convinced that He is the "perfect Coach" who corrects us only to get us back on the path of attaining a significant and secure life.

PRAYER: *Father, thank You that I can keep confessing and starting over so that You can "coach" me to a higher level of joy and fulfillment.*

CJ

DESPERATELY SEEKING HAPPINESS

Psalm 16:11 – *You make known to me the path of life; you will fill me with joy in your presence, with eternal pleasures at your right hand.*

My wife, Danette, and I were married in 1994. Together, we've had some pretty remarkable experiences. We've traveled around the world, walked along tropical beaches, visited the White House, and even met our share of famous people along the way. These uncommon adventures have been a blast, and I couldn't imagine sharing these moments with anyone else.

While these experiences serve as wonderful memory makers, they pale in comparison to the satisfaction Danette and I feel as we strive to accomplish the important things in life. Indeed, raising our children, developing meaningful friendships, serving people, and advancing the Gospel have generated greater joy than we could have ever imagined.

I'm sure many of you feel the same way about the important people and passions in your life. But if you are like us, you still feel the world attempting to pull you into its definition of happiness. It's a constant back and forth. Though we're far from perfect, we've discovered that lining up our priorities with God's purpose and plan makes all the difference.

Let go of the world's definition of happiness and find the joy connected to investing in those things that will last forever.

PRAYER: *God, help me today to find joy in eternal pursuits.*

SP

WASKULLY WABBITS

1 Peter 1:7 – *So that your genuine faith, which is more valuable than gold that perishes when tested by fire, may result in praise, glory, and honor when Jesus, the Messiah is revealed.*

I come from a long line of rabbit hunters—specifically my dad who has raised some of the best beagle dogs in his county for years. As he has grown older, he doesn't like to carry a big gun, so he shoots at rabbits with a small .22. My dad is the Clint Eastwood of rabbit hunters.

And then there's me—I hunt with the largest rabbit gun available by law because I'm the Elmer Fudd of rabbit hunters. When the beagles see that I'm going hunting, they get this look on their faces that says, "Great…Mr. Miss is here."

And I miss way more often than more than I connect. When I am off-target, I tend to maximize the difficulty of the shot in my explanations to my dad. "Didn't have a clear shot," or "The rabbit was too far away, so I just tried to throw a Hail Mary shot at it." In other words, I try to cover.

Sometimes, we miss spiritually. In those moments, our honesty helps others grow integrity, as well. It's my nature to cover my flaws. However, it's for God's glory (because it highlights our need for Him) and others' good (because they feel less pressure to be perfect) when I am vulnerable.

PRAYER: *Spirit, thank You for convicting me when I sin, when I miss spiritually. Today, I want to start over again and walk with You. Forgive me for where I have failed and help me to grow in Your power.*

DF

September 23rd

SCARED STRAIGHT

Luke 16:19-28 – *... Lazarus who died and the angels carried him to Abraham's side (Heaven). The rich man also died. In Hell he looked up and saw Abraham far away, with Lazarus by his side. So he called to him, 'Father Abraham, send Lazarus to dip the tip of his finger in water and cool my tongue, because I am in agony in this fire.' Abraham replied, "between us and you is a great chasm, so those who want to go across cannot..."*

I was watching a show called *Beyond Scared Straight* where troubled kids are taken to an actual prison and get "talked to" by the inmates. It's amazing to see their transformation from arrogant youths to being completely intimidated and afraid. At the end of the show, viewers get to see footage of the kids back at home armed with a whole new outlook.

If God, Jesus, and Heaven are real, then Hell is also real. Thinking about the reality of Hell and all that it entails can actually give us a better perspective on our lives.

If you are unsure of your eternal destiny, invite Christ into your heart. If you are concerned for another, encourage him or her to receive Christ. Your words may change someone's eternity.

PRAYER: *Father, thank You for rescuing me from a horrible torment. Use me to lead others to Your gift of Heaven by putting their faith in Christ.*

CJ

GIVE YOUR ATTENTION TO THE WHITEBOARD

1 Chronicles 16:11 – *Look to the Lord and his strength; seek his face always.*

In my first college religion class, the following statement was written on an oversized whiteboard at the front of the lecture hall:

> In quiet moments, worship God.
> In painful moments, trust God.
> In happy moments, praise God.
> In difficult moments, seek God.
> In every moment, thank God.

I can't recall the name of the professor who passed along such worthwhile instructions, but I certainly remember feeling challenged and encouraged by what was written.

We serve a God who is always accessible. He desires to walk with us through every season of life. Be quick to offer Him the praise, the worship, and the thanks He deserves. And when life gets tough, seek His face and trust His strength. He'll always be there for you.

PRAYER: *Father, help me today to focus on You in every circumstance that comes my way. Remind me to call upon You in life's quiet, glorious, and painful moments.*

SP

YOU GOTTA HAVE FAITH

Ephesians 2:8-9 – *For it is by grace you have been saved, through faith—and this is not from yourselves, it is the gift of God—not by works, so that no one can boast.*

Salvation is received by grace and through faith. There are different uses of "faith" in the Bible. Sometimes, it's used with the definite article "the." For instance, Jude 3 says, "contend for *the* faith...." Sometimes, the Bible adds a "your," such as when Jesus said to the Disciples, "Where is *your* faith?" Thirdly, faith is used as an expression of belief, but in Eph. 2, faith is more than just believing facts. It's "actively trusting."

But do you trust Him—when a group of friends are baiting you into a critical, gossip conversation? How about when your spouse is in a bad mood and pushes your buttons to start a fight? Can you actively trust God to defend you, instead of defending yourself?

Maybe you're the favorite/unfavorite kid in the family. You tend to do most things right, but you have a sibling who tends to do most things wrong. And the worse your sibling gets, the more attention, affection, and support he or she receives. You want your parents' approval too, but you never seem to get it. Can you actively trust Jesus for your ultimate approval?

Salvation means that you trust God to do (in you) what you cannot do (in you). It's His work, not our work, so that we can't take the credit—so that we cannot boast.

PRAYER: *God, I don't want to try to take Your place. I'm trusting You to do in me right now what I can't do in me right now. Change me, renew me, and take all of the credit.*

DF

SLOBS

2 Chronicles 3:5-6 – *Solomon paneled the main hall with pine and covered it with fine gold and decorated it with palm tree and chain designs. He adorned the temple with precious stones...*

The Bible reveals that God wanted specific decorations for the beautiful temple that Solomon built. Some say this gorgeous interior is a reflection of the inner beauty that the Father can create in those who receive Christ.

I'm not exactly sure how this temple-decorating thing works, but I do know that appearances do affect people's perception. A sloppy house and unkempt attire may not affect how God sees us, but it does affect how others look at us. For instance, I've walked into big houses in expensive neighborhoods where the owners had stuff laying around everywhere—what a mess!

When I was out on my own for the first time, I was a growing Christian who wanted to be a positive influence. Unfortunately, I was one of those "slobs." A wise man talked to me about how my dirty apartment and messy attire affected how I was perceived by others, including others I wanted to help. While having fancy décor in my apartment wasn't going to happen, having a clean and organized home made me feel better and helped others not be tempted to discard me.

PRAYER: *Father, help me to be grateful for and take care of the possessions You have given me.*

CJ

FASHION, FAME, AND FORTUNE

1 Peter 4:10 – *Each of you should use whatever gift you have received to serve others, as faithful stewards of God's grace in its various forms.*

Diane was an up-and-coming fashion designer. She had a top-tier job in one of New York's premier fashion houses. She had money, notoriety, and the admiration of her colleagues—she was living the dream.

One day without notice, Diane walked into her creative director's studio and informed him that she was leaving. The decision shocked her co-workers and left her friends speechless. Diane was wildly successful, and those closest to her couldn't believe she was walking away from it all.

A month later, Diane was working on the mission field in the remote, jungle villages of South America. She had traded fame and fortune for the opportunity to roll up her sleeves and serve others. Her faith in Jesus was real, and though her friends didn't understand, she desired to make an eternal impact on people's lives.

Is God calling you to serve Him today? Are you willing to abandon everything in order to pursue His purpose for your life? Consider letting go of the trappings of this world and using your gifts and abilities to make a difference in the lives of others.

PRAYER: *God, help me today to see Your calling on my life. Help me to care less about my personal gain and more about Your people.*

SP

SEALED WITH A KISS

Ephesians 1:13 – *...you were marked in him with a seal, the promised Holy Spirit...*

In the 1940s, Flora Klein showed promise as a make-up artist at the age of fourteen. An older, influential woman recognized Flora's talent. Flora did the lady's make-up daily, making the older woman feel unique and special, covering her minor flaws.

Her problem—Flora was a prisoner of the Third Reich.

The older lady's husband was the Commandant of the concentration camp that held Flora, her mother, and her aunt. Sadly, Flora's family members fell prey to Hitler's extermination orders. However, Flora's talent kept her from meeting the same fate.

After the war, Flora came to America, married and had a son, Eugene. He shared Flora's creative gifts in cosmetics. He also possessed some of the passionate flaws that can accompany artistic gifts. Still, Eugene showed a unique work ethic that matched his creative abilities. He sold his small make-up company in his late twenties for $10 million to pursue his first love—music. Actually, he brought music and make-up together.

See, when Flora Klein came to the United States and married, she became Flora Simmons. And her son, Eugene Simmons, brought his unique brand of artistry in music and make-up to create the band KISS.

As a Christian, God's Spirit has sealed you for eternity. And, just like Flora and Eugene, God has also given you many gifts and talents. You can leverage that security and those gifts for your own Kingdom or God's Kingdom.

PRAYER: *God, help me today to live from this reality that my future, my eternity, is secure with you. Your Spirit is proof of Your life in me. Spirit, please empower my gifts for Your glory and not my own.*

DF

PUNCHED IN THE EMOTIONAL FACE

Psalm 147:3, 5 – *He heals the brokenhearted and binds up their wounds...His understanding has no limit.*

We all go through times of heartbreak and disappointment, and those wounds can create loneliness, discouragement, and hopelessness. Life can hurt, and it can feel like we're being "punched right in the nose" of our emotions.

The challenge is to not just try to escape the pain. Instead, we need to confront it. Sure, we may have those key people whom we can go to for comfort or advice. But going to our all-powerful yet intimate God is the key to true healing. That is where we find true comfort. As today's verse tells, us, "His understanding has no limit."

I recall a time of my getting hurt deeply by someone. Confused and empty, I decided to go for a car ride with God. That drive was a huge breakthrough for me. I talked aloud to God and poured out my heart. Then, I simply listened.

Over the years, this type of communication with my all-understanding God grew my relationship with Him to another level. I even would have fantastic counseling sessions with Him over dinner at Pizza Hut (I didn't talk aloud there, as Mr. Hut and the waitresses would think I had flipped out).

PRAYER: *Lord, remind me to go to You first with my hurts. Thank You that You completely understand and completely care.*

CJ

OPEN ARMS

Luke 15:32 – *But we had to celebrate and be glad, because this brother of yours was dead and is alive again; he was lost and is found.*

Several years ago, a husband and wife spoke to me about their twenty-five-year-old daughter who had turned her back on the Lord. Their daughter's poor choices broke their hearts, and to make matters worse, they had not seen her in over a year.

The more we talked, the more I was moved by the couple's unconditional love for their daughter. And though they spoke of their daughter's missteps, they spoke even more of their love for her. The mother told me how she meticulously counted each day that her daughter was gone. Furthermore, the father spoke of how he routinely sat on the front porch, hoping to see her drive up the gravel lane.

Within a few months of our conversation, the young lady returned home after living for more than a year as a prodigal daughter. Her parents welcomed her home with open arms. Today, she is walking with Jesus.

Make no mistake about it; the best course of action is to avoid living like a prodigal. However, if you find yourself broken by the despair of your sin, know that you can return home. Pick yourself up, turn from your sin, and run to Jesus. You are forgiven.

PRAYER: *Father, today I turn from my sin and return to You. Thank You for the chance to come home—for welcoming me with open arms.*

SP

THE DEVIL MADE ME DO IT

2 Peter 1:3 – *His divine power has given us everything we need for a godly life through our knowledge of him who called us by his own glory and goodness.*

Today's title was made famous by comedian Flip Wilson. He created a pastor's wife character, who was routinely forced by the devil to spend money frivolously. The tough part about explaining the existence of evil is not just that you see God's enemies at work in the world, but you also see it in yourself.

Our typical explanation for that is something such as, "Well, people have bad things happen to them, so they do bad things." Basically, evil is a product of evil. Here's the problem with that—a child at three months old cries shrill sobs of despair in his or her little crib, so the parent rushes in and picks the child up! And the child smiles.

What just happened? At three months old, that child just manipulated their parents. Who taught that child to lie? Nobody. You and I come into this world "sin included." Part of Christian doctrine is depravity—that even though we want to do what's right at times, we are built to do what's wrong.

All of that said, the Bible is clear that we have everything we need to grow in Christ. So, we can't blame the evil outside of us or the sin inside of us. We have the power and the love of God to apply to our lives right now.

PRAYER: *Jesus, I want to apply Your Cross, Your love, Your example to my life in this moment. I don't want to wait until later today, tomorrow, or next week. I believe that now is the time for me to grow spiritually.*

DF

I WANT TO BE A STAR

Philippians 2:14-15 – *Do everything without complaining or arguing, so that you may become pure children of God, living in a crooked and depraved generation, shining like stars in the universe.*

As we go through the day, listen to all of the complaining and grumbling. Not many seem to be content, and not many spend much time looking at the other side's point of view.

Why? Because it feels good to gripe and paint ourselves as the expert.

On my first real job after college I was pulled aside by my boss who was a respected and wise man. Graciously, he pointed out that I came across to others as if I "had all the answers." He advised me to take on a "healthy self-doubt."

As I talk with others, I need to ask myself, "Could I be wrong here? Could I be misunderstanding the whole picture? Could there be a variable I'm missing? What are they really trying to say to me?"

So outside of the essentials, such as faith in Jesus being the only way to salvation, I've become much more thoughtful and open to others' points of view. Not surprisingly, it has boosted my social skills.

PRAYER: *Heavenly Father, I want to shine in this dark generation by not complaining and arguing. Give me understanding, tact, and compassion as I interact with others.*

CJ

STOP COUNTING SHEEP

Philippians 4:6 – *Do not be anxious about anything, but in every situation, by prayer and petition, with thanksgiving, present your requests to God.*

Steve couldn't sleep. Financial difficulties, job worries, and parenting concerns consumed his heart and mind. For one reason or another, tonight was worse than normal, and he couldn't turn off his brain. He tried reading, listening to white noise, and counting sheep—nothing seemed to work.

By 2:30 in the morning, Steve was miserable, and his tossing and turning had interrupted his wife's rest. Understanding the stress her husband was under, she rolled toward him and said, "If you can't sleep, stop counting sheep and talk to the Shepherd."

Truth be told, we have all probably lost way too much sleep worrying about tomorrow. When we are overwhelmed, it is important to remember that peace is a byproduct of prayer. When we speak to God, we enter into the presence of One who comforts and calms. He looks forward to hearing about our worries and concerns. Furthermore, He desires to fill us with His peace.

PRAYER: *God, help me let go of my anxious thoughts and turn them over to You. Help me to pray more and worry less. Grant me peace.*

SP

OUR SACRED SECULAR LIFE

Colossians 3:23 – *Whatever you do, work at it with all your heart, as working for the Lord, not for human masters.*

Years ago on a family trip, we made a stop to eat at a Chili's restaurant in Oak Ridge, TN (home of the Oak Ridge Boys, which is totally irrelevant unless you loved the song "Elvira" as much I did). It was my kids' first time to eat at Chili's, and they loved it!

My six-year-old son liked it so much that he said, "Dad, when I grow up, I want to work at Chili's." My sarcastic response was, "Son, you don't know how proud that would make Mom and me."

In the prior year, he had told my wife that he wanted to be a pastor when he grew up, which is my calling. So, after Chili's comment, Angie said, "Well, buddy, what about being a pastor?" He responded, "Well, you don't have to work all of the time to do that—I mean, Sundays I guess."

On average, Americans spend 90,000 hours at work or one-third of their lives. It makes absolutely no sense then to divide what we think is the sacred part of our lives (i.e. Sunday church attendance) from the rest of our lives.

There is no separation for the Christian between the sacred life and the secular life. All of life belongs to our King.

PRAYER: *Father, as I go to work or stay at home to work today, help me to see my work time as Your time. I invite You into my work today. I want to do it for You and with You!*

DF

I SEE YOU; STILL I LOVE YOU

Proverbs 15:3 – *The eyes of the Lord are everywhere, keeping watch on the wicked and the good.*

My college roommate and I pulled continual pranks on each other. One time I was hiding in our dorm room closet to scare him, and I saw him creep into the room. I heard his little chuckles as he was rigging up my bed with clothes hangers and weights (I never did know where he was going with that). Then I jumped out, scaring him as planned.

We tend to act differently if we know we are being watched. We would probably not do those "secret sins" as much. Yet, on the upside, knowing that God is watching helps us to also know He understands exactly what we are going through and is there for us.

Comedian Brian Regan once said, "I would have been a lot better off if I'd studied more when I was growing up. But you know where it all went wrong was the day they started the spelling bee. Because up until that day I was an idiot, but nobody else knew."

God knows us, He watches us, and still He loves us.

PRAYER: *Lord, I know You long to be involved in my life. Thank You that You are patiently watching and waiting for me to confess wrongs and call on You for strength, direction, and comfort.*

CJ

BROKEN BARN DOOR

James 1:22 – *Do not merely listen to the word, and so deceive yourselves. Do what it says.*

The last thing I heard my mom say was, "Be sure to look before you back out of the barn. Sometimes the door rolls back down, and you won't know it—double-check before you back out."

Moments later, I felt the crunch of aluminum against the truck's tailgate and heard the unmistakable sound of our barn door being ripped off its tracks. Unfortunately for me, I had listened to my mother's words but failed to follow them.

As followers of Jesus Christ, we have a two-fold responsibility to God's Word: we are called to be attentive listeners *and* active doers. Of course, it is important to know the precepts and principles of the Bible—to hide the truth of God's Word in our heart. But it doesn't stop there. We must actively practice everything we have learned—choosing to do what the Word of God says.

James 1:22-24 warns us not to deceive yourself into a false sense of spirituality. It's not enough to hear about generosity, evangelism, and the pursuit of righteousness. We have to give our resources, share our faith, and make good choices. Listening and doing are connected to genuine faith. Chase after it today!

PRAYER: *God, remind me today to put my faith into action. Help me take what I know and become an active doer of Your Word.*

SP

October 7th

THE SURVEY SAYS

Matthew 6:5 – *And when you pray, you must not be like the hypocrites. For they love to stand and pray in the synagogues and at the street corners, that they may be seen by others.*

This verse is not politically correct. According to Jesus, there are not different types of prayer—Jewish prayer, Muslim prayer, Hindu prayer, Christian prayer, and so on. He says that there's biblical prayer and everything else.

According to a survey from Lifeway Research, here are the top reasons Americans pray:

1) Friends and family; 2) Personal problems (when 1 and 2 are the same thing, the ranking REALLY goes up); 3) Future prosperity; 4) To win the Lottery (21%); 5) For their favorite team to win a game (13%); 6) To find a really good parking place (7%)

Think about the bottom half of that list. Your odds of hitting the Lottery? 1 in 292,201,338. So, if multiple people are praying this consistently, our "effectual fervent prayers" are not "availing much."

Your only conclusion from reason number five is that the best team must have the best players and the best prayers? I really cannot criticize number six. I have done that!

Jesus says that prayer is not an audition. You don't need to pray loudly. It's not a competition. You don't need to pray proudly. Instead, prayer is an invitation, where the relationship determines the request. Talk to God a lot. Ask Him anything. It will change you. And you just may get a good parking place every now and then.

PRAYER: *Father, today is an opportunity to get to know You minute-by-minute. Help me to go with You and not leave You here at a moment in the morning. I want to talk to You at 12:00pm, just as I do at 8:00am.*

DF

I HATE SHOTS

Isaiah 40:29 – *He gives strength to the weary, and increases the power of the weak.*

Being totally self-sufficient sounds good, but just doesn't work. Try having a close friendship with a person who doesn't accept change and has a "my-way-or-the-highway" personality. It's a recipe for a miserable social life.

As a child, I was in the hospital a lot because of circulation problems. It seemed as though I was always getting shots, and I hated them! However, my mentality was to be tough, so I'd tighten my little butt cheeks (they were little back then) and the nurse would "stab" me and leave. Boy, did it hurt!

Finally, a caring nurse informed me that if I would just relax and not flex, then the needle would easily go in with little pain. I figured her suggestion was worth the try, but it felt as though I was being told to relax while an angry savage threw a spear into my backside.

Yet, it worked. It was a major breakthrough to my most feared enemy—the needle.

The experience helps me to understand that our natural reflex isn't always the best. We need to relax our "self-sufficiency muscle" and allow God to come alongside us.

PRAYER: *Father, I can't do life alone. Remind me continually to ask for Your guidance and power to live effectively.*

CJ

A CONVERSATION WITH LILLY

James 1:12 – *Blessed is the one who perseveres under trial because, having stood the test, that person will receive the crown of life that the Lord has promised to those who love Him.*

Lilly Rutherford passed away at the age of ninety-six. She was a follower of Jesus Christ and a woman of deep faith. Her family and her church admired Lilly's commitment and marveled at her perseverance.

On the day of Lilly's memorial service, hundreds of people gathered to celebrate her life and faith. Recounting her life, the pastor spoke of the fact that Lilly had become a widow at the age of thirty-five. Furthermore, he shared how she had lost her youngest son in Vietnam and her oldest daughter to cancer. The more the pastor shared of Lilly's story, the more it became apparent that her life was full of adversity.

As the pastor closed his message, he described to those assembled his final conversation with Lilly. He had asked her about all the trials and tests. He had also asked her how she'd managed to endure the pain and heartbreak. With a lump in his throat, the pastor shared Lilly's final words to him: "My reward in Heaven is greater than my suffering on earth."

Some will face trials. Others will face testing. God promises a great reward for those who persevere. Lean on the promises of Scripture and approach each challenge with eternity in mind.

PRAYER: *Father, remind me today that You are with me as I face the challenges of this life. Help me to persevere and rest in the hope of Your reward.*

SP

DO YOU HAVE THE RING?

2 Corinthians 5:5 – *Now the one who has fashioned us for this very purpose is God, who has given us the Spirit as a deposit, guaranteeing what is to come.*

This chapter uses a word to refer to believers that meant *immigrant*—someone who is part of one country but resides in another—in the original reader's culture. So, Christians are immigrants from Heaven. Heaven is truly our home country.

As a reminder of our true home, God gave us a "guarantee," or a down payment. That word meant *engagement ring*.

The engagement ring is still part of our culture today. When two people love each other, one person spends an exorbitant amount of money to prove his love by spending his hard-earned cash on a ring. And to prove her love, she receives this ring with joy (if the clarity, color, and size are right).

What does the engagement ring prove? A wedding is on the way.

When I was a kid, my mom made a seven-layer applesauce stack cake from scratch. It was my favorite cake then and still is now. I could walk into the house and smell it—just the aroma—and I knew what it was. My wife makes the cake for me every year on my birthday. When I walk in the house, I know it—the aroma means the cake is right around the corner.

The work of God's Spirit in your life is also a guarantee of what is on the way. In fact, it's a down payment that the best is yet to come.

PRAYER: *Jesus, because of Your love, I believe that this is not all there is—the best is yet to come. I look forward to better days of being with You forever.*

DF

October 11th

I DID IT, AND I WAS WRONG

1 John 1:9 – *If we confess our sins, he is faithful and just and will forgive us our sins and purify us from all unrighteousness.*

As a high school principal, it was very important for me to ask students who were sent to my office, "What did you do wrong?" If the students gave excuses and made things up, I'd ask again, "What did you do wrong?" If they started the confession with, "I guess I..." I then would say, "Please don't guess. Just tell me what you did wrong." I also made sure the students knew that this honest confession was more important than avoiding the consequences.

Now, I'm not sure if God works exactly in the same way, but I do know that it was priceless to see the relief on the students' faces who confessed their specific offenses. I always praised them for their courage, and they received a lesser punishment. There is power in confession.

PRAYER: *Heavenly Father, help me to have the courage to confess without excuses and admit my specific wrongs. Thank You for the freedom and change that develops when I do. In Jesus' name. Amen.*

CJ

DEAR GOD

Isaiah 61:10 – *For he has clothed me with garments of salvation and arrayed me in a robe of his righteousness...*

Dear God,

Today I put my faith and trust in Your Son, Jesus. And in the blink of an eye, everything has changed.

I have been handed a robe of righteousness—a covering for my sin. It's like nothing I have ever felt or experienced before. The righteousness of Your Son has been credited to my account. It's as though I never sinned. I am not worthy of such grace and mercy.

Jesus, Your righteousness has been given to me, and my sin has been given to You. You allowed Yourself to become sin so that I might be declared righteousness.

Jesus, You allowed Yourself to be sacrificed. I know it cost You everything. Your horrific death on the cross paid the debt of my sin. Your suffering paid the penalty my sin deserves. Your misery clothed me in this eternal robe of righteousness. I can never thank You enough.

PRAYER: *Father, today I thank You for Your Son, Jesus. Help me to walk worthy of His righteousness.*

SP

October 13th

FATHER KNOWS BEST

Romans 8:15 – *The Spirit you received brought about your adoption to sonship. And by Him we cry, "Abba, Father."*

The great theologian Jim Gaffigan once said, "You want to know what it's like having a fourth kid? Imagine you're drowning, then someone hands you a baby."

Sometimes we project onto God what we see in our earthly fathers. In the process, we make God out to be a version of the common father, whom we've experienced.

As a result, "colonel god" demands perfection, because he is keeping score—not to mention that we should salute when he approaches. You may get a medal or a dishonorable discharge. "Grandpa god" is just the opposite. Even though he is a little slow and hard of hearing, he will get you whatever you want. Not very off is "Obi-Wan Kenobi god." He's kind of impersonal, maybe a "higher power" out there. But for sure, he doesn't have a name, and we certainly can't know who he is. He is a force in a galaxy far, far away.

It's interesting that the Bible knows nothing of these portrayals. Rather, God is a perfect, heavenly Father who loves you exactly as you are. And He loves you too much to leave you the way you are. He's not formal, but He is holy. He's not a pushover, but He is compassionate. He's never far, far away, because He is always near.

PRAYER: *God, You are right here with me today. You're present every second. Help me to see You, listen to You, and follow wherever You lead.*

DF

October 14th

GPS

Psalm 32:8 – *I will instruct you and teach you in the way you should go; I will counsel you and watch over you.*

GPS devices were made with people like me in mind. I get lost just pulling out of my own driveway. There was even a time I entered onto a freeway from a two-lane road, and the next thing I know, I'm in a parking lot.

Wouldn't it be great to have a GPS to navigate us through our daily lives? We just plug in our question, and it tells us what to do and think.

"What job should I pursue?" "What did my wife really mean when she told me she didn't need my help on a project?" "What is my boss thinking?" "What was I thinking?!" "Why are they mad at me?" "What do I need to change about dealing with people?" "How can I help others and not be so selfish?"

The truth is that God wants to be our instructor, teacher, counselor, and overseer. We just need to continually ask! We must also continually look for wisdom and answers in the Bible, from wise advisers, and from our circumstances.

PRAYER: *Father, remind me to keep asking and to keep seeking.*

CJ

JUST THINKING

SPEECHLESS

Romans 8:26 – *In the same way, the Spirit helps us in our weakness. We do not know what we ought to pray for, but the Spirit himself intercedes for us through wordless groans.*

A few years back, I found myself sitting on a modestly crafted chair under a massive shade tree in the middle of a remote village in Malawi. To my left sat one of our ministry's pastors, on my right was one of our translators, and in front of me was a man whose heart was broken.

The day before, he had buried his wife of sixteen years. The depth of his sorrow was written on his face and heard in his voice. The widower expressed concern over the fact that he sometimes tried to pray but found himself speechless before the Lord. For the next hour, I listened as our ministry pastor offered comfort and tried to help this grieving man see that God knew his heart.

When we are weak and don't know the words to pray, we have One who takes over and speaks on our behalf. In moments of sorrow and trouble, when we can't articulate our thoughts and our needs, the Holy Spirit intercedes for us. Rest in His work.

Trust the Holy Spirit's work and know that God hears you when you are unsure of your next word.

PRAYER: *God, I thank You today for the work of the Holy Spirit in my life.*

SP

ON THE MENU

Psalm 34:8 – *Taste and see that the Lord is good; blessed is the one who takes refuge in him.*

In the Old Testament, God established Cities of Refuge as places where people could run for safety and justice. These cities both served the people of Israel and were also a foreshadow of Christ being our Refuge.

Because of the extent of God's grace, humans have an amazing capacity to feel entitled to God's maximum blessing, while simultaneously offering back to God the minimum levels of our time, talent, and treasure.

What if I walked into the house and said to my wife, "I want you to know that I am making a commitment to talk to you for five minutes every day. When we talk, I am going to tell you what I need from you and what you can do for me that day. After these five minutes of conversation, we will not speak anymore throughout the day...unless I need something."

Some men are reading this right now and thinking, "What's the problem with that? What's the illustration—I don't get it."

We don't come to God to get him to shake the Blessing Tree for us. We come to Him because we have tasted and seen with our own lives that He is our good Refuge.

PRAYER: *God, I am coming to You today because You have shepherded me as a Father, died for my sins in the person of Jesus, and filled me with Your presence in the person of the Spirit. You are the Refuge to which I run!*

DF

October 17th

ANKLE WEIGHTS

Luke 6:27-28 – *Love your enemies, do good to those who hate you…*
pray for those who mistreat you.

Are you kidding! Is this a misprint in the Bible? "Do good to those
who hate you?"

As a high school athlete, I was trying to get faster, and using ankle
weights was the big craze at the time. You basically tied lead bars
around your ankles and ran around like a crazy man.

There are probably safer methods, but when I took those babies off,
I felt as if I were floating. That's how I see today's verse. It's about
getting better by doing something that is harder, or "heavier," than
what we are used to.

Care about an enemy, do good to a hater, or pray for someone who
messes with us. This will increase who we are as a people and also
increase our dependence on God. We will be doing something that
doesn't come "naturally;" rather, it has to happen "supernaturally."

This can be challenging even with a loved one, especially after
being mistreated or frustrated by one. In fact, this can be the most
difficult time to apply this verse!

PRAYER: *Father, bring names into my head of people who are hard to
pray and do good for. I need Your strength and perspective. Thank You
for the blessings that will follow.*

CJ

VARSITY BLUES

Matthew 6:33 – *But seek first his Kingdom and his righteousness, and all these things will be given to you as well.*

My flight was almost ready to board, and still, I decided to stop and purchase a chili cheese dog from The Varsity in Atlanta's airport. I simply could not deny my taste buds the experience of such a culinary masterpiece.

There is nothing dignified about hustling through the airport with a hot dog in your mouth. Nevertheless, I was relieved to reach my gate in time. Unfortunately, a few minutes after boarding the aircraft, my stomach started to rumble. At that moment, I fully realized the error of my ways.

While humorous now, this ridiculous story illustrates how foolish it is to prioritize the temporary over the important. And though we don't always think about it, we face decisions every day that reveal whether we're interested in the temporal or committed to the eternal.

Spiritually speaking, we are called to let go of earthly pursuits and replace them with spiritual priorities. God desires that we chase after that which is important to Him—His Word, service to others, and the Gospel. At the same time, He promises to provide for those who are obedient much more than we could ever imagine. Seek Him first, and He'll provide the rest!

PRAYER: *God, help me today to pursue You and make Your priorities my priority.*

SP

NO SPEEDING

Psalm 23:1 – *The Lord is my shepherd, I lack nothing.*

God is my Shepherd and I am His sheep. It sounds comforting—but only if you really believe that YOU are a sheep.

Sheep are not dynamic creatures. What was the last movie you remember about a dynamic lamb? Dogs have Lassie…horses have Seabiscuit…mice have Jerry…dolphins have Flipper…spiders—even SPIDERS—have Charlotte, but sheep? Nothing. Nada.

Actually, sheep are great followers. They follow a shepherd, or they follow the herd. If the sheep leading the pack walks across a street in front of oncoming traffic, they will all take the same walk.

Because people are like sheep, we have the tendency to follow the herd, particularly when it comes to busyness. However, hurry is not a substitute for intimacy. Just because everyone else lives fast does not mean that you have to live at the same pace. It's not a schedule issue; it's a heart issue. Life has appropriate speed limits, but I'm afraid of slowing down because someone may pass me.

In one week of my life, I turned thirty-three and negotiated a deal on a minivan on the same day. I felt as though I was one step from mowing the lawn in shorts and black dress socks. Life goes by so quickly, so I guess your options are that you can slow down OR crash.

PRAYER: *Father, thank You for being MY Shepherd. Today, I want to follow You wherever You lead, instead of trying to lead You where I think is best. I trust that You have what is best for my life.*

DF

JESUS IS DROPPING BY TO CHAT

Psalm 5:3 – *Morning by morning, I lay my requests before You and wait in expectation.*

Prayer is actually communicating with the God of the universe. But sometimes we just throw our "requests" into the air out of habit or for good luck. When praying with others, we tend to say words that we think will impress or, at least, not make us sound bad (It's kind of like comedian Brian Regan says: "I'm just trying to go through life without looking stupid.")

I asked some college students what they'd do if Jesus Himself walked through the door, put His arm around you, and said, "What can I do for you today? How can I help?" Their eyes lit up with expectation because they could picture their prayers being heard by the living Deity who can and will act.

The Bible tells us to pray in just that way. He is really right beside us, listening.

PRAYER: *Heavenly Father, thank You that You are at my side listening and desiring to work for me, through me, and in spite of me. In Jesus' name I pray. Amen.*

CJ

October 21st

GATE CHANGE GRATITUDE

Proverbs 16:9 – *In their hearts humans plan their course, but the Lord establishes their steps.*

Due to a last-minute gate change, I was now sprinting through the airport. At one point, I hurdled a stroller and sidestepped a man carrying two Auntie Anne's pretzels. I reached the gate just in time to see the plane backing away from the jetway.

Furious, I pulled out my phone and booked myself on the next flight. Walking to my new gate, I bumped into an old friend from college. We talked for a while, and he told me about his marriage struggles. Before he boarded his plane, I had the chance to pray with him. Walking away, he said, "Hey, I'm glad I ran into you. I needed that."

This crazy airport experience reminded me that God is sovereign and has the right to alter my plans to accomplish His goals and objectives. My job is to relax and trust His decisions.

It's good to make plans. Just be flexible when God steps in and makes a minor or major adjustment. It may not always feel like it, but He has your best interest at heart. If you can trust Him for your eternal home in Heaven, you can trust Him with your momentary plans on earth.

PRAYER: *God, help me today to welcome Your interruptions and find joy in Your purpose.*

SP

I FORGET

Revelation 2:4b – *You have left your first love.*

My wife and I have some friends named Austin and Sophia. For their wedding, they had written their own vows, which they planned to recite to each other from memory. It was right out of a Hallmark movie. The plan was that each of them would give a copy of their vows to the officiant in case the emotion of the moment was overwhelming.

If you watch their wedding video, there was a song right before the vows, and you can see Sophia asking the pastor for her copy of the vows. Then, you can see the pastor shaking his head at her to say that she never gave him a copy.

It would have been better if Austin would have stuttered through his vows, perhaps missed or confused a few words. But he didn't. He quoted those beautiful vows like a professional orator. Then, it was Sophia's turn.

A deer staring into bright headlights had a better chance of survival than she did of remembering those vows. But the show must go on, so she made them up on the fly. Sophia looks at him and begins, "Austin (long pause)…I just love you…."

Sometimes, it's easier to do ministry for God than remain in love with God. Don't forget your first love.

PRAYER: *Father, forgive me for taking You for granted as though You need me. I love You because You love me first…created me…died for my sins…and have promised me an eternal home.*

DF

BE A FOUND NEMO

Matthew 18:12 – *If a man owns a hundred sheep, and one of them wanders away, will he not leave the ninety-nine on the hills and go to look for the one that wandered off?*

In today's verse, Jesus is explaining God's personalized love for every one of us, and this parable of the lost sheep reminds me of the popular movie *Finding Nemo*.

Finding Nemo is an animated story of a father fish who has lost his son, Nemo. During the film, the dad sets out to bring his son back home to safety, and he risks his life over and over for his missing offspring. Because of the father's unfailing love, he was willing to die before he would give up his hunt!

Sometimes we feel as though God is this impersonal deity in the sky who is too busy to be bothered. On the contrary! He not only cares about us, but He also longs to come alongside us as we attempt to tackle our most intimate issues, desires, and needs.

PRAYER: *Lord, I want You to be my Lord and friend. Thank You that You yearn to have me back when I stray. Remind me to let You in on my most intimate concerns, dreams, and feelings.*

CJ

WORTH PASSING ALONG

Ephesians 1:3 – *Praise be to the God and Father of our Lord Jesus Christ, who has blessed us in the heavenly realms with every spiritual blessing.*

The ministry I lead has a secondary school (high school) in Malawi. Once a year, I'm privileged to speak to the two hundred wonderful students and twelve remarkable teachers who make our school thrive.

In 2016, while visiting the campus, I noticed the following list beautifully written on the chalkboard in one of the classrooms. It encouraged my soul, and I believe it's worth passing along:

I Am
I Am Chosen - 1 Thessalonians 1:4
I Am A Child Of God - John 1:12
I Am A New Creation - 2 Corinthians 5:17
I Am One In Christ - John 17:21
I Am The Temple Of The Holy Spirit - 1 Corinthians 6:19
I Am A Citizen Of Heaven - Philippians 3:20
I Am Forgiven Of My Sins - Ephesians 1:7
I Am Fearfully And Wonderfully Made - Psalm 139:14
I Am Redeemed - Galatians 3:13
I Am Set Free - John 8:32

As Christians, we are blessed with eternal riches. Remembering who we are and what we have in Jesus Christ brings hope. Take time today to dwell on God's goodness.

PRAYER: *God, I praise You and thank You today for Your love.*

SP

TRUTH, THE TALIBAN, AND TAPEWORMS

John 3:3 – *Jesus replied, "Very truly I tell you, no one can see the kingdom of God unless they are born again..."*

Big moments are the culmination of small faithfulness. In 2000, a young lady named Heather went to serve as a vocational missionary in Afghanistan. The Taliban seized their offices in 2001 because they heard that sixteen Afghans had become Christians. Heather and her co-worker Dayna were kidnapped by the Taliban and held for over three months.

Heather recalls one night in a prison where she felt as though she had a cold and coughed uncontrollably. She awakened the next morning to realize she had coughed up an eighteen-inch tapeworm.

Most of us want the talk show interview, but few of us are willing to go to prison. In the same way, religion rarely leads to authenticity. Let me offend your religion for a minute. If you're Baptist, walking down an aisle won't save you. If you are Catholic, keeping the sacraments won't save you. If you are Methodist or Lutheran, going to confirmation classes doesn't mean you are a Christian. If you are Nazarene, keeping all the rules doesn't get you into Heaven. If you are Pentecostal or charismatic, having an emotional experience doesn't mean you are a believer.

God's Word says that you "must be born again." Check out Appendix I of this book if you are ready to take that step.

PRAYER: *Father, thank You for salvation that You have so graciously provided in Jesus. Jesus is MY way, My truth, and MY life. I'm eternally grateful that You have made me new!*

DF

BE MY PERSONAL TRAINER

Romans 15:5 – *May the God who gives endurance and encouragement give you the same attitude of mind toward each other that Christ Jesus had.*

Once I watched a show about overweight teenagers, and every kid received a personal trainer.

One girl who weighed 263 pounds had an outstanding trainer. He gave her clear guidelines while also verbally pushing and encouraging her. He said things such as, "You can do this...I know it's hard, but you will break through...I'm so proud of you...It's okay that you failed today because we'll start over...You'll be so glad you kept going...You are important...."

Notice that his approach wasn't negative. He never uttered the words, "This is why you're so fat...Let's go...What's wrong with you?" I'm sure the girl received plenty of that harshness from her own self-talk.

In the end, she lost 79 pounds and was so glad that she'd allowed this guy to impact her life. When God "trains" us, He is very much like this positive trainer. Tapping into His power and perspective gives us the much needed "endurance and encouragement" for living.

PRAYER: *Lord, remind me to continually depend on Your endurance and encouragement. Train me in life. Thank You for the amazing blessings that will follow.*

CJ

October 27th

JULIET'S GLORY

2 Corinthians 4:17 – *For our light and momentary troubles are achieving for us an eternal glory that far outweighs them all.*

Juliet felt overwhelmed. In the last two months, her husband received a cancer diagnosis, and she lost her job at the bank. Struggling to get through each day, Juliet felt like everyone and everything was working against her. She wondered why God would allow her circumstances to become so difficult and painful.

As she had done so many times before, Juliet turned to God's Word for hope. Searching Scripture, she found both hope and perspective.

As Christians, it is important to remember that God is not working against us when we face trials and troubles. God's perspective is not our perspective, and where we see a struggle, He sees eternal glory for you. God constantly weighs the temporary against the everlasting, and He always has your eternal best in mind.

When we suffer, God empathizes with us. At the same time, He allows us to experience momentary trials to increase our eternal glory. The idea here is that as you overcome trials and suffering, your eternal glory increases. It's not always easy to accept this truth in the midst of trouble. However, it should encourage our souls to know that our eternal glory will ultimately outweigh our temporary trials.

PRAYER: *Father, give me strength today to endure hardship. Help me see my suffering through Your eyes. Come quickly.*

SP

GETTING YOUR EXERCISE

2 Timothy 1:6a – *For this reason I remind you to fan into flame the gift of God.*

Two of my friends, Kelly and Marc, and I coached our sons in a flag football league. The league was for first through third graders. In talking about the league, we knew our coaching/motivational skills. We thought of ourselves as Belichick, Parcells, and Lombardi.

Our team had no third graders, more first graders than second graders, and only two of our kids had ever played prior to the season. At one point in the year, we were 0-5, we hadn't scored a touchdown, and we had only made two defensive stops—in the whole season.

In all of my years of kids' sports coaching, I had never gotten a call from the league director because of how badly my team was playing. However, the league director did call me to ask if we needed help! The league saw us more as Mo, Larry, and Curly than Belichick, Brady, and Lombardi.

When the league director asked if we needed help, my response was, "Yeah, we'd like a couple of lightning fast third graders." The other teams were better because their boys were older and had exercised their gifts. Today is an opportunity to exercise your gifts. You will get better the more you train.

PRAYER: *Father, thank You that You have gifted me. I want to serve Your Kingdom and make a difference in Your name. Empower me by Your grace.*

DF

BE PLAY-DO

2 Corinthians 4:16 – *…inwardly we are being renewed day by day.*

One day I was watching a movie where actor Paul Rudd was trying to make Reese Witherspoon swoon. In order to do so, he gives her a small canister of Play-Doh as a birthday gift and explains that he has kept this for years as a reminder of how life can work out.

He continues to melt her heart with the story of how Play-Doh was originally invented with the purpose of cleaning wallpaper. The inventors were going out of business until they tweaked the product and sold it as a toy for kids. Instantly, the company made millions.

His character's point was to tell his love interest that she is an amazing woman who is just going through some hard times and is just a few "tweaks" away from being where she needs to be.

God has made each of us unique and special. Now He longs to make some slight "tweaks" to give us a more fulfilled life as we begin to look more and more like Christ.

PRAYER: *Lord, point out my much-needed adjustments with relationships, in what I do, with how I view daily life, and especially with who I am. I can't do life on my own.*

CJ

LET IT RIP

Job 12:12 – *Is not wisdom found among the aged? Does not long life bring understanding?*

I ski with pretty good pace and precision. However, my children are insanely fast on their snowboards. Several years ago, on a beautiful day in Breckenridge, we decided to race.

Getting off the lift, I knew that if I were to beat either of them, I would have to let it rip. So, I did. One-third of the way down, we were neck and neck. By the halfway point, they started to pull away, and my skis began to shake violently. It was decision time. Should I put the hammer down and try to catch them, or should I let up and survive the run? The fact that I am alive and well today should serve as an indicator of my decision.

I desperately wanted to show my children that their dad could still fly down the slopes, so I certainly did not enjoy coming to grips with my age that day. However, there was something satisfying about tapping into a pocket of wisdom that probably kept me from leaving Colorado with a concussion and broken leg.

Getting older isn't always fun. Gaining wisdom, on the other hand, is priceless. Tap into it and pass it along to others.

PRAYER: *God, help me today to exercise the wisdom You have provided over the years.*

SP

BLESSED DISOBEDIENCE

1 John 3:1 – *See what great love the Father has lavished on us, that we should be called children of God! And that is what we are!*

Every parent/teacher/coach asks at some point, "Am I a good coach? A good teacher? Should God have allowed me to reproduce? I feel like a terrible parent. Just look at my kid!"

What only makes that feeling worse is that we inevitably run into another parent who says, "Your daughter was at our house recently. She is so easy-going…easy to talk with…it's like talking to an adult!" The parent is thinking, "You've got the wrong kid."

Or someone will say, "Your son spent the night at our house last week." You are awaiting the laundry list of corruption that your son brought into their home. What comes next? "Your son has such great manners. He takes his dishes to the sink…looks me in the eye when he talks to me…what a great kid!"

When I was eighteen, my dad said to me, "You're going to be amazed at how much smarter I get in the next six years."

He was right, per usual. Our kids often give us, their parents/ teachers/coaches, their worst and save their best for everyone else. At times, I wonder if God ever sees us in the same way.

He's our perfect Heavenly Father. But do we give Him our best or save it for other people and our own personal interests?

PRAYER: *Father, I want to give You my best today. You deserve it. You died on the Cross for me, so I want to live for You. Grant me the grace to give You first place in my life.*

DF

BOO!

Deuteronomy 31:6 – *Be strong and courageous. Do not be afraid or terrified because of them, for the LORD your God goes with you; He will never leave you nor forsake you.*

An old German proverb states, "Fear makes the wolf bigger than he is."

When I was a young kid, my older sister would often tell me scary things about the night so that I would snuggle in bed with her (I guess I was cute at one point in my life). Needless to say, I grew up being terrified of the dark, as my young mind would imagine all of the dangerous possibilities that loomed about.

To be honest, my fears were paralyzing. It wasn't until I accepted Christ at college that I could start to cope with the dark. We all have fears that can paralyze us to some degree: rejection, taking risks, talking to new people, being without a friend nearby, losing loved ones, death, making a mistake, clowns, running out of money, and the list goes on and on.

How are we to deal with our fears? There's an old saying that can help us: "Feed your faith and your fears will starve to death."

PRAYER: *Lord, make me* strong and courageous. *Hold my hand as my Friend and Protector as I face and work through my fears.*

CJ

INCOMPLETE AND EMPTY

Colossians 2:8 – *See to it that no one takes you captive through hollow and deceptive philosophy, which depends on human tradition and the elemental spiritual forces of this world rather than on Christ.*

Several years ago, I met a man named Michael. Despite having everything he needed and most of what he wanted, his heart wasn't satisfied. He was searching for answers to profound philosophical, societal, and spiritual questions.

Hollywood, mainstream media, and elite educators only offered abstract and agnostic answers. By ignoring spiritual matters, their solutions seemed incomplete and empty to Michael. He was looking for something greater than human traditions and ancient philosophy. By his own account, he was searching for faith.

Serious thoughts rattle around the brains of men and women everywhere. The deep questions of life and hope are embedded in their hearts and souls. And while the world tries to prove otherwise, we know the answers to these questions are rooted in Jesus Christ and are discoverable in Scripture.

As Christians, we encounter people every day who are searching for something to believe in. They seek truth, peace, love, and purpose. We know the source and have the answers. It's our job to set aside the world's empty response, share the truth, and point them toward Jesus Christ.

PRAYER: *God, help me be aware of the seekers around me today and give me the opportunity to point them toward Jesus.*

SP

YOUR HUMILITY FILTER

James 4:6 – *God opposes the proud, but shows favor to the humble...*

In Proverbs 3, James 4, and 1 Peter 5, God says, "I will Heisman stiff-arm the proud, and welcome the humble." Okay, that's my translation, but the Bible gives us the same verse three different times. Why is humility so important?

Andrew Murray defines humility as saying to God, "I need you." Pride is humility's enemy.

After owning our first home for a year, my wife Angie came to me and confessed that she was struggling to keep our house clean. No matter how much she dusted, there always seemed to be a dirty film on our furniture. So, I thought I could give her some pointers on proper dusting techniques—husband fail #1.

After mentioning this to my dad, he asked how long it had been since I changed my furnace filter. I responded, "There's a furnace filter?" Husband fail #2. Oddly, I still have that dirty filter wrapped in a garbage bag in my basement to remind me about humility and pride.

I believe the reason the Bible calls us to humility using the same verse not once, not twice, but three times is that humility should filter everything that comes into our lives. If not, our lives will be covered with pride, and God will hold us at arm's length.

PRAYER: *God, I need You today. I don't want to succeed in my own strength. I know that is only a set up for a greater failure. I don't want success without You.*

DF

THE DIVINE DAMP HEATED CLOTH

Psalm 19:12 – *Who can discern their own errors? Forgive my hidden faults.*

I once got a staph infection and applied ice to calm the pain. However, the cold pushed the infection deeper into my body. One hospital stay and one month later, I was able to function almost normally again. A nurse later told me that if I'd put damp heat on it, I would have avoided all these complications because the infection is drawn toward the heat.

We can also have "infections" in our thinking, actions, or words. Ignoring these errors and hidden faults is like applying ice to the infection: it drives it deeper into our spirit, causing more serious problems or even death to our character.

On the other hand, bringing these flaws to light by confessing them to God and continually asking Him to help us confront them is like applying the damp, heated cloth. The infection comes to the surface and leaves our body, so we can experience life to its fullest.

PRAYER: *Lord, help me to confront and confess and not ignore the "infections." Bring them to the surface and heal me. Convince me that it's worth cleaning out our pet sins.*

CJ

GLORY DAYS

Philippians 3:13-14 – *Forgetting what is behind and straining toward what is ahead, I press on toward the goal to win the prize...*

When I thumb through middle school or high school yearbooks from the 1980s, I cringe a little. Actually, I cringe a lot. Acid-washed jeans, parachute pants, and shoulder pads were all the rage. Girls had big hair, boys had bad hair, and rock-n-roll bands had a combination of both.

All kidding aside, I enjoyed being a teenager in the 80s. I have a lot of fond memories from high school, and I genuinely appreciate the people who invested in my life when I was younger. I believe it was Bruce Springsteen who referred to these formative years as our "Glory Days."

Truth be told, we all look in the rearview mirror from time to time. The danger of spending too much time looking backward is that you can get stuck living in the past. Spiritually speaking, if we are not careful, we end up basking in the glory of our past victories and wallowing in the guilt of our previous failures. Both activities have the power to keep us from building our faith today.

Let go of the past, live in the present, and press toward a vibrant and growing relationship with Jesus Christ.

PRAYER: *Jesus, help me pursue and serve You today with the same passion and enthusiasm I had when I first came to faith.*

SP

THE SCRAMBLE

2 Corinthians 5:14 – *For Christ's love compels us, because we are convinced that one died for all, and therefore all died.*

My golf tension is: 1) I really like to golf periodically and 2) When I golf only periodically, I don't like it anymore by the sixth hole. However, there's an answer to this dilemma—the Scramble.

In case you are not familiar with the Scramble, a group (most often a foursome) picks the best shot of the group—for EVERY shot. So, that effectively eliminates all of my bad shots and allows me to feel like Arnold Nicklaus-Ballesteros-Woods, whenever the group chooses my good shot.

Scramble golf only has one requirement for enjoyment. Every group needs only one thing: a ringer, an A-player. This player is someone who loves golf so much that they practice!

This metaphor is almost too easy. The Bible is clear that all of our spiritual shots are bad. We are out of bounds the majority of the time. We are barely D-players on our best days. We could never measure up to God's standard of holiness and perfection. But Jesus is quite simply our A-player. He makes perfect shots every time.

He substituted His perfection for your failures and mine, and this sacrificial love of Jesus changes us.

PRAYER: *Jesus, Your love has the power to change me, control me, and give me purpose and motivation. The more I focus on it, the more it gives back to me. I love Your love.*

DF

DUMB SHEEP

Psalm 23:4 – *Even though I walk through the darkest valley, I will fear no evil, for You are with me; Your rod and Your staff, they comfort me.*

In the Scriptures, shepherds had the tough job of leading and protecting sheep all day in the hot sun because sheep are dumb animals that can't make it on their own.

Imagine a self-sufficient sheep: "Listen, Mr. Shepherd. I can take care of myself from those lightning fast wolves with sharp teeth. If I get stuck in a tough situation, I will use my slow, uncoordinated, awkward body to escape." Baaaad idea. (Dad joke!) That scenario is basically us trying to live without tapping into God's help, guidance, and protection.

Shepherds also use a staff, and on one end, the staff has a hook to pull the dumb sheep out of holes, bushes, or other messes. The other end was pointed and used to fend off attacks from predators. God is also our Shepherd, as He uses His staff to pull us out of the bad situations we get ourselves into. In addition, He uses it to protect us from a world of people who want to take advantage of us.

PRAYER: *Father, help me to depend on You to guide, protect, and watch over me. I need Your staff to comfort me.*

CJ

UNDERCOVER AND UNINTERESTED

1 John 2:15 – *Do not love the world or anything in the world. If anyone loves the world, love for the Father is not in them.*

A few years ago, I met Carlton and Madison (not their real names) at a missions conference in Virginia. The couple was raising support to serve in a country that didn't allow Christian missionaries. They referred to their mission point as a "creative access country."

When they explained their goals and objectives, it became obvious that they were going to have to make great personal and financial sacrifices to live in their target country. When I asked about this reality, Madison said, "It's okay with us. The world's stuff is uninteresting. We just want to tell people about Jesus."

Listening to the couple, I thought about how the pursuit of comfort, wealth, power, and pleasure is such a driving force for so many people. It was refreshing to see young people who were choosing a different path.

The Bible teaches that people's love for the world can diminish and crowd out their passion for God. The testimony of Scripture and our personal experience reminds us that it is hard to serve two masters. Like Carlton and Madison, let go of the temporary and embrace the eternal. Use what you have to make a Gospel impact.

PRAYER: *God, help me today to resist the world's trappings. Help me let go of the temporary comforts of this world and chase after You.*

SP

HOPE ON A ROPE

Hebrews 11:1 – *Now faith is confidence in what we hope for and assurance about what we do not see.*

Faith is not primarily a feeling. Rather, it *leads* to feelings. Faith begins with testing our confidence based on the evidence.

We can not judge God by our feelings. Instead, we ought to judge our feelings by God and what He says. This kind of thinking is *counter* to what you will *encounter* in life. For example, you will hear things such as, "It doesn't matter what you believe, as long as you believe it with all your heart."

Let's say Mr. X and Mr. Y are repelling down a mountain. Mr. X confidently belays himself to a rope that is absolutely too weak to hold his weight. Conversely, Mr. Y, even though he is fearful, ties himself to a rope that's definitely strong enough to bear his weight.

So, one man is climbing with great faith in a weak rope, and one man is climbing with weak faith in a great rope. What is the outcome? Mr. X will fall, and Mr. Y will be safe.

It has nothing to do with the strength of their faith—it is only the strength of the rope that matters.

You can believe strongly in the wrong thing and easily fall. Or you can believe just enough to act in something that is right, and you will be as solid as rock. God is the only true thing.

PRAYER: *God, I don't just believe in You today. I believe You. I believe that Your Words are true, so I'm acting on them, following them, and applying them today to my every situation.*

DF

"FILL 'ER UP!"

Ephesians 3:19 – *...that you may be filled to the measure of all the fullness of God.*

An older, shabbier car that is filled with gas is much more useful than an empty 2020 Saab. While the owner may have the new car's manual memorized and can rebuild the engine, without gas, he is stuck.

God longs to be our fuel. Many times we try to work out our circumstances with our own resources. To do so is like pushing a brand new car from the rear bumper. Sure, it's easier if we get others to help us push, but it's still not better than using a gas powered motor.

As Christians, we need to ask God to empower us throughout the day, to fuel our work. As a matter of fact, that is the foundation of what the Bible explains as trust and faith—we rely on God, not ourselves. That is also why He left us with the Holy Spirit, and as Ephesians 5:18 says, we are to "be filled with the Spirit."

Another benefit of using this "divine fuel" is it can turn an old jalopy into a high-powered driving machine. The more we fuel up with God, the more He can refurbish our whole being.

PRAYER: *Lord, fill me with Your Spirit. Empower me as I live my life.*

CJ

A TALE OF GENEROSITY AND GREED

Luke 12:34 – *For where your treasure is, there your heart will be also.*

With her backpack in hand, Emily smiles as she boards the crowded bus in Accra. Serving on a nutrition assistance team, she is on another trek into the rural areas of Ghana to help hungry families. At the age of 33, Emily has few possessions of her own, yet she gives of her own resources to make a difference. Emily is building a legacy of generosity and love with the people she serves.

Her older brother Eric, on the other hand, is on the opposite end of the spectrum. Tight-fisted wouldn't even begin to describe his lack of benevolence. Eric has an obsession with his possessions and never entertains the idea of giving to those in need.

As Christians, we are called to a life of generosity. Giving to the poor and offering our resources to advance God's Kingdom should replace hoarding and greed. Our possessions will pass away, but our generosity can make an eternal impact.

Emily and her brother Eric have two very different perspectives, each driven by their heart's desire. Emily's heart pounds to serve people while Eric's pounds to serve himself. It's okay to have things. The question is, "How will you choose to use them?"

PRAYER: *God, create within me today a heart to for serving others and a spirit of extravagant generosity.*

SP

BRINGING A KNIFE TO A GUN FIGHT

Philippians 4:8 – *Finally, brothers, whatever is true, whatever is honorable, whatever is just, whatever is pure, whatever is lovely, whatever is commendable, if there is any excellence, if there is anything worthy of praise, think about these things.*

At the beginning of World War I, the Turks were advancing in the Middle East. They were dug into a trench in the village of Khevsurs and armed with rifles, grenades, and cannons. But they knew an enemy army was advancing.

The Knights of Ave Matre Dei showed up on the battlefield—armed in coats of mail, with lances and swords. The Knights were easily picked off one-by-one by the Turks' snipers.

These Knights had been sequestered in the Caucasus Mountains for seven centuries. They were fighting (at least in their minds) the Crusades at the bequest of Pope Innocent, circa 1202. They had no idea that a "rifle" even existed, let alone the cannons and grenades that would seal their fate.

Christians are also in a battle, and it begins with your mind. What are you feeding your mind, your soul? What kind of thoughts is that "food" producing? Angry thoughts? Scared thoughts?

If we aren't careful, we will show up to a spiritual gunfight with a knife in hand. God wants to renew your mind. This means we need a steady diet of God's Word and other resources to plant good seeds and reap a great harvest of godly thinking.

PRAYER: *Father, I submit my mind to You right now. Help me to grow in awareness that I am both in a battle today and that I have everything I need to fight in You.*

DF

FROGGER ARCADE GAME

Proverbs 13:8 – *A man's riches may ransom his life.*

Do we own things or do our things own us? I believe our inner peace is a good indicator.

As a young college student, back in the days when annual tuition wasn't as pricey as a large yacht, I saved up enough to buy a sweet Corvette. I remember driving my prized possession through downtown Washington DC. To be honest, you actually don't drive through DC; you "dodge and escape," as if playing a real life video game. I was a mess!

I compare that stressful experience with my Corvette to my first car when I was a poor newlywed. It was a really old, black Toyota Celica with "custom dents." I was actually surprised every time it started, and my biggest concern was which junkyard would charge me the least to take it away after it died.

One time, I backed that car into a large pole. My initial reaction was panic until I remembered what I was driving. I simply checked to see if the wheels were clear of any gnarled car body and then drove away carefree down the road.

PRAYER: *Father, help me to use things without being owned by them. Give me the peace to focus on and enjoy relationships instead of possessions.*

CJ

FRUSTRATIONS DISAPPEAR IN BOSTON

Romans 8:28 – *And we know that in all things God works for the good of those who love him, who have been called according to his purpose.*

Charlotte was stranded on the side of the road. As smoke poured out from under the hood of her rental car, she realized that she was going to miss her flight home. Frustrated, she called for a cab to pick her up and take her back to the hotel.

Walking through the hotel lobby, Charlotte overheard a gentleman named Jacob describe to a friend that his flight had been canceled and he was going to have to stay another night in Boston. As he concluded his call, Charlotte overheard Jacob say, "I guess all things work together."

Recognizing the front end of a Bible verse, she spun around to catch a glimpse of the man who had made the statement. Their eyes met, and after a brief moment of awkwardness, they struck up a conversation. At that moment, the frustration of canceled and missed flights seemed to disappear for both of them. Twelve months later, Charlotte and Jacob were married at her church in Washington, DC.

In His divine care, God arranges the events in our lives to bring about both earthly and eternal good. Trust Him during times of difficulty, frustration, and suffering. He always has a plan.

PRAYER: *God, help me trust You today. Remind me that You are in control and You have my best interest at heart.*

SP

AUCTION-EARS

Matthew 6:20-21 – *But store up for yourselves treasures in heaven, where moths and vermin do not destroy, and where thieves do not break in and steal. For where your treasure is, there your heart will be also.*

My father was a part-time auctioneer. He and my mom worked together to do some local estate sales. And during their years, they made some good buys. But like any collector, they had to make *many* deals for *some* winners.

When my dad was in his eighties, he held an estate auction. Our family filled six flatbed trailers full of what seemed like ancient farm tools. In addition, we had to include wagons, horse tack, and farmhouse contents.

When the six-and-a-half hour sale was complete, the barn felt very empty. And the aftermath of the auction spoke to me.

For my parents (who I believe did an incredible job of storing up *eternal* rewards), a lifetime of accumulating good deals in this life was gone—vaporized in a single auction.

That was a good reminder to me, especially since I'm an Enneagram 3, an achiever. A friend once encouraged me, "All of your hours overworking will eventually benefit your wife's next husband."

Live today wisely and generously.

PRAYER: *Spirit, help me to hear the lives of people who have died before me. They could not accumulate enough wealth to make them happy or change their eternal destinies. I won't either, so I want to walk with You in generosity today.*

DF

ARE YOU TALKIN' TO ME?!

Judges 6:12 – *When the angel of the LORD appeared to Gideon, he said, "The Lord is with you, mighty warrior."*

God was commissioning Gideon to lead His people and take back their freedom from the nasty Midianites.

At first, I pictured Gideon as this Arnold Schwarzenegger-like dude. But Gideon's reply in verse 15 tells us sometimes else: "Pardon me, my lord, but how can I save Israel? My clan is the weakest in Manasseh, and I am the least in my family."

Gideon was basically responding with, "You can't possibly be talking to me. My family is an unimpressive, unnoticed bunch, and I am kind of the skinny loser of my family. There's no way You want this Charlie Brown to lead an uprising."

But the Lord wasn't teaming up with Bruce Willis or Vin Diesel. He was asking someone along the lines of Napoleon Dynamite's brother, Kip, to lead. Needless to say, God used Gideon to dominate the Midianites.

How could this be possible? Because God was with him!

PRAYER: *Father, when I am feeling insignificant and weak, remind me that Gideon conquered the enemy because You teamed up with him. Team up with me today.*

CJ

MY HANDWRITTEN GIFT

2 Corinthians 9:15 – *Thanks be to God for his indescribable gift.*

A group of Malawian pastors and I gathered in a circle to bid each other farewell. Earlier in the day, we had worked together to hold an outreach service in a village located deep within the remote areas of southern Malawi. Before we headed back to our respective villages, one of the pastors had a gift he wanted to share with the rest of us.

Opening his Bible, he pulled out a stack of 3 x 3 inch papers. Each piece had been carefully torn to size and included a handwritten list of things he was thankful for that day.

Though it was written in the Chichewa language, my interpreter translated the list for me as follows:

> Today I Am Most Thankful
> For Grace
> For Mercy
> For Forgiveness
> For Salvation
> For Jesus Christ

I still have my scrap of paper. It is taped in the Bible I had with me that afternoon and reminds me to thank God each day for the gift of salvation.

PRAYER: *Father, remind me each day of Your great salvation. Help me today to express my thankfulness for the work of Your Son, Jesus.*

SP

LISTEN UP

2 Corinthians 1:4 – *Who comforts us in all our troubles, so that we can comfort those in any trouble with the comfort we ourselves receive from God.*

In 2000, Robert Putnam published a book about the necessity of human relationships called *Bowling Alone*. Putnam led some Harvard researchers to conclude that people with lesser health habits (tobacco use, higher than average alcohol use, poor dietary habits) but who had more friends lived significantly longer than people with better health habits who were isolated.

In other words, it's better to have a Coke with friends than drink kombucha alone.

On a flight back to central Ohio from Phoenix, I sat next to a doctor who was flying home to see her mother, who had recently been diagnosed with liver cancer. I commended her for visiting her mom, and she asked me what I did for a living. Normally, that makes conversations a little weird, but on that day the opposite happened.

She started talking and never took a breath! She revealed that she herself had cancer, but her mom had gone on vacation to Egypt instead of coming to be with her. They hadn't spoken in two and half years, and she cried as she shared that experience with me.

Right before we landed, she said, "Thanks so much for talking with me," which was odd because I didn't say a word from Phoenix to Dayton! You can encourage others today if you *listen* for the opportunity.

PRAYER: *Father, please bring people across my path today who are broken, hurting, or just need some of my time. Remind me how many people feel isolated and alone. Help me to point them to You.*

DF

AVOID INNER STRIFE

Philippians 3:15 – *Let the peace of God rule in your hearts.*

After realizing I only needed a three-day hotel stay, I tried to cancel the last day of my original four-day hotel reservation. However, the booking service would only allow me to drop the last day for a larger fee than the actual price of the room. I calmly debated why they should make an exception to the policy due to the fact that I use their service all of the time.

Unfortunately, they would not budge. I chose to just end the phone call before I blew up, even though my gut felt unsatisfied that I didn't rip into them. Still, my peace deep inside had remained intact.

When I arrived at the hotel, the guy at the desk realized I only needed three days and mentioned that he would talk to the outside booking service for me. He eventually did work it out. I'm sure the service company wouldn't have been so willing to accommodate the request if I would've "vented" on them.

PRAYER: *Heavenly Father, help me to walk in peace with You and with those around me, so that I can have Your inner peace. In Jesus' name I pray. Amen.*

CJ

PICK A TEAM

1 Kings 18:21 – *How long will you waver between two opinions? If the Lord is God, follow him; but if Baal is God, follow him.*

At the conclusion of my message, a high school student approached me and began describing his relationship with God as "lukewarm on a good day." Furthermore, he characterized himself as someone who lived for God on Sunday and the devil on Monday. But before he left, he smiled and said, "Today I made a decision. I decided I couldn't stay in the middle any longer. It was time to choose, and I chose Jesus."

As followers of Jesus Christ, we sometimes find ourselves wavering between our commitment to live for Him and giving in to the pull of this world and all it has to offer. In I Kings 18, the prophet Elijah calls the people of Israel to commit to one side or another. He's aware of their fluctuating allegiance and demands that they choose between the one true God and the false god of their day.

A Word of Challenge: There isn't room in this dark and dying world for followers of Christ to have one foot in each camp. It's time to pick a team, live for Jesus, and never look back.

PRAYER: *God, help me make choices today that demonstrate my love and commitment to You.*

SP

FAMILY MATTERS

Ephesians 6:1-3 – *Children, obey your parents in the Lord, for this is right. "Honor your father and mother"—which is the first commandment with a promise—"so that it may go well with you and that you may enjoy long life on the earth."*

Thanksgiving and Christmas are fall highlights for every family. Still, I wonder how many people think about going to see their relatives and say, "Maybe my family is not the perfect picture of mental/emotional health?" I asked that question at church one time, and people began raising their hands. One lady raised two hands!

The Bible, not surprisingly, has a lot to say about family dynamics, and in today's verses, it speaks to kids and dads. In the United States, forty percent (4 out of 10) of children go to bed every night without a dad. One-third of all kids born leave the "father" blank on their birth certificate.

Interestingly, there is another dynamic at work in American homes. It's not so much "under-parenting" by fathers, as it is the opposite. Some parents over-parent their children. They are too involved and fail to give their child space to develop mentally, emotionally, and physically. These dads are a referee's worst nightmare.

How do we solve this parenting dilemma? Look at how God parents His children. He walks with us every step of the way, while giving us the opportunity to choose. We say at our church—prepare your kids for roads, not the roads for your kids. Love God personally and point your kids His direction.

PRAYER: *Father, thank You for my kids, for my family's children, for my friends' children, for the children that I have the opportunity to impact for eternity's sake. Help me to see today as a gift, instead of a nuisance.*

DF

BE A SMOKEY THE BEAR

James 3:5 – *The tongue is a small part of the body, but it makes great boasts. Consider what a great forest is set on fire by a small spark.*

There are two types of people: those who carry a bucket of water and those who carry a bucket of gasoline.

When a juicy piece of gossip, a complaint, or a criticism comes up, there are those who pour water on it to help protect others and squelch it. Then there are those who pour gasoline on it to keep it destructively going.

Our words affect lives. They can hurt others and ourselves. They also have the potential to give much-needed encouragement and help.

I once learned a valuable lesson as a kid, after I'd turned an innocent looking mud puddle into an instant six-foot high "land torch" (long story), that messing around with gasoline can literally backfire. The warning throughout James 3 is that even a small spark WILL backfire, as it burns up our insides and damages others.

PRAYER: *Lord, remind me to confess and start over when I pour gasoline on situations. Help me to pour water to protect and lift up others with my words. Get me through the temptation to join in.*

CJ

CAN I GET A WITNESS?

Acts 1:8 – *But you will receive power when the Holy Spirit comes on you; and you will be my witnesses in Jerusalem, and in all Judea and Samaria, and to the ends of the earth.*

Mike Rathburn had never been in a courtroom. However, he'd seen enough television to know that he was now the key witness in a massive criminal case.

Though Mike wasn't involved, he did witness the alleged crime. Concerned about making a blunder on the witness stand, he sought out an attorney who reminded him, "It is a privilege to be a witness in a case of this magnitude. Your responsibility is to tell the court about everything you discovered and encountered. Do this, and you'll satisfy your duties as a witness."

As a Christian, you serve as a witness to the life-changing and soul-saving power of Jesus Christ. Consider the following: When you discovered that Jesus' death, burial, and resurrection was enough to provide for your salvation, you became aware of the most significant truth of all-time! As a witness to this truth, you have the awesome opportunity to tell others.

Furthermore, when you accepted Jesus as your Lord and Savior, you had a personal encounter with the Creator of the universe! As a firsthand witness to this supernatural transformation, you have the incredible opportunity to speak to others about Jesus' gift of love, grace, and mercy. What a privilege!

PRAYER: *Jesus, give me boldness as I share my faith. Give me opportunities today to speak with people about my encounter with You.*

SP

"SUB!"

John 10:11 – *I am the good shepherd; the good shepherd lays down His life for the sheep.*

In 2015, NBA All-Star Kyrie Irving and Pepsi teamed up for some basketball drama. Irving dressed up as an old man, affectionately named Uncle Drew. He showed up disguised at public basketball courts around the country.

To make it even more interesting, he started slowly. However, he eventually turned on the NBA skills and left the youngsters with their mouths hanging open.

I played in a weekly basketball game until I was forty-five years old. I was no Uncle Drew. As a matter of fact, the way that I knew I should hang up the high tops was that I was yelling, "Sub!" more than I was actually playing.

The Scriptures are clear that when we could not pay for our own sins, Jesus was our Substitute. He stood in our place on the Cross, making peace between us and God. It's human nature to attempt to earn God's good favor. However, we will eventually wear out at some point because of our imperfect nature. It's great to be able to cry out, "Sub!"

PRAYER: *Jesus, I am grateful today that You gave Your life for me. You didn't just die for me, because You had to—You chose to die for me because You wanted to make a way for me to get to the Father. I want to live for Your glory today!*

DF

BLOODY, BRUISED, AND BROKEN

Acts 14:19-20 – *They stoned Paul and dragged him outside the city, thinking he was dead. After the disciples had gathered around him, he got up and went back into the city.*

Paul was ministering in Lystra where the fickle crowd went from worshipping him to being persuaded to stone him. The experience reminds me of how some sports fans act when things aren't going their way.

After being stoned by the people, Paul lay on the ground bloody, bruised, and broken. They thought he was dead, but then he woke, stood up, and went back into the city. He had a focus, a passion, and a lot of guts.

There are days we feel pummeled. We're hit by figurative stones from bosses, friends, co-workers, illness, and the heaviest stones are from those we love.

Why did Paul go back? How did Paul do it? He was absolutely convinced that better times were ahead with great rewards if not in this life, then in eternity.

Paul also tapped into God's strength. The prayer, "I can't, but Lord, You can," comes to mind, and it needs to be paramount in our thinking. Feelings didn't control Paul. His perspective, mission, and God's energy did.

PRAYER: *Father, give me Your perspective and energy. Thank You for heaven.*

CJ

November 26th

ILL-ADVISED DEEP DIVE

Psalm 69:15 – *Do not let the floodwaters engulf me or the depths swallow me up or the pit close its mouth over me.*

There is no doubt about it—I had bitten off more than I could chew. As I stood atop a thirty-foot lava cliff in Hawaii, it was finally my turn to jump.

Though I had seen dozens of people make the dive, resurface, and swim to shore, a momentary dread came over me. Nevertheless, I jumped. And as sure as I am sitting here today, I'll be happy never to do it again.

I have a friend who is fond of saying, "If you live long enough, you are bound to find yourself in the deep end." Living in this dark and dying world, we are bound to face adversity. Waves of grief and doubt, followed by oceans of hardship and trouble, are all a part of our experience on planet Earth.

In Psalm 69, David is in a tough spot. He is in trouble and is begging for help. In a moment of desperation, he cries out to God. In the same way, when you find yourself sinking in the depths of trouble and despair, ask the Lord for help. Reach up and take God's hand of rescue.

PRAYER: *God, help me today to look to You in times of trouble. Help me put away my pride and resist the temptation to go it alone. Rescue me.*

SP

SCARED TO A SCORE

Hebrews 12:1 – *Since we are surrounded by such a great cloud of witnesses, let us throw off everything that hinders and the sin that so easily entangles. And let us run with perseverance the race marked out for us.*

In my last game of my last season of pee wee football, I was converted from tackle to wing back due to injuries. The game was a battle of no-win teams, and in the fourth quarter, the score was tied 0-0, a real nail-biter.

That's when our QB made a terrible read on the option. He pitched the ball to me. Kicking into turtle turbo, I ran wide with a defender yelling my name, as he chased me down the sideline. I fell into the end zone thirty yards later, and we won our only game of the season 6-0.

My only question as I lay in the end zone—oxygen deprived—and being dogpiled by my teammates was, "Who was so slow that they couldn't catch me running down the sideline?"

When I stood up, I saw that my pursuer was actually my father. He had been standing on the fence on that sideline, and he ran with me the whole thirty yards…yelling my name. He was the witness in my cloud.

Early that season, when I was the second team offensive tackle on a team of fourteen players, my dad looked at me one day and said, "You're getting fast." I'll never forget that moment.

Heaven is cheering for you today. Run well.

PRAYER: *God, I believe that You believe in You in me today. I'm encouraged that I'm loved by You as my Father, redeemed by You as my brother, and filled by You as my Helper. I want to run with perseverance today.*

DF

November 28th

FREE OF CHARGE...NOT!

Proverbs 16:11 – *Honest scales and balances belong to the Lord.*

I once ordered a Whopper at Burger King, and the workers accidentally put a second one in my bag. For a high school boy who ate like a tree chipper, it was as though I'd won the lottery. However, as I started to understand my relationship with God, I realized that honest scales are important.

We have the tendency to think we are standing alone when we choose to be honest, but God notices and blesses us. Even my own children look at me strangely when I return money if I'm given too much change at a store or when I go out of my way to pay the entrance fee at a ball game when I easily could've walked in the back entrance "free of charge." While honesty in the small things might not seem that significant to some, it matters to God.

White lies, stealing something left unattended, illegal downloading, not paying someone back...all of these can seem "free of charge" in the short term, but guilty feelings and hardness of heart grow like a fungus on our inner peace.

PRAYER: *Father, help me walk daily with a sense of Your constant presence and care, so that I won't feel the need to get things that seem "free of charge."*

CJ

IT ALL CAME CRASHING DOWN

Psalm 63:8 – *I cling to you; your right hand upholds me.*

On its maiden voyage, my son's remote control airplane found its way onto the roof of our neighbor's garage. Without hesitating, I got out a ladder and made the climb onto their roof. Getting up was easy. Getting down was not.

Making the transition from the garage roof down to the top rung of the ladder, I lost my balance, and the ladder swung out from under me. Falling, I reached up and grabbed hold of the gutter. For a moment, I was safe. A second later, the gutter tore away from the garage, and I crashed to the ground. A day in the life of yours truly.

People reach for things they believe will solve their problems or enhance their lives. They put their trust in money, fame, fortune, comfort, and pleasure. Scripture teaches that such luxuries are temporary and will not last. If you latch onto them, at some point, they will break, and you'll find yourself crashing to the ground.

Instead, reach for something eternal. Come to faith in Jesus, live according to His Word, and serve others. Put your trust in things that will last. Let go of the world and cling to the promises of Jesus.

PRAYER: *Jesus, help me today to put my trust in You, cling to the eternal, and let go of that will not last.*

SP

November 30th

A NAME CHANGE

Revelation 3:12b – *I will write on him the name of my God, and the name of the city of my God, the new Jerusalem, which comes down from my God out of heaven, and my own new name.*

When my nephew was five years old, he learned that he could constantly talk to Siri, and Siri would respond to his requests. He acquired the habit of saying, "Hey Siri, call me _____." He would then make up a random name that the iPhone would use to refer to its owner.

By that, I mean Siri would change the owner's name in his/her contacts. So, my sister-in-law (his mom) began getting emails from Walmart.com that said, "Hey! This is Syd Winston from Walmart, and I'm excited to reach out to you, Mrs. Booty Butt-Butt."

I have another "friend" who changes people's names in their phones if folks leave them lying around. There's nothing like being in public when Siri apologizes to you with, "I'm sorry, Deuce-Dropper."

Throughout the Scriptures, God changes people's names, and it signifies a life-changing moment—Jacob to Israel, Saul to Paul, Abram and Sarai, and Simon to Peter.

However, God is not done yet. Revelation 19 hints that not only will God reveal Himself with a new name, but both Revelation chapters 2 and 3 foreshadow that God's children will receive a new name, as well.

Today, God sees more in you than you see in yourself. We must choose who we will believe.

PRAYER: *Father, thank You that You see my potential in Christ over my sin. You could ask me to earn Your love, but instead You give it freely to me. Help me to believe that what You say and see about my life are real.*

DF

FROM ABOVE

2 Kings 6:17 – *Elisha prayed, "Open his eyes, Lord, so that he may see." Then the Lord opened the servant's eyes, and he looked and saw the hills full of horses and chariots of fire.*

We all have the tendency to look at life from our own point of view and fail to consider the views of others.

One day, I was driving through the mountains of West Virginia on my way back to school in North Carolina (I was taking a "shortcut" that ended up adding hours to my trip). Along the way, those twisty roads seemed to get narrower and narrower. Add to it an occasional semi-truck, and you have one mortified, college-aged driver.

From my limited perspective of the road, I nervously had to be ready to react every second to anything that might come my way. However, if I'd had the ability to look at my route from above, my trip would be so much easier. I may have even enjoyed the scenery.

The experience taught me two life lessons…

#1: Don't take "shortcuts" through the mountains!

#2: When I'm being selfish, I can only see what's around me and life is nerve-racking. But if I'm depending on God, I can start to see from His perspective. In essence, I begin to see things from above.

PRAYER: *Lord, open my eyes that I may see life through Your eyes.*

CJ

TWO TYPES OF PEOPLE

1 Corinthians 15:58b – *Always give yourselves fully to the work of the Lord, because you know that your labor in the Lord is not in vain.*

Serving two seasons as the team chaplain for a local high school football team, I have heard some remarkable pre-game speeches. One of my favorites started like this:

"There are two types of people in this world—people who talk about getting things done and people who roll up their sleeves and actually get things done. Now let me ask you one question: Which person are you going to be?"

Indeed, these are applicable words for a football team about to face its rivals on the Friday night gridiron. At the same time, they apply to each of us as we consider our service to the Lord. Truth be told, it's easy to talk about serving God, but it's not always easy to carve out the time or summon the energy needed to give of ourselves.

God desires for all of us to be involved in personal ministry. He has a purpose and a plan that requires us to use our gifts and abilities to help carry them out. It's time to get off the bench, step onto the field, serve God, and impact the lives of the people around you.

PRAYER: *God, today I ask You to create in me a greater desire to serve You. Use me to carry out Your purpose and Your plan.*

SP

SANDPAPER PEOPLE

1 Thessalonians 5:11 – *Therefore encourage one another and build each other up, just as in fact you are doing.*

We all have people who rub us the wrong way. Talking with them is like unexpectedly stepping on a Lego in the dark.

How do we deal with difficult people? First, we have to understand that others see us as difficult people at times. No one is perfect—including you and me. Second, everyone is created by God for God.

Job is a fantastic example of how to deal with difficult people. He has three "friends" who come to visit, while Job is in misery. Job doesn't speak for seven days and neither do his friends. Dr. John Phillips says the custom in their world was that the guest could not speak until they were first spoken to by the host, and Job didn't speak for a week!

When Job finally caves after seven days, you realize why he had been silent. One friend only talks about his own personal experiences. The second hints around that Job needs to figure out why God is against him. And the third? Mr. Know-it-all basically says, "If God charged people a fee for every sin, Job, you would be a poor man."

Yet, at the end of the narrative, Job prays for his friends. We also have the example of Jesus who prayed for His crucifiers. Why? Because they are imperfect people, created in the image of God, and in need of a Savior.

PRAYER: *Father, I will come into contact with people today who I don't like. But while I don't like them, You love them. You created them for Your glory. Help me to encourage and build them up however possible.*

DF

Z PACK FOR INNER VICTORY

1 Corinthians 15:56-57 – *The sting of death is sin, and the power of sin is the law. But thanks be to God! He gives us the victory through our Lord Jesus Christ.*

My doctor will be calling in my prescription for an antibiotic any minute now for an upper respiratory infection. This sickness has lasted for days and has stopped me from exercising, sleeping, and just feeling well. Thankfully, as soon as the medicine enters my system, it will begin to fight off infections that could possibly lead to death if left untreated.

Spiritually speaking, our wrongful actions, thoughts, and words cause our inner peace and well-being to corrode and die if left untreated. What are some symptoms of our inner sickness? Impure thoughts, worry, confusion, stress, hate, discontent, helplessness, hopelessness, just to name a few.

When we suffer from this inner sickness, we must hand it over to God and confess our sins. When we do, it works as a most powerful antibiotic! Remember, He has already given us the victory!

PRAYER: *Heavenly Father, I hand You each wrong I have done today. Fill me with Your peace. It's comforting to know You allow me to continually start over. Thank You for Your victory.*

CJ

DON'T BE SURPRISED

1 Peter 4:16 – *However, if you suffer as a Christian, do not be ashamed, but praise God that you bear that name.*

Sayid grew up in the Middle East. The son of an oil field worker, he routinely moved throughout the region while his father pursued employment. At the age of nineteen, Sayid met a Christian missionary posing as an English teacher in his country. Within a matter of weeks, the missionary shared the Gospel with Sayid, and he became a follower of Jesus Christ.

When Sayid's family learned of his newfound faith, they immediately disowned him. As word spread, Sayid felt the sting of persecution in his community. Sometimes the abuse was subtle, but often it was open and harsh. Sayid paid a heavy price for his faith.

As Christians, we shouldn't be surprised by the pushback we receive because of our faith. As people in our country become less tolerant of Jesus Christ, we should expect opposition. Quite simply, in a nation and in a world that is increasingly hostile toward Christ-followers, we should live in anticipation of persecution.

A word of hope: Millions of martyrs and persecuted saints who came before you have suffered because of their faith. Stand firm and count it a privilege to be harassed, oppressed, or mistreated because of your faith. You're in good company.

PRAYER: *God, help me today to stand firm in my faith. Help me to find peace in the company of those who suffered for Your namesake.*

SP

December 6th

HOLY HUDDLES

Matthew 28:19 – *Therefore go and make disciples of all nations, baptizing them in the name of the Father and of the Son and of the Holy Spirit.*

Imagine Patrick Maholmes in the huddle preparing to call the first play of the most important game of his career: "That was a great huddle. Kelce, way to keep our lines straight in the huddle. Beautiful! Guys, what if we just stay in the huddle, because it's kind of brutal out there—dangerous! Those Raiders across the line of scrimmage want to hit and tackle us. They could hurt us." That's not how you win Super Bowls.

The point of the huddle is not the huddle. The point of the huddle is to play—to get into the game!

All individuals, families, businesses, and ministries will fight the huddle mentality at some point. We all have the tendency to turn inward, to be selfish, and to live with a me-first attitude. However, Jesus went to Cross to pay for our sins and showed us what it is to live with an others-first mentality. Before He ascended to Heaven, He broke the huddle. He commissioned us to make an eternal difference in the world.

We have all heard of the no-huddle offense. There's no such thing as a no-offense huddle. So, break the huddle today, use your gifts, speak up when you would normally be silent, and shine light into darkness.

PRAYER: *Father, help me see beyond myself today…beyond my own selfish desires. I want to see others the way that You see them. Give me Your vision for my life.*

DF

WASH THE DISHES

Matthew 23:25-26 – *You clean the outside of the cup and dish, but inside they are full of greed and self-indulgence. First clean the inside of the cup and dish, and then the outside also will be clean.*

In today's verse Jesus was talking to the Pharisees about their wrong perception of what God expects. He was pointing out that they needed to work on their insides and not just on what they do or how they appear.

I recall my first semester in graduate school seminary. My wife and I were moving into our apartment, and we needed a hand with a couple pieces of furniture. I asked several seminary students ("want-to-be pastors"), and their rejections were polite: "I have exams next week" and "I don't have time", "I'm preparing a sermon" (I wonder if the sermon was about helping others in need?)

It made we wonder if I was like that? Was I truly allowing God to change me on the inside in preparation to help others? I knew I needed to start the battle of allowing Him to change me to my deepest core.

Billy Graham once said, "A real Christian is a person who can give his pet parrot to the town gossip."

PRAYER: *Lord, I give You my inner, private person to work on. Change me from the inside out. Remind me to confess and keep starting over. Thank You that this "cleaning" is worth it!*

CJ

SALT AND SUGAR LOOK THE SAME

Psalm 55:21 – *His talk is smooth as butter, yet war is in his heart; his words are more soothing than oil, yet they are drawn swords.*

In high school and college, Maria struggled to find genuine friends. More often than not, she found herself surrounded by people who verbalized their friendship but ultimately proved to be hurtful, fake, and phony.

Mark's small business was on an upward trajectory until he partnered with a slick-talking colleague who he admittedly didn't know very well. Within months, everything he had worked for had fallen apart.

Some time ago, I heard a preacher say, "Be careful whom you trust. Salt and sugar look the same." I certainly agree. Fake friends and bad business associates love to flatter, gossip, and take advantage. People like this are masterful with their words and uncanny in their ability to make us blind to their true intentions.

Allow time to pass before you go too deep into your friendships and business partnerships. By doing so, you open the door for discernment concerning these new people in your life. Consequently, you create the chance to observe whether or not their actions match their words. Furthermore, you allow yourself to see if they are genuine in their motives and have your best interest in mind.

PRAYER: *God, help me today to be patient and discerning as I enter into new relationships. Protect me from those who wish me harm.*

SP

NOTHING BUT THE TRUTH

Ephesians 4:25 – *Therefore each of you must put off falsehood and speak truthfully to your neighbor, for we are all members of one body.*

When Paul says, "put off the *false*," he literally says, "put off the *pseudo*." The reality is that I/we all live in pseudo-kingdoms, and I think I'm king.

As a young man, I remember thinking about what it would be like to be married. I was certain that I would come home at 5:00 p.m. each day with my three children awaiting my arrival at the door thanking me for how I have tirelessly sacrificed to provide for their needs.

I'd see my spouse in an apron because of the freshly baked bread she had made for our dinner that's on the table. I'd even see my slippers by the remote control in the easy chair, so I can relax after a hard day.

Is that how things work at your house? Not mine either. Even though I think I'm the king—that I'm in control, it's imaginary control…a total mirage. While I am blessed with a great family, I am supposed to serve them, not be served by them.

Paul says we need to live in "truth." It's the word "integra," where we get our word for integer. It means "whole." Don't settle for a partial life—partial joy—partial contentment—partial self-control. Live whole.

PRAYER: *Father, thank You so much that I do not have to settle for less-than living. I want to live the full and free life that You have designed for me.*

DF

BLOW UP MY BALLOON

2 Thessalonians 1:11 – *We constantly pray for you that by His power He may fulfill every good purpose of yours and every act prompted by your faith.*

We tend to separate our "spiritual life" from our regular life, but the key to fulfilled living is allowing the two to collide. Lasting satisfaction only comes when we let God weave into our passions, work, sports, relationships, dreams, and desires. Plus, God loves when we continually hand them over to Him.

One time, my daughter was playing in a basketball event, and she looked at me and said, "Basketball isn't fun anymore." Now, understand that she loves basketball and works extremely hard at the sport. I told her that basketball is like a balloon: if the balloon is flat, basketball will grow stale, but if you inflate it with God, it can be very fulfilling.

Every area of our lives can be "inflated" through our prayers, as we ask God for His **power**, His **perspective**, and His **purpose.**

PRAYER: *Father, invade every area of my life so that by Your power I can pursue what I enjoy while also finding Your purpose and fulfillment. In Jesus' name. Amen.*

CJ

THE OTHER SIDE

2 Corinthians 5:17 – *Therefore, if anyone is in Christ, the new creation has come: The old has gone, the new is here!*

Jack and Charlie tore through their college years. Together, they epitomized what it meant to live hard and fast. There wasn't a line drawn that they didn't cross.

After graduation, they moved to different parts of the country to pursue their careers. Time and distance made it impossible for the two friends to remain close. Ultimately, they drifted apart.

At the age of thirty, Jack tracked down Charlie's address and sent him a heartfelt letter. In it, he referenced the "good old days" and thanked Charlie for his friendship. Furthermore, Jack wrote about his newfound faith in Jesus Christ—referencing the fact that he had become a new man. With profound sincerity and for the better part of two pages, Jack explained to Charlie that he was now on the other side of their rip-roaring college days. And without an ounce of judgment, Jack pleaded for Charlie to join him there.

When we come to faith in Jesus Christ, we turn from our past and become a new creation. As a part of that transformation, we develop a desire for others to experience life as we now know it. Take time today to let someone know about life on the other side.

PRAYER: *God, thank You for making me new. Give me an opportunity today to tell someone about my transformation.*

SP

December 12th

DON'T FALL FOR THE FAKE

John 8:32 – *Then you will know the truth, and the truth will set you free.*

The Man Who Never Was tells the WWII story of the English invasion of Italy. The best place for the English to invade was through Sicily, but the Germans were too strong. So, the English created a "shadow mission."

Churchill approved this covert mission known as Operation Mincemeat. First, the Brits dropped a body out of a plane off the coast of Spain. Although Spain was neutral in the war, they sympathized with the Germans. The body (known as Col. William Martin) needed to have died of pneumonia to ensure enough moisture in the lungs to fool an autopsy, so the Brits found a young man who had passed away from pneumonia.

He had a uniform and various kinds of papers, including love letters from a fictitious woman. He washed up on the Spanish shoreline with all of those belongings, and it appeared as though he'd been soaking in the ocean for a few hours. Spain found him; the Germans examined his papers and found a letter which contained a specific line, "PS: Looking forward to having some *sardines* with you." The Germans moved their troops to Sardinia, and the English basically walked through Sicily without casualty.

Often, we give our hearts to empty realities that won't last forever: beauty, finances, notoriety, you name it. Don't fall for the fake.

PRAYER: *Father, You are what is real. Forever home with You is real and authentic. I want to live for that eternal day, instead of only living for what I can see.*

DF

UPSIDE DOWN THINKING

Matthew 20:26 – *...whoever wants to be a great among you must be your servant.*

There are many times when we read things in the Bible that seem to contradict our cultural mindset. I call this "upside down thinking." Here are some examples: to live we need to die (to self), to gain we need to give, and in today's verse, to be great we need to serve.

The Merriam-Webster Dictionary defines the word "counterintuitive" as "contrary to what one would intuitively expect." Today's Bible passage is clearly one of God's "counterintuitive" ideas.

However, if we think about it, the best leaders (teachers, bosses, coaches....) in our lives have been those who really care about us and would go out of their way to help us. They're not just in control nor do they lord their power over us.

Mother Teresa spoke at a Harvard graduation one year. When she spoke, the place was silent as they hung on her every word. Why? People who serve earn authority! At another time while receiving the Nobel Peace Prize, she was asked, "What can we do to promote world peace?" Her response was, "Go home and love your family."

PRAYER: *Heavenly Father, develop who I am through opportunities to serve and help those around me.*

CJ

December 14th

WHO TURNED OFF THE LIGHTS?

Psalm 119:105 – *Your word is a lamp for my feet, a light on my path.*

I woke up freezing and in absolute darkness. It was 6:00 a.m. in the middle of February, and an overnight ice storm had knocked out the power. A cold shave and shower followed by a dimly lit attempt at getting dressed made me realize how much I depended upon electricity for the proper execution of my morning routine. As you might imagine, my morning was off to a rough start.

It's frustrating when you have to start your day without power. There's nothing worse than stumbling around in the dark and wishing you could turn on the lights.

From time to time, I jump into my day and fail to tap into the power source—I fail to turn the lights. Invariably, these are the days when I spend more time listening to talk radio or checking social media updates than I do reading my Bible. What a waste of time.

God's Word is described in Psalms 119:105 as a lamp and a light. It can move you out of darkness and into light. Reading the Bible illuminates your heart and mind with the very words of God. Choose to tap into this power source every day.

PRAYER: *Lord, help me let go of time wasters and build a routine that includes spending time in Your Word each day.*

SP

POETRY IN MOTION

Acts 15:28a – *It seemed good to the Holy Spirit and to us.*

In my senior English class, poetry writing was not my strong suit, so I went to my teacher, Mr. Wheeler, and bemoaned the difficulty of writing a fourteen-line Shakespearean sonnet.

He encouraged me, "Dean, just write about something you love." And that, friends, is when the magic happened.

I gave birth to the well-known Thespian piece, "The Fast Break of Life." I'm sure you've heard of it, read it, and some have it committed to memory. (Actually, I feel like Matt Foley (aka Chris Farley) would have looked at me and said, "A real Bill Shakespeare.")

The sonnet turned on one critical line, "On the break, you may drive, or you may dish. Choose the right option to score, if you wish." Those words have brought tears to many eyes.

Today, you will make some decisions—big ones and small ones. In some, you will be confident. In others, you will have questions. Remember that we make two mistakes when attempting godly choices: 1) Not considering God at all 2) Not regularly seeking biblical wisdom.

In the early church, the Apostles had a tough decision. How did they decide? "We believe this is what God wants, and we see the wisdom too."

You can stand on a solid foundation for your choices today.

PRAYER: *Father, help me to listen to You today. I want what You want. In areas where I'm unsure, I want to want what You want.*

DF

December 16th

GOOD JOB

2 Corinthians 13:10 – *When I come I may not have to be harsh in my use of authority—the authority the Lord gave me for building you up, not for tearing you down.*

When my seventy-year-old friend visited his ninety-five-year-old dad, he noticed the small, rickety TV his father was watching, and he decided to help his dad by installing a big, new one.

Now, my friend grew up under this father who only corrected and criticized him. So, the next day when he received a call from his dad, he expected his never-pleased-father to tell him all of the mistakes he'd made setting up the TV.

But he heard for the first time, "Thank you, son for the new television. You did a great job!" My seventy-year-old friend told me that he has longed to hear those words all of his life!

Coaches, teachers, bosses, and parents mostly tend to use words of correction. But without a foundation of encouragement, true learning is stifled.

We need to look to encourage and compliment those around us.

PRAYER: *Father, thank You for Your patience with me. Help me to pass that on to those whom I interact with.*

CJ

STRAIGHT TALK

Romans 6:23 – *For the wages of sin is death, but the gift of God is eternal life in Christ Jesus our Lord.*

In high school, I often spent the night with a good friend of mine. Though we had a midnight curfew, we were confident we would be able to sneak into the house if we were running late. We were wrong.

For the better part of thirty minutes, we were on the short end of a parental tirade that would make a marine blush. I don't remember everything that was said, but I do remember it started with the words, "I'm going to give it to you straight."

In homage to the opening statement from my friend's father—which was obviously crafted to denote clarity, allow me to share some straight talk with you concerning four important truths:

> Death Is Certain
> There Are Consequences To Sin
> There Are No Exits In Hell
> Only Jesus Can Save Your Soul

Romans 6:23 highlights a number of these truths and should move us to be thankful that Jesus saved us from the penalty of our sin. At the same time, the reality of each truth should compel us to tell others about the gift of Jesus Christ. Thank Jesus today for your salvation and tell the world about His great love.

PRAYER: *God, remind me today of all that You have saved me from and burden my heart for those who do not know Your Son.*

SP

FIRST-CLASS MORON

James 5:16a – *Therefore confess your sins to each other and pray for each other so that you may be healed.*

I recall catching a Monday morning flight: the sprint to the airport, the long security lines, and me with a backpack and rolling carry-on. Fortunately, I made it through the security with just enough time to hit Starbucks.

Coffee and a blueberry muffin redeemed the morning. My hands were full as I rushed to the gate, and I could see the plane boarding and the first-class passengers in line.

Nothing against you, if you fly first class. It's just that moment when the stewardess comes to pull the curtain closed, and she gives everyone in coach the look that says, "Maybe if you just worked a little harder."

Anyway, as I waited to board the flight, a TSA officer approached the counter with a rolling carry-on bag, and I thought, "That looks exactly like my bag." I had gotten distracted by my coffee/blueberry muffin combo and had left my bag at Starbucks.

The officer yelled out, "Someone (code for 'Moron') forgot their bag!" All the first-class people rolled their eyes at each other. What could I do? I just had to humble myself, walk up there, and say, "That's my friend's bag—what a moron." I kid. I kid.

Living in vulnerability is healthy for you and others. Confessing our sins reminds us that we are not God. We need healthy opportunities to live in community. Your humility will encourage others.

PRAYER: *God, your Word says that when I am weak, then I am strong. Help me to find opportunities today to appropriately be vulnerable to help my soul and others as well.*

DF

A STEP FURTHER

1 John 3:18 – *Let us not love merely with words or tongue but with actions...*

People need to hear that they are cared about, but even taking it a step further is what God is telling us. In other words, we are to make an effort to do something for someone in the midst of needing a helping hand ourselves. By doing this, we are saying to God, "I believe that You are real and will take care of me when I help others."

Rarely do I feel like running to the store for my wife, helping my son clean up the broken glass from his dropped candle, pulling out my jumper cables for someone when I'm in a rush to get home, moving a friend's couch (the ol' "bad back" excuse only works so many times), or giving the dreaded ride to the airport.

However, we can view these as opportunities to allow God's invasion into our hearts and for Him to bring His fulfillment. As Henry David Thoreau once penned, "There are few who do not love better to give advice than to give assistance."

PRAYER: *Lord, help me to seize the "opportunities" to put my faith into action. Thank You for the blessings that will follow.*

CJ

WHATEVER YOU DO, DON'T STOP

2 Thessalonians 3:13 – *And as for you, brothers and sisters, never tire of doing what is good.*

Several years ago, after I'd wrapped up a speaking session at a student ministries conference, a young man named Tony approached me and said, "Hey, I'm tired of doing the right thing." Intrigued by his lead-in, I stopped and listened.

For the next half hour, Tony talked about being ridiculed by his peers. He mentioned feeling unappreciated by those he served. Finally, he expressed doubt as to whether or not his obedience even mattered. After listening, I took the next few minutes and tried to encourage his soul.

As Christians, when thoughts like these enter our brain, it is important to remember that the world's ridicule is bound to fall upon those who follow the principles and precepts of God's Word. Additionally (and unfortunately), we have to know that even well-intentioned people don't always adequately express their appreciation. Furthermore, we have to believe the Bible when it tells us that our obedience matters to God.

Over the years, I have discovered it is very easy to give up on the things that require significant effort to accomplish. Don't quit—these are the endeavors that are important and make a lasting impact on people's lives. Don't stop doing good.

PRAYER: *God, help me today to obey You and serve others regardless of the outcome.*

SP

PREACHER'S KIDS

James 1:2 – *Consider it pure joy, my brothers and sisters, whenever you face trials of many kinds.*

There are only two options that make sense of pain without God: a religious answer and an irreligious one.

The religious answer is that morality means justice. "If you live a good life, you'll have a good life." In other words, if you are moral, God gives you what you want.

So, if my kids are happy, it's because I'm a good parent. If I'm successful at work, it's because I'm a harder worker. See the problem? When tragedy occurs, it's because someone isn't righteous enough.

The alternative is an irreligious answer, which suggests that an inequity of suffering means that God is either mean or not in control. This answer ends in despair. If there's no God, then our only hope is to, "Take a tough pill."

When my youngest child was three years old and said to me, "Daddy, I learned a new song today. 'When you're sittin' on the john and toilet paper's gone, be a man (clap, clap) and use your hand.'" My small group leaders' kids taught her that song. (See, it's not always the preacher's kids.)

Neither view—the religious or the irreligious—is correct. The Bible tells us we can *count* trials as joy because they help us grow. Jesus simultaneously lived the most morally pure and excruciatingly painful life. Trials, even though they hurt, can make us more like Christ.

PRAYER: *God, I'm praying that You change painful circumstances in my life today. However, if my circumstances don't change, please change me in the middle of those situations. I trust You today.*

DF

THE WATERBOY

1 John 2:6 – *Whoever claims to live in Him must walk as Jesus did.*

Being a basketball coach, I think even winter can be an exciting time of the year. A question I have often pondered is, "What would Jesus be if He were a part of a basketball team?"

Though He would make the best coach, would be the best athlete (it wouldn't even be fair if He were the athletic trainer or team doctor), I think He would be the manager. If not the manager, He would be a player that hung out and helped the manager.

What's the role of the manager? The team manager is the person who serves the team, oftentimes without even being acknowledged. The manager organizes the water bottles and uniforms and makes sure all of the equipment is ready. It's truly a thankless position that most players completely ignore.

It's a fantastic exercise of our faith to humbly look for opportunities to help someone without being noticed. Talk about "walking like Jesus"! The power and peace will infuse into our hearts as we serve as He did.

PRAYER: *Father, give me eyes to see those who are taken for granted and those who are serving behind the scenes. Help me to encourage and assist them as I quietly help others.*

CJ

WHITEBOARD WISDOM

1 Peter 3:15 – *Always be prepared to give an answer to everyone who asks you to give the reason for the hope that you have.*

A week before their graduation, I addressed a group of men who had spent the better part of the last year training to be pastors in the remote villages of Malawi and Mozambique. To gauge their preparedness, I said to them, "Tell me about Jesus."

Without hesitation, a young man stood and said, "He is the Son of God." I wrote his answer on the whiteboard. The next young man stood and said, "He is the Light of the world." Again, I wrote his response down. This process continued until I finally ran out of space.

Pointing to the whiteboard, I asked one more question: "With this in mind, tell me, what is Jesus' impact on your life?" Before I could get the words out of my mouth, a student shot to his feet and said, "He is the only hope for my salvation."

As Christians, we have the incredible opportunity and awesome responsibility to tell people about the hope that Jesus provides. Be ready and willing to speak to others about who He is and what He has done for you. If you do, you are bound to make an eternal impact on someone's life.

PRAYER: *Jesus, help me today to develop a passion for speaking to others about who You are and how You changed my life.*

SP

December 24th

A LITTLE EINSTEIN

James 1:5 – *If any of you lacks wisdom, you should ask God, who gives generously to all without finding fault, and it will be given to you.*

Albert Einstein taught more than just physics. In Einstein's earlier years, he traveled around the European countryside giving a lecture, and his chauffeur was the one person who went with him. So, the chauffeur had heard him give the same lecture every night—over one hundred times.

Finally, the chauffeur said to Einstein, "You know, I've heard you give that lecture so often, I think I could give it." Einstein responded, "Well, then, why don't you?" So, long before the days of Instagram, they agreed to switch roles. And the next night, this chauffeur pretended to be Einstein, while Einstein dressed up like a chauffeur.

The chauffeur made his way all through the lecture, and it all went very well. However, both Einstein and the chauffeur had forgotten there was always a Q&A time post-lecture.

Somebody stood up and asked a very complex question about quantum physics, and the chauffeur (dressed as Einstein) stood motionless for a minute. He didn't even understand the question, let alone have an answer. Then he responded, "That question is so easy, I'm going to let my chauffeur answer it!"

Wouldn't it be great to have a little Einstein travel with you all of the time to answer the hard questions? The Bible says that we do have unlimited access to eternal wisdom. We only have to ask.

PRAYER: *For everything I'm facing today, God, I'm asking for wisdom. Thank You that no matter the answer, You will give it to me generously as I seek to follow You with all of my life.*

DF

DOLLAR STORE COFFEE MUGS

Philippians 4:11 – *For I have learned to be content whatever the circumstances.*

My wife, Danette, and I were broke in the days leading up to our first Christmas together. We had only been married a few months, Danette was still looking for work after relocating to Ohio, and my job didn't pay much.

After purchasing a few modest gifts for friends and family, our bank account was depleted. Despite being broke, we still wanted to exchange gifts with each other, so we did the one thing we could afford—we made a trip to the dollar store. Content to purchase only one item each, we went shopping. Three days later, we sat in our pj's and laughed as we opened the $1 ceramic coffee mugs we'd bought for each other. It was the best Christmas ever!

Being content is critical to one's sanity and essential to a vibrant walk with God. If we spend our lives comparing ourselves to everyone or wishing we had more, we'll end up jealous of others and bitter towards God.

Letting go of earthly pursuits and replacing them with spiritual priorities is fundamental to finding contentment. Choose to trust God's plan for your life, serve Him, pursue righteousness, and love the people around you. Contentment will soon follow.

PRAYER: *God, remind me today of Your many blessings and help me find contentment in the pursuit of spiritual priorities.*

SP

FRIEND

Exodus 33:11 – *The Lord would speak to Moses face to face, as one speaks to a friend!*

I have always been intrigued with today's verse and the idea that Moses would go into a special tent and actually talk to God. What must that have been like?!

While I do understand that things worked a little differently in the Old Testament, the description of how Moses and the Lord conversed blows me away—*as one speaks to a friend*! How amazing that this is how the Bible describes their relationship!

This verse has changed my prayer times. It has also changed how I view God. Sure, God is a holy, all-powerful Deity. Yet, He is my friend too.

During some of life's really stressful times, I have gotten into my car to go for a drive. I'll take that time in the car in order to get alone and pour my heart out to my Friend. It is a very comforting thing to do, and how blessed are we that we can even do it.

PRAYER: *Lord, teach me to be Your friend. In Jesus' name. Amen*

CJ

LOVE IS BLIND

Proverbs 30:18-19 – *Three things are too wonderful for me; four I do not understand: the way of an eagle in the sky, the way of a serpent on a rock, the way of a ship on the high seas, and the way of a man with a woman.*

If Solomon (the wisest person ever) says something is confusing, then we need help. I have often wondered what aliens would say about dating and marriage. Kids are the closest beings we have. Their observations were caught in the 1970s TV show called *Kids Say the Darndest Things.*

"What do most people do on a date?" Martin–age 10: "They just tell each other lies and that usually gets them interested enough for a second date." Martin has a bright dating future.

"How do people typically fall in love?" Wendy–age 8: "When a person gets kissed for the first time, they fall down and don't get up for at least an hour." Wendy has high expectations.

"What should you look for in a husband?" Christine–age 9: "Well, beauty is only skin deep, but how rich you are can last a long time." Christine will be dating on Wall Street.

"What is a surefire way to make someone fall in love with you?" Camille–age 9: "Shake your hips and hope for the best." Camille should begin counseling now.

Human intimacy is a desire to be fully known and fully loved. We first find that in Christ's love for us as shown on the Cross.

PRAYER: *Jesus, right now I'm declaring that I'm living out of Your love for me today. My source will not be the person I'm dating or the person I'm married to. I'm grateful to be living from Your sacrifice for me on the Cross!*

DF

YOU CAN'T HANDLE THE TRUTH

Ephesians 4:25 – *Therefore each of you must put off falsehood and speak truthfully to your neighbor, for we are all members of one body.*

Recently I was flying home from Atlanta, and the gentleman next to me was watching the film *A Few Good Men* on his tablet. As the movie became more intense, I was intrigued by my seat neighbor's facial expressions. He was really into it!

With his headphones on, he started to whisper the lines from the movie's pivotal scene. He didn't realize it, but with each word, his voice became louder. Finally, as the film reached its apex, my seat neighbor exclaimed, "You can't handle the truth!" When he realized how loud he'd been, his face turned as red as the Delta triangle painted on the side of the plane.

Discovering a character's dishonesty is the primary plotline of the movie that had captured my seatmate's attention. Unfortunately, for many, failing to tell the truth has become the story of their lives.

God's Word demands honesty and truthfulness. As Christians, we know the Lord's expectation but still struggle to tell the truth. Lying ultimately leads to a lack of trust, broken relationships with people, and a fractured relationship with God. Honor the people you encounter and honor the Lord you worship by speaking truth.

PRAYER: *God, help me today to be truthful in all that I say.*

SP

WEDDED BLISS

1 John 4:18 – *There is no fear in love. But perfect love drives out fear.*

I have led my fair share of weddings, where weird stuff happened. Members of the wedding party have passed out. The would-be husband has stood up front for five to seven minutes *waiting* on the bride to walk down the aisle (presumably because the bride was having second thoughts). Uninvited animals have crashed the ceremony.

A pastor friend once shared with me a story from one of his pastor friends who was performing a ceremony. At this particular wedding, the uncle of the bride sent in a request since he could not attend. He asked someone to read 1 John 4:18 which says, "There is no fear in love; instead perfect love drives out fear."

Unfortunately, the reader quoted John 4:18 at the wedding: "For you have had five husbands, and the man you now have is not your husband."

There are times when we want to communicate one thing, but we communicate something entirely different. Those are moments for humility instead of insecurity, as insecurity will cause you to jump into damage control mode out of fear. But God's love—the kind that allows us to be humble as we approach one another—casts fear to the side. Live out of God's love today!

PRAYER: *Spirit, let Your love guide my decisions and my interactions today. I need Your empowering voice to allow me to live honestly and authentically, when I fail. I have everything I need from Your perfection, so I don't have to try and earn my own status.*

DF

December 30th

APPLE CIDER VINEGAR

James 1:15 – *After desire has conceived, it gives birth to sin; and sin, when it is full-grown, gives birth to death.*

When we invite Christ into our lives, we receive the Holy Spirit. Now we have the ability for God to develop and enhance us, and this may entail cleaning up some ugly habits.

My son had this horrible wart growing on his knuckle for years. We would attempt quick fixes and cures from the drug store. However, all this did was create a "super wart." We even tried cutting it out, but it only came back stronger (and looked like a sixth finger).

Finally, we discovered that when apple cider vinegar is taped to the wart every night for several weeks, the virus will slowly die. My son gave up after one attempt, but I encouraged him to persist. Slowly the "monster" turned black and died after continual and consistent treatment.

Our deep, embedded habits take time for the Holy Spirit to erode away. "Treatments" may involve continually confessing (admitting our wrongs), asking Him to change us, and starting over when we give up.

PRAYER: *Father, do the work in me so I can experience life to the fullest. Thank You that I can keep restarting.*

CJ

BEHIND THE SCENES

Ephesians 6:18 – *And pray in the Spirit on all occasions with all kinds of prayers and requests. With this in mind, be alert and always keep on praying for all the Lord's people.*

When my oldest daughter began doing theater in high school, I learned to enjoy musicals. With an incredible teacher, our school's presentations were Cadillac productions on a Pinto budget.

However, some of my favorite moments occurred, when there were microphone miscues. A student would accidentally leave his/her mic on backstage, and the unscripted teenage talk was incredible—unless it was your kid on the hot mic!

One tension in the Christian life is that God's enemy becomes our enemy by default. And just like God, our enemy is invisible in this physical world.

Right now, we have to be aware that there are things going on behind the scenes of this world. So, maybe your *perceived* problem is not your *actual* problem. Maybe it's designed by God's enemy to trip you or trap you.

It can be a maddening rabbit hole to go down, so "don't go there."

Instead, "pray in the Spirit." You have a hot mic straight to Heaven, and He has already won the eternal victory. Even though it feels as though it's a battle we cannot win, this battle is ultimately one that God will not lose.

PRAYER: *God, right now, I recognize that I have already won an eternal battle. I am not working for a victory: I am living from Your victorious resurrection today.*

DF

APPENDIX I
WE CAN HAVE ETERNAL LIFE

"I write these things…so that you may <u>know</u>
that you have eternal life" (1 John 5:13)

God also tells us in the Bible:

THE BAD NEWS
We "*all have sinned…*" (Romans 3:23): wrongful actions, thoughts, or words.
That's what made us "*…separated from God…*" (Isaiah 59:2).

BUT…

THE GOOD NEWS
God's love made a way to hand us eternal life: heaven, daily help, a full life.
"*…the gift of God is eternal life…*" (Romans 6:23).

THE CONCERN
A gift can't be earned. If so, it wouldn't be a gift.
"*…this* (salvation) *is not from yourselves* (no matter how good or bad we've been), *it is the gift of God…*" (Ephesians 2:8-9).

THE SOLUTION
God came down as the man, Jesus. He died on the cross and rose from the grave for us.
"*Christ died for sins once for all…to bring you to God…*" (1 Peter 3:18).

THE INVITATION

To bridge the separation, receive the gift of eternal life, and connect personally to God,
pray this in your own words:

I Admit that I sin, forgive me.
I Believe that You died on the cross for me.
Come into my life.
Amen.

"…(Jesus speaking) I stand at the door (of your heart) and knock. If anyone...opens the door, I will come in…" (Revelations 3:20).

[Watch Billy Graham's "Steps to Peace" message at stepstopeace.org. It's less than three minutes, and it's very impactful.]

APPENDIX II
-PRAYER GUIDE-

Dean, Sean, and Chris all use an acrostic like *"APPTS"* (appointments) to help round out a good prayer meeting alone with God.

A - "Admit."
Confess wrongful actions, words, and thoughts. Ask Him to *Change* us.

P - "Praise."
Thank Him that He *Reigns* (He's bigger than our problems) and that He *Renews*.

P - "People."
Pray for *Family*, *Friends*, and to *Forgive our Foes* (This is cleansing).

T - "Thanks."
Appreciate the *People* and *Possessions* in our life and also our *Position* in life.

S - "Self."
Give Him our *Dreams*, *Desires*, *Disappointments*, *Direction*, and *Daily needs*.

Colossians 4:2 – *Devote yourselves to prayer, being watchful and thankful.*

Being ***devoted*** to prayer is different from just trying to pray. For example, Chris' wife is ***devoted*** to jogging and makes sure she is running the streets of their neighborhood five days a week. One of their sons was ***devoted*** to basketball and shot 4,000 practice shots a week in the off-season. That's what ***devotion*** looks like.

When it comes to praying, we see being ***devoted*** to prayer in two ways. First, it means to "breathe" quick prayers throughout our busy day. Second, it means having a set time to pray where we can focus our hearts on God.

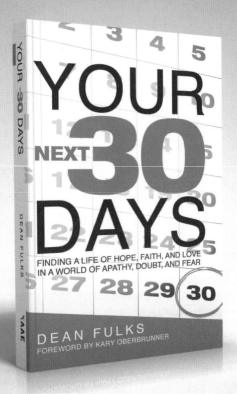

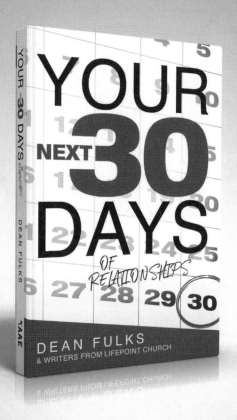

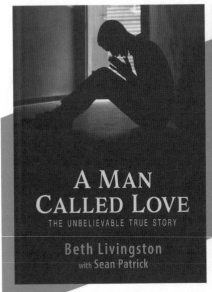
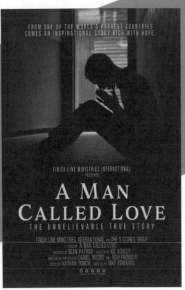